SUBMISSION IN SUFFERING

SUBMISSION IN SUFFERING

AND OTHER ESSAYS ON EASTERN THOUGHT

BY

H. H. ROWLEY, D.D., F.B.A.

CARDIFF

UNIVERSITY OF WALES PRESS

1951

PRINTED IN GREAT BRITAIN AT
THE UNIVERSITY PRESS
ABERDEEN

DEDICATED TO

MY FORMER COLLEAGUES AND STUDENTS

IN CHEELOO UNIVERSITY, TSINANFU

IN WHOSE FELLOWSHIP I GAINED

AN UNDYING LOVE

FOR CHINA AND ITS PEOPLE

PREFACE

THE three essays which together make up this volume have all appeared separately, the first as a monograph published in 1942 by the University of Wales Press Board, the second as a reprint from the *Bulletin of the John Rylands Library* of October 1940, and the third as a reprint from the *Bulletin of the John Rylands Library* of November 1948. Several requests for republication of the first essay have led to this new edition in combination with the others, and the opportunity has been taken to revise them all. For permission to include the second and third essays I express my thanks to Professor E. Robertson, Librarian of the John Rylands Library, and Editor of the *Bulletin*.

The preponderant interest in Chinese thought which marks these studies is the enduring fruit of my years of service in China, and though the pressure of my duties in other academic spheres leaves me little time to maintain that interest, whenever opportunity offers I turn to this field as a recreation. In the first study I enter a wider field, for which my excuse must be that for a few years I was responsible for the teaching of the History of Religion in the University College of North Wales, Bangor, and so was compelled to engage in research in this field in order to equip myself for the routine work of teaching. The lecture on 'The Chinese Sages and the Golden Rule' was delivered as a public inaugural lecture to mark the beginning of the teaching of the subject in the College. In all of the essays my aim is to develop a truly comparative method. This is sometimes understood to mean an unfavourable comparison of other religions with Christianity; at others to mean the collection of superficial similarities between religions. Only the shallow are misled by verbal similarities to the assumption of identity of thought, or by similarities of practice to the assumption of identity of significance. It is always important to examine words and practices in the context of all that is known of the individuals or groups from whom they are taken. It is such an examination which I have undertaken here,

vii

striving to get behind the sayings and the attitudes which fall to be considered to the essential thought of men. To all I have tried to bring the spirit of sympathy and the desire to understand, and at the same time to exercise that critical faculty which is of the essence of all academic study.

The List of Works Consulted makes no profession to be complete, and merely records the titles of the works I have used in the preparation of these essays. As a bibliography of the subject it is most incomplete in the Biblical field, where it would be easiest for me to multiply titles. Yet as these studies are primarily in non-Biblical thought, it is fitting that the literature on the Bible here cited should be restricted. Everywhere I have sought especially to consult texts—in the original where I could read it or could get access to the works, and in a variety of translations where I was forced to rely on translators.

H. H. ROWLEY.

MANCHESTER UNIVERSITY.

CONTENTS

SUBMISSION IN SUFFERING

A COMPARATIVE STUDY OF EASTERN THOUGHT

THE problem of suffering is no new or simple one. It has often been treated as part of the wider problem of evil, both physical and moral, and men have wrestled with its profound mystery, yet without finding any complete or convincing solution. The present study is not a new attempt to reach a solution, and is only incidentally concerned with speculative discussions of the problem. It is primarily concerned with innocent suffering, or suffering that appears to be innocent, and with the response to suffering inculcated in some of the religious systems of the world. It is limited to a study of the relevant material in the principal Asiatic religions. Nor can the treatment even here be anything like exhaustive.

Many religions and religious teachers have taught that the wise response to suffering, whether innocent or deserved, is submission. But that submission differs widely in spirit and in character, and all that is here attempted is to illustrate these differences. Within the teachings of a single religion, or even of a single teacher, some variety may be found. Nor should it occasion any surprise. For the recognition that the problem of suffering is complex, and that its explanation and its purpose may not be in all cases the same, means that the response may rightly be varied in character, even though it is always in terms of submission.

I

There is much in the teaching of the Bible, and especially of the Old Testament, which suggests that there is no innocent suffering, but that justice is invariably done. One of the fundamental teachings of Deuteronomy is that the nation always reaps the just reward of its own policy, and the compilers of the historical books of the Old Testament had this principle ever before their eyes. The prophets, too, proclaimed that the nation that flouted the will of God in its internal social and religious life, and that ignored Him in its foreign policies, was bound to reap a harvest of disaster. In the relentless course of events the will of a righteous God must appear. The object of these teachers, however, was not to make speculative denial of the possibility of innocent suffering, but to issue a practical call to the nation to heed the will of God. Nor can it be denied that there is a substantial measure of truth in their teaching, or that history and experience do in the large support the view that the God Whose hand is seen in human affairs is a God of justice.

In the life of the individual, too, there is much to support the view that righteousness and godliness are profitable, while iniquity brings a harvest of sorrow. Hence amongst the Proverbs, which reflect observation rather than speculation, we read: 'The reward of humility and the fear of the Lord is riches, and honour, and life',[1] and 'He that soweth iniquity shall reap calamity'.[2] Similarly, the Psalmist observes, 'I have been young, and now am old; yet have I not seen the righteous forsaken, nor his seed begging their bread',[3] and 'I have seen the wicked exultant, and rearing himself like a cedar of Lebanon. But I passed by, and lo! he was not; I sought him, but he could not be found'.[4] Nor is it surprising that Babylonian singers struck the same note. 'Who is planning sin, his horn thou destroyest. The man thinking of bribery, his ground is changed. The wicked judge thou causest to see imprisonment. The man receiving bribes, not guiding aright, thou causest to bear punishment.'[5]

In this last utterance there is more than a hint of exact retribution, and frequently we find this principle stated yet more precisely. 'The doings of a man's hand shall be rendered unto him',[6] and 'As thou hast done, it shall be done unto thee'.[7] Similarly, in the New Testament we find, 'They that take the sword shall perish with the sword',[8] and 'Whatsoever a man soweth, that shall he also reap'.[9] With these we may compare

---

[1] Prov. xxii. 4. [2] *Ibid.*, 8. [3] Psalm xxxvii. 25.
[4] *Ibid.*, 35 f., following the text of the Septuagint.
[5] Quoted in Widengren, *The Accadian and Hebrew Psalms of Lamentation as Religious Documents*, 1937, p. 50. [6] Prov. xii. 14.
[7] Obad. 15. [8] Matt. xxvii. 52. [9] Gal. vi. 7.

an Indian proverb, 'Who plants mangoes, mangoes shall he eat; who plants thorn-bushes, thorns shall wound his feet'.[1]

As one of the great principles of the universe, valid in the world of nature and in that of experience, this is undeniably sound. It only becomes mischievous when it is elevated into a hard and invariable law, so that suffering is believed to be the proof of sin. 'Accidents or suffering', says Widengren, in treating of Babylonian religious ideas, 'must have been merited by previous actions'.[2] Iniquity does bring a harvest of trouble, and many are the examples of 'poetic justice'. But it cannot be inferred from the sin that the 'poetic justice' followed, nor inferred from the suffering that a corresponding iniquity entailed it. In the book of Jubilees it is said of Cain that 'his house fell upon him and he died in the midst of his house and he was killed by its stones: for with a stone he had killed Abel, and by a stone he was killed in righteous judgement'.[3] and in 2 Maccabees it is said of Antiochus Epiphanes, 'he that had driven many from their own country into strange lands perished himself in a strange land . . . and he that had cast out a multitude unburied had none to mourn for him, nor had he any funeral at all, or place in the sepulchre of his fathers'.[4] On the other hand it is recorded that the gentle Hillel saw a skull floating on some water, and reversing the process of inference, he observed, 'Because thou drownedst they drowned thee, and at the last they that drowned thee shall be drowned'.[5]

[1] Quoted in Cave, *Redemption, Hindu and Christian*, 1919, p. 181.

[2] *Op. cit.*, p. 52. The only direct evidence he can present (pp. 165 f.) in support of this, however, is a passage whose reading he admits to be very uncertain (cf. p. 331, No. 33): 'I have sinned and therefore I am sick'. Sometimes the sufferer was quite unaware what transgression he could have committed, yet supposed that somehow he must have sinned. Cf. Böhl, in *De godsdiensten der wereld*, ed. by van der Leeuw, i, 2nd ed., 1948, p. 159. For a study of Babylonian texts dealing with the suffering of the innocent, cf. Stamm, *Das Leiden des Unschuldigen in Babylon und Israel*, 1946, pp. 14 ff. The assumption that one's own sufferings must necessarily be the fruit of sin may bring much needless agony, but may also minister to humble submission of spirit; but it is more particularly the assumption that the sufferings of others are the proof of their sin that is fraught with mischief and cruelty.

[3] Jubilees iv. 31. See Charles, *The Book of Jubilees*, 1902, p. 42.

[4] 2 Macc. v. 9 f.

[5] Pirqe Aboth ii. 7. See Danby, *The Mishnah*, 1933, p. 448. The same incident is recorded in the Babylonian Talmud, Sukkah 53*a*; see Slotki, *The Babylonian Talmud translated into English*, Seder Mo'ed, vi, 1938, p. 253.

Any such attempt to maintain the complete and rigid justice of God in all experience breaks on the hard rock of experience, and exposes the very justice of God to question. The friends of Job built on such a foundation, and argued on the ground of Job's misfortunes the enormity of his sins, until Eliphaz roundly charged him with heartless oppression and impious scorn of God.[1] While this may have been the orthodoxy of a particular age, or of particular circles, it was never the orthodoxy of the Old Testament. For innocent suffering was from the first recognized to be one of the facts of experience.

In the earliest of the main documents on which the Pentateuch rests there is recorded the story of Joseph, who for his very piety and faithfulness was cast into a prison. Ultimately, it is true, he attains position and honour, but his sufferings are still left without explanation in terms of justice. Moreover, Israel's traditions told how innocent suffering, unredressed by subsequent honour, made its appearance in the first human family in the murder of Abel. Further, prophets continually complained of the sufferings brought on the innocent by the oppression of the wicked, and psalmists in their hours of pain and sorrow repeatedly protested their innocence. When, therefore, the book of Job maintained that there is innocent suffering in the world, it was not propounding any new doctrine, but only enunciating afresh what experience had always proclaimed, and what had only been obscured by a false theological deduction from the justice of God.

In the ancient Chinese writings we frequently meet with statements that would seem to imply that justice is invariably meted out to men, and that all suffering is self-entailed. 'Good and evil do not wrongly befall men', we read in the Shu Ching,[2]

For much other Rabbinical material on the principle of retribution, see Schechter, *Studies in Judaism*, First Series, 1938 reprint, pp. 213 ff., and Bonsirven, *Le Judaïsme palestinien au temps de Jésus-Christ*, ii, 1935, pp. 53 ff.

[1] Job xxii. 5 ff.

[2] Shu Ching IV, Book VI, ii. 5, translation of Legge (*The Chinese Classics*, iii, Part i, 1865, p. 216). Couvreur (*Chou Ching*, 1916, p. 110–numbered III, vi. 5) renders: 'Les biens et les maux ne descendent pas sur les hommes suivant le caprice du hasard; mais le ciel les distribue suivant les mérites'. Old (*The Shu King*, 1904, p. 102–numbered III, vii) has 'It is by no means that success and failure are indiscriminately dispensed to mankind, but Heaven sends down distress and blessings according to merit'.

the oldest of the Chinese classics,[1] 'because Heaven sends down misery or happiness according to their conduct'. Again, 'In its inspection of men below, Heaven's first consideration is of their righteousness; and it bestows on them accordingly length of years or the contrary. Heaven does not cut short men's lives;—they bring them to an end themselves';[2] and 'There is not any cruel oppression of Heaven; people themselves accelerate their guilt and its punishment.'[3]

Combined with this, however, we find the recognition of the fact that the innocent are often involved in the calamities brought down by the guilty. 'The king of Hsia extinguished his virtue and played the tyrant, extending his oppression over you, the people of the myriad regions. Suffering from his cruel injuries, and unable to endure the wormwood and poison, you protested with one accord your innocence to the spirits of heaven and earth. The way of Heaven is to bless the good and to punish the bad. It sent down calamities on the House of Hsia, to make manifest its crimes.'[4] In the Shih Ching, too, we find complaints against the injustices that prevailed in the affairs of men:

> Beneath the great wide Heaven
> The king owns every land.
> Go round each border—everywhere
> His servants at his bidding stand.
> Scant justice yet to me his chiefs have shown;
> For I must work as were all wit my own. . . .

[1] Cf. Forke, *Geschichte der alten chinesischen Philosophie*, 1927, p. 6. Modern study has, however, detracted something from its antiquity. Cf. E. R. Hughes, *Chinese Philosophy in Classical Times*, 1942, p. 3.

[2] Shu Ching IV, Book IX, 3 (Legge, i, p. 264). Couvreur (*op. cit.*, p. 137) numbers the passage III, ix. 3. Old (*op. cit.*, p. 132) numbers it III, xv. His rendering begins: 'Although Heaven judges the inferior people, and according to their handiwork determines to them either long life or short. . . .' The word 'inferior' gives a wrong impression to the English reader, and still more the rendering 'handiwork'. The Chinese here has the word *i*, which is normally rendered *righteousness*.

[3] Shu Ching V, Book X, 11 (Legge, ii. p. 409). Couvreur (*op. cit.*, pp. 208 f.) numbers IV, x. 11, while Old (*op. cit.*, p. 201) numbers IV, xii.

[4] Shu Ching IV, Book III, ii. 3 (Legge, i, p. 186). Couvreur (*op. cit.*, pp. 94 f.) numbers III, iii. 3, and Old (*op. cit.*, p. 82) numbers III, iii. The latter's rendering is again questionable. He has: 'The way of Heaven, which blesses the good and punishes the wicked, has brought down calamities on Hia in order to illustrate his wickedness', where *illustrate* does not convey the meaning of the Chinese *chang*. Cf. Couvreur: 'il a . . . montré par là que ce prince était coupable'.

Some live content in tranquil ease;
Some for their country their full vigour spend.
Some rest recumbent on their beds;
And some have journeyings that know no end.

Some know not clamours and alarms;[1]
And some have miserable toil and pain.
Some idly roost, or lie supine;
Some serve their king, and scarcely bear the strain.[2]

Or again:

Don't escort the big chariot;
You will only make yourself dusty.
Don't think about the sorrows of the world;
You will only make yourself wretched.

Don't escort the big chariot;
You won't be able to see for dust.
Don't think about the sorrows of the world;
Or you will never escape from your despair.[3]

Don't escort the big chariot;
You'll be stifled with dust.
Don't think about the sorrows of the world;
You will only load yourself with care.[4]

Mencius once observed, 'Calamity and happiness in all cases are men's own seeking',[5] and he frequently taught, with the same moral earnestness as Deuteronomy and the Old Testament prophets, that evil policies must bring a harvest of trouble. To King Hsüan, of Ch'i, he once asserted that his policy was more foolish than climbing a tree to look for fish. 'If you climb a tree to look for fish', he said, ' although you

[1] Waley (*The Book of Songs*, 1937, p. 321) renders this line, 'Some senselessly yell and bawl', taking the words *pu chih* adverbially. Legge (*The Chinese Classics*, iv, 1871, Part ii, p. 361) and Couvreur (*Cheu King*, 3rd ed., 1934, p. 270) take them as Jennings above. Karlgren (*The Book of Odes*, 1950, p. 158) renders 'Some never hear any calling or summons.'

[2] Shih Ching II, vi. 1, translation of Jennings (*The Shi King*, 1891, pp. 238 f.).

[3] Legge (*op. cit.*, p. 363) renders 'You will not emerge from imperfect views', and Jennings (*op. cit.*, p. 239), similarly, 'That can lead to nought more bright'; while Couvreur (*op. cit.*, p. 271) has: 'Votre intelligence en serait troublée, obscurcie'. Karlgren (*loc. cit.*) renders 'You will not be able to come out in the light'.

[4] Shih Ching II, vi. 2, translation of Waley (*op. cit.*, p. 321).

[5] Mencius II, i. 4, translation of Legge (*op. cit.*, ii, 1861, p. 74; 2nd ed., 1895, p. 198).

do not get the fish, you will not suffer any subsequent calamity. But doing what you do to seek for what you desire, doing it moreover with all your heart, you will assuredly afterwards meet with calamities.'[1] Twice Mencius quoted[2] a passage from the Shu Ching,[3] which is also quoted in the Li Chi:[4] 'Calamities sent by Heaven may be avoided, but from calamities brought on by oneself there is no escape'.

Yet Mencius no more than Deuteronomy supposed that justice is invariably done in the affairs of men. He was often moved with the thought of the sufferings of the innocent folk through the evil policy of the state, and could describe them hearing the royal music with aching heads, and knit brows, and saying to one another, 'That's how our king likes his music! But why does he reduce us to this extremity of distress? Fathers and sons cannot see one another. Elder brothers and younger brothers, wives and children, are separated and scattered abroad.'[5]

Hsün-tzŭ, who led the right wing of Confucianism,[6] and who flourished slightly later than Mencius, also taught that calamity and happiness are self-attained, but saved the accuracy of his observation by carrying his realm of absolute justice beyond the eye of man. 'The person who has tried to see into man's

[1] Mencius I, i. 7, translation of Legge (*op. cit.*, ii, pp. 21 f.; 2nd ed., pp. 145 f.).

[2] Mencius II, i. 4 (Legge, *ibid.*, p. 75; 2nd ed., p. 199) and IV, i. 8 (Legge, *ibid.*, p. 175; 2nd ed., p. 299).

[3] Shu Ching IV, Book V, ii. 3 (Legge, *op. cit.*, iii, 1865, Part i, p. 207).

[4] Li Chi xxx. 16. For text and translation cf. Couvreur, *Li Ki*, ii, 1899, p. 526; for translation only, see Legge, *Sacred Books of the East*, xxviii, 1885, p. 359.

[5] Mencius I, ii. 1, translation of Legge (*op. cit.*, ii, pp. 27 f.; 2nd ed., pp. 151 f.). Wilhelm (*Mong Dsi*, 1921, p. 12) renders: 'Weshalb doch bringt die Liebe unseres Königs zur Musik uns in diese äusserste Not, also dass Vater und Sohn sich nimmer sehen, dass Brüder, Weib und Kind getrennt und zerstreut sind?' Cf. Lyall, *Mencius*, 1932, p. 17.

[6] Cf. Forke, *Geschichte der alten chinesischen Philosophie*, 1927, p. 218: 'Hsün-tse hat auf die Überlieferung und Erklärung der konfuzianischen Klassiker einen grossen Einfluss ausgeübt, jedenfalls einen sehr viel grösseren als Mencius.' E. R. Hughes, *Chinese Philosophy in Classical Times*, 1942, p. 226, observes that Hsün-tzŭ 'was in many respects the greatest, as he was in all respects the most philosophical, of the Confucianists.' Cf. E. R. and K. Hughes, *Religion in China*, 1950, p. 38: 'There can be no question but that Hsün Ch'ing reinforced that side of Confucianism which tended to rationalistic humanism'.

hidden parts . . . knows that there is no one who in his purposes despises moral principles, who is not inwardly anxious, . . . and inwardly fearful. When the mind is anxious and fearful, though the mouth be holding meat, it will not recognize the flavour thereof; though the ears hear bells and drums, they will not recognize the sound thereof; . . . for he may enjoy the goodness of all things, yet he cannot be contented.'[1] This is something quite other than the idea that inner worth and outer fortunes are invariably matched. Like the teaching of Deuteronomy, it is motivated by the practical desire to inculcate virtue but it substitutes for the material pragmatism of Deuteronomy the thought of the inner working of conscience, with its canker gnawing at the heart of the prosperity of the wicked.

Again Mo-tzŭ, the founder of a heretical school, sometimes spoke as if absolute justice was wrought in human experience. 'When the emperor practises virtue Heaven rewards; when the emperor does evil Heaven punishes.'[2] 'When man does not do what Heaven desires, but does what Heaven abominates, Heaven will also not do what man desires, but do what he abominates. What man abominates are disease and calamities. Therefore not to do what Heaven desires but to do what it abominates is to lead the multitudes in the world to calamity.'[3] Yet he was far from failing to recognize that the sphere of injustice and of innocent suffering is wide. 'When the emperor has done good, Heaven rewards him. When the emperor has committed wrong, Heaven punishes him. When the emperor is unjust in reward and punishment and not judicious in hearing lawsuits, Heaven visits him with disease and calamities, and frost and dew will be untimely.'[4]

It should, however, be observed that while the purpose of such teachings, whether in Israel or in China, was the encouragement of virtue, they were liable to have religious consequences

---

[1] Hsün-tzŭ xxii. 14, translation of Dubs (*The Works of Hsüntze*, 1928, p. 298).

[2] Mo-tzŭ xxvii, translation of Mei (*The Ethical and Political Works of Motse*, 1929, p. 141).

[3] Mo-tzŭ xxvii (Mei, p. 144). Cf. Forke, *Mê Ti*, 1922, p. 324. The version of Tomkinson (*The Social Teachings of Meh Tse*, 1927, p. 89) is widely different.   [4] Mo-tzŭ xxviii (Mei, p. 152).

quite other than those designed. He upon whom misfortune and suffering came might acknowledge that it fell deservedly upon him, and humble himself before God, but he to whom prosperity came, unmarred by the working of an evil conscience, would be liable to indulge in self-righteous pride, and to regard himself as favoured by God because of his moral worth. Submission in suffering, but self-righteousness in prosperity, would be apt to follow—and, as Xenophon observes, 'It seems harder to find a man who can bear good fortune well than one who can bear misfortune well'.[1]

Moreover, it offered little message of comfort to the innocent sufferer. For while in its denunciation of oppression it recognized the possibility of innocent suffering, it did not stress this aspect to the sufferer. To him the suffering brought only the message of guilt. If he was conscious of his sin, he might accept his suffering with submission and repentance, but if he was not conscious of it, he could only be tortured with doubt as to what he had done. In the text known as 'The Babylonian Job' the sufferer, who describes his agonies in detail, is conscious of his piety and uprightness. 'I took thought only for prayers and supplication. Prayer was my rule, sacrifice my order, the day of God's honouring was my heart's joy.'[2] He can only torture himself with the thought that what he had taken to be well-pleasing to his god was for some wholly inscrutable reason offensive. 'That which seemeth good to oneself is evil with God, and that which in one's heart is rejected is good with God. Who can understand the counsel of the gods in heaven? The plan of the gods full of darkness, who shall establish it? How shall pale-faced men understand the ways of the gods?'[3] But this is scarcely distinguishable from the view that suffering is the arbitrary dispensation of fate. It accepts the calamity with submission as somehow deserved, but deserved only by the

---

[1] *Cyropaedia* VIII, iv. 14, translation of Miller (*Xenophon's Cyropaedia* (Loeb Library), ii, 1914, pp. 382 f.).

[2] See Rogers, *Cuneiform Parallels to the Old Testament*, 1912, p. 166 ; H. Gressmann, *Altorientalische Texte zum Alten Testament*, 2nd ed., 1926, p. 275; Jean, *Le Milieu Biblique*, ii, 1923, p. 249; Langdon, *Babylonian Wisdom*, 1923, pp. 39 f.; Pritchard, *Ancient Near Eastern Texts relating to the Old Testament*, 1950, p. 435 *a*.

[3] See Rogers, p. 167; Gressmann, p. 275; Jean, p. 249; or Langdon, p. 41.

workings of an arbitrary and incomprehensible standard, and it can lead to no amendment of spirit whereby the divine will may be better satisfied.[1]

II

Some Jewish Rabbis seized on the verse 'visiting the iniquity of the fathers upon the children, and upon the children's children',[2] as offering the explanation of innocent suffering. Thus we read, 'Moses said before God, "Lord of the world, why is there a righteous man who enjoys prosperity, and a righteous man who is afflicted with adversity? Why is there a wicked man who enjoys prosperity, and a wicked man who is afflicted with adversity?" He replied, "Moses, the righteous man who enjoys prosperity is the righteous son of a righteous father; the righteous man who is afflicted with adversity is the righteous son of a wicked father; the wicked man who enjoys prosperity is the wicked son of a righteous father; the wicked man who is afflicted with adversity is the wicked son of a wicked father".'[3]

In the Indian Laws of Manu we find the same extension of the working of the principle of retributive justice to include the children. 'If the punishment falls not on the offender himself, it falls on his sons; if not on the sons, at least on the grandsons.'[4]

This shifting of responsibility for troubles to the previous generation is found in the period of Jeremiah and Ezekiel, and it called forth the protest of both prophets. 'Our fathers have sinned, and are not; and we have borne their iniquities', moaned the people.[5] 'They shall say no more, The fathers have eaten sour grapes, and the children's teeth are set on edge. But every one shall die for his own iniquity',[6] cried Jeremiah, and with this may be compared Ezekiel's 'Behold, all souls are

---

[1] For a comparison between Job and the Babylonian ideas, cf. Stamm, *Das Leiden des Unschuldigen in Babylon und Israel*, 1946, p. 79, where the difference is traced to the richer view of God in Israel.

[2] Exod. xxxiv. 7.

[3] Babylonian Talmud, Berachoth 7*a* (cf. Cohen, *The Babylonian Talmūd*: *Tractate Berākōt*, 1921, p. 38).

[4] Laws of Manu iv. 173, translation of Bühler (*Sacred Books of the East*, xxv, 1886, p. 156).

[5] Lam. v. 7.   [6] Jer. xxxi. 29 f.

mine; as the soul of the father, so also the soul of the son is mine: the soul that sinneth, it shall die'.[1] In their desire to bring home to the conscience of their own generation their responsibility for their own plight, they formulated what could only be understood as the principle of rigid individual retribution.

In the New Testament we find both their view and the one they contested rejected as canons of judgement. 'Now there were some present . . . which told him of the Galilæans, whose blood Pilate had mingled with their sacrifices. And he answered and said unto them, Think ye that these Galilæans were sinners above all the Galilæans, because they have suffered these things? I tell you, Nay . . . Or those eighteen, upon whom the tower in Siloam fell, think ye that they were offenders above all the men that dwell in Jerusalem? I tell you, Nay.'[2] 'And his disciples asked him, saying, Rabbi, who did sin, this man or his parents, that he should be born blind? Jesus answered, Neither did this man sin, nor his parents.'[3]

Actually, of course, there is a measure of truth in both these rejected views. There is, as has been said, a principle of retribution in the world, and iniquity does bring a harvest of sorrow. It is also true that children suffer for the sins of their fathers. But neither principle is so rigid in its working, or so sufficient as a solution of the problem of evil, that it can be inferred from a particular suffering that it is the just reward of the individual's sin, or the sin of his parents.

To our modern individualism there may seem something inconsistent with the principle of justice in the children paying for the sins of their fathers, though life abounds with examples of it. In truth, we are not merely individuals, but members of a society, linked in countless ways to those who have preceded us and to those who will follow us, as well as to our contemporaries, and justice is wider than retribution. The entail of the father's sins may fall upon the children, but so too will much that the fathers have achieved in culture and character become the inheritance of the children, to be preserved or squandered. But Israel, with its emphasis rather on the social character of man, was not troubled by the thought of the

---

[1] Ezek. xviii. 4.   [2] Luke xiii. 1.   [3] John ix. 2 f.

injustice of this principle, and it was not to counteract any
such speculative difficulty that the prophets spoke. It was
rather to counteract the paralysing quality of the submissiveness to which this view led. It bred a submissiveness touched
with smugness in those who could avoid the troubles they saw
about to descend on others, and in those who bore the troubles
a sense of impotence in the face of sorrows for which they felt
no responsibility, yet which they somehow believed to be
deserved. When Hezekiah was told that his treasures should be
carried away to Babylon, and his children made eunuchs in
the service of an alien king, he replied, 'Good is the word of
the Lord', and added, 'Is it not so, if peace and truth shall be
in my days?';[1] while the dull hopelessness of those who believed
they were paying for their fathers' sins is well exemplified in
Lamentations v, with its final cry, 'Thou hast utterly rejected
us, Thou art very wroth against us'.[2]

III

In Indian thought a rigid causal nexus between sin and
suffering is postulated, but since it is linked with the doctrine
of metempsychosis the sin and its penalty may not fall within
the span of the same incarnation. In this way the problem that
confronted the 'Babylonian Job' is eliminated. Absolute justice
is held to be meted out to all, and since the suffering in one
incarnation may be the fruit of the sin in another, the absence
of any consciousness of the sin is of no moment. The doctrine
therefore contains both a warning against iniquity and a
message of judgement to every sufferer. The man upon whom
calamity and misfortune fall has no complaint against God,
and none against his fellow-men. He is but paying the just
price of his own misdeeds, in this or a former life.

It is in the Upaniṣads that this doctrine of *karma*[3] is first

---

[1] 2 Kings xx. 19=Isa. xxxix. 8.   [2] Lam. v. 22.

[3] Farquhar, *The Crown of Hinduism*, 1913, p. 137, thus defines *karma*:
'The word *karma* means literally action, but in the doctrine means the inevitable working out of action in new life. The idea is that a man's body,
character, capacities, and temperament, his birth, wealth, and station, and
the whole of his experience in life, whether of happiness or of sorrow, together
form the just recompense for his deeds, good and bad, done in earlier existences. Every act necessarily works itself out in retribution in another birth.

enunciated, and the word appears for the first time on the lips of Yājñavalkya,[1] concerning whom Geden says, ' If the name represents a real individuality, and is not merely a title under whose shelter many convergent thoughts and reasonings have found expression, Yājñavalkya may claim a place with the greatest thinkers of the world or of any age.'[2] Belief in *saṁsāra*, or the round of rebirths, is enunciated more clearly in Chhāndogya v. 3-10, and in Bṛhadāraṇyaka vi. 2.[3] In the latter passage it is said that 'those who know' are freed from the round of rebirths. 'A spirit comes near them, and leads them to the worlds of the Brahman. In these worlds of Brahman they dwell exalted for ages. There is no returning for them.'[4] On the other hand, 'they who conquer the worlds by means of sacrifice, charity, and austerity' pass through various states, and then 'when this (the result of their good works on earth) ceases, they return again to the ether, from ether to the air, from the air to rain, from rain to the earth. And when they have reached the earth, they become food, they are offered again in the altar-fire, which is man, and thence are born in

The expiation works itself out not only in the man's passive experience (*bhoktṛitvam*) but in his actions also (*kartṛitvam*). Then these new actions form new *karma*, which must necessarily be expiated in another existence.' Ranade (*A Constructive Survey of Upanishadic Philosophy*, 1926, pp. 145 ff.) claims that traces of the doctrine are to be found in the Vedas, but recognizes that its explicit formulation is first found in the Upaniṣads, and in particular in the *locus classicus* cited in the text above. Both McKenzie (*Hindu Ethics*, 1922, p. 15) and Griswold (*The Religion of the Ṛigveda*, 1923, p. 318) agree that the germ of the doctrine is found in the Ṛigveda. In treating of the Vedas, Dasgupta (*History of Indian Philosophy*, i, 2nd ed., 1932, p. 22) says: 'Sacrifice was regarded as almost the only kind of duty, and it was also called *karma* or *kriya*'. The word *karma* here is not used in the sense it has in the Upaniṣads and later literature (cf. Griswold, *op. cit.*, p. 340).

[1] Bṛhadāraṇyaka iii. 2 (see *Sacred Books of the East*, xv, 1900, p. 127, or Hume, *The Thirteen Principal Upanishads*, 2nd ed., 1934, p. 110). Deussen (*The System of the Vedânta*, 1912, p. 375) says that in this passage 'we seem to have the very birth of the doctrine of transmigration before our eyes'. Dasgupta, however, says there is fairly conclusive evidence that the transmigration doctrine had originated among the Kṣattriyas (*op. cit.*, p. 34; cf. Hume, *op. cit.*, p. 54).

[2] Hastings' *Encyclopædia of Religion and Ethics*, xii, 1921, p. 542b.

[3] See *Sacred Books of the East*, i, 1879, pp. 76 ff., and xv, pp. 204 ff. (translated by Max Müller), or Hume, *op. cit.*, pp. 230 ff., 160 ff.

[4] Hume, *op. cit.*, p. 163, renders: 'A Person consisting of mind goes to those regions of lightning and conducts them to the Brahma-worlds. In those Brahma-worlds they dwell for long extents. Of these there is no return.'

the fire of woman. Thus they rise up towards the worlds, and
go the same round as before.' Similarly in Kaṭha iii. 7 f.:[1] 'He
who has no understanding, who is unmindful and always
impure, never reaches that place, but enters into the round
of rebirths. But he who has understanding, who is mindful and
always pure, reaches indeed that place, from whence he is not
born again.'

Deeply embedded in all this is the belief that life itself is
evil, and that the great end of being is to get out of life, as an
individual existence, and to be absorbed in the great under-
lying reality behind all the illusion of phenomena. 'Suffering
cannot be abolished' says Radhakrishnan,[2] 'so long as spiritual
life has to be lived under human conditions. Until the whole
being is made an offering to God, the process of gradual rise
through suffering cannot cease. "Man verily is the sacrifice"
says the Upaniṣad. Life is a perpetual dying till we are face
to face with God. Life is a place of torment, where the human
spirit writhes to possess the eternal. Veil after veil is to be
withdrawn. The illusions of life are to be torn away and our
cherished dreams dispersed before the life divine can be
reached.'

Until that goal is reached man is caught in the wheel of
saṁsāra, and his fate is self-determined. 'He binds his Self by
his Self, as a bird with a net, and overcome afterwards by the
fruits of what he has done, he enters on a good or bad birth.'[3]
'By means of thoughts, touching, seeing, and passions the incarnate Self assumes successively in various places forms, in
accordance with his deeds, just as the body grows when food
and drink are poured into it. That incarnate Self, according to
his own qualities, chooses many shapes, coarse or subtile, and

[1] *Sacred Books of the East*, xv, p. 13. Cf. Hume, *op. cit.*, p. 352, Rawson,
The Kaṭha Upaniṣad, 1934, p. 123, and Otto, *Die Kaṭha-Upanishad*, 1936,
pp. 19 f. 'The whole of the Kaṭha', says Ranade (*op. cit.*, p. 28), 'is surcharged
with lofty ideas about the Immortality of the Soul, as well as suggestions for
the practical attainment of Ātman'. For a French translation of a part of the
Kaṭha Upaniṣad by Masson-Oursel, cf. *Histoire générale des religions*, iii,
1945, pp. 25 ff.

[2] *Indian Philosophy*, i, 1929, p. 244 = *The Philosophy of the Upaniṣads*,
1924, p. 120.

[3] Maitrāyaṇīya iii. 2 (*Sacred Books of the East*, xv, p. 237; cf. Hume, *op.
cit.*, p. 418).

having himself caused his union with them, he is seen as another and another, through the qualities of his acts, and through the qualities of his body.'[1]

'According to the principle of *karma*', says Radhakrishnan again,[2] 'there is nothing uncertain or capricious in the moral world. We reap what we sow. The good seed brings a harvest of good, the evil of evil. Every little action has its effect on character. . . . We cannot arrest the process of moral evolution any more than we can stay the sweep of the tides or the course of the stars. The attempt to overleap the law of *karma* is as futile as the attempt to leap over one's shadow. It is the psychological principle that our life carries within it a record that time cannot blur or death erase.'

Examples of the same teaching from the later literature could be multiplied. 'Influenced by acts men are placed in different situations of life. Acts, therefore, produce consequences that are inevitable: emancipation is desired from mere folly. . . . The Supreme Lord and ordainer of all ordaineth everything in respect of the weal and woe, the happiness and misery, of all creatures, even prior to their births, guided by the acts of each, which are even like a seed. . . . As a wooden doll is made to move its limbs by the wire-puller, so are creatures made to work by the Lord of all. . . . Like a bird tied with a string, every creature is dependent on God. . . . Like a pearl on a string, or a bull held fast by the cord passing through its nose . . . every creature followeth the command of the Creator.'[3] 'The diseases from which men suffer are undoubtedly the result of their own *karma*. . . . Every man is thus helpless, overcome by misery and illusion, and again and again tossed and overpowered by the powerful current of his own *karma*. . . . The actions done in a previous existence are seen to fructify in our present life. . . . In the world of men no man reaps the consequences of another man's *karma*. Whatever one does, he is sure to reap the consequences thereof; for the

---

[1] Śvetāśvatara v. 11 f. (*Sacred Books of the East*, xv, pp. 258 f.; cf. Hume, *op. cit.*, p. 407).

[2] *Indian Philosophy*, i, pp. 244 f. = *Philosophy of the Upaniṣads*, pp. 120 f.

[3] Mahābhārata, Vana Parva xxx, translation of Pratāpa Chandra Rāy (1884, pp. 86 f.).

consequences of the *karma* that is once done, can never be obviated.'[1] 'Man with his subtle original body created by God, lays up a great store of virtue and vice. After death he quits his frail body and is immediately born again in another order of beings. He never remains non-existent for a single moment. In his new life, his actions follow him invariably as his shadow, and fructifying makes his destiny happy or miserable. The wise man, by his spiritual insight, knows all creatures to be bound to an immutable destiny by the destroyer, and incapable of resisting the fruition of his actions in good or evil fortune.'[2] 'Amongst creatures, the measure of weal or woe is dependent on the acts of a previous life. Indeed, every creature comes into the world, taking with him his own measure of weal and woe. The son is not bound by the acts of the sire, or the sire by those of the son. Bound by their own acts good and bad, all have to travel by this common road.'[3]

This rigid determinism would seem calculated to stifle all moral effort. Such is not the case, however. Just as the Jewish Rabbi Akiba could say, 'All is foreseen, but freedom of choice is given',[4] and Christian theologians could combine belief in predestination and freewill, so Hindu philosophy could combine this determinism with faith in the power of moral initiative. '*Karma* rightly understood', says Radhakrishnan,[5] 'does not fetter the mind or chain the will. . . . Man is not a mere product of nature. He is mightier than his *karma*. . . . The law of *karma*, which rules the lower nature of man, has nothing to do with the spiritual in him. The infinite in man helps him to transcend the limitations of the finite. The essence of the

---

[1] Mahābhārata, Vana Parva ccix (pp. 647 f.).

[2] *Ibid.*, clxxxiii (p. 544).

[3] *Ibid.*, Çanti Parva cliii, translation of Pratāpa Chandra Rāy (i, 1890, p. 502).

[4] Pirqe Aboth ii. 16, translation of Danby (*The Mishnah*, p. 452).

[5] *Indian Philosophy*, i, p. 246 = *Philosophy of the Upaniṣads*, p. 122. So, too, in the Jaina view, *karma* is not incompatible with freedom. Cf. Dasgupta (*History of Indian Philosophy*, i, p. 206): 'It may not be out of place to mention that though the *karmas* of man are constantly determining him in various ways, yet there is in him infinite capacity or power for right action, so that *karma* can never subdue this freedom and infinite capacity, though this may be suppressed from time to time by the influence of *karma*. It is thus that by an exercise of this power man can overcome all *karma* and become finally iberated'.

spirit is freedom. . . . Man oscillates between nature and spirit, and so is subject to both freedom and necessity.'

Were this not so, Hindu philosophy would offer only an explanation of what is, and not a way of escape to what may be. For no greater futility could be imagined than the unfolding to men of the path that leads through virtue to release from the weary round of rebirths, if entrance upon that path were irrevocably barred to them. Nor could a mere determinism offer an adequate explanation even of the present. For if the iniquity of yesterday determined the sorrow of to-day, and left man no freedom to amend his way for a fairer morrow, the iniquity of yesterday would be left with no explanation beyond an endless chain of necessity, for which the self could not be ultimately responsible. In the very doctrine that to-day's experience of life, with all its miseries, is the fruit of the self's initiative in the past, there is implied the power of initiative to-day.[1] In the passage already referred to, in which Yājñavalka first uses the word *karma*, it is followed by the observation, 'a man becomes good by good work, and bad by bad work'.[2] Goodness is therefore a matter of becoming, and not merely of being. So too, in Chhāndogya v. 10,[3] immediately after it has been said that 'those whose conduct has been good will quickly attain some good birth, the birth of a Brāhmaṇa, or a Kshatriya, or a Vaiśya; but those whose conduct has been evil will quickly attain an evil birth, the birth of a dog, or a hog, or a Chaṇḍāla', it is added, 'Hence let a man take care to himself'. Similarly, in the later Mahābhārata[4] we read: 'Passing through thousands of births . . . our spirits wander about, secured by the fetters of our own *karma*. . . .

[1] This is equally true of Buddhism. Cf. Tachibana, *The Ethics of Buddhism.* 1926, pp. 90 ff., esp. p. 92: 'Our present different births are the results of the accumulated Kammas performed in our previous existences, and our present different dispositions are also predestined by our previous Kammas, the Buddhist doctrine of Kamma on the one hand being a fatalism; but at the same time we must understand that we are moulding our own fate in the next birth through our actions, because we are free to do or not to do as we please.' Macnicol (*Indian Theism from the Vedic to the Muhammadan Period*, 1915, pp. 229 ff.) observes that in the introduction of the element of ethical freedom a nobler ethical order is correcting the less noble legal one.

[2] *Sacred Books of the East*, xv, p. 127. Cf. Hume, *op. cit.*, p. 110.

[3] *Sacred Books of the East*, i, pp. 82 f. Cf. Hume, *op. cit.*, p. 233.

[4] Vana Parva ccix (tr. of Pratāpa Chandra Rāy, pp. 648 f.).

If, casting off their fetters, they purify themselves by their
actions . . . they attain the Elysian regions.' Or again,
'One sinful act proceeds from another. Therefore . . . avoid
all evil acts and do not thus set thy heart upon grief.'[1]

Nevertheless, Radhakrishnan is surely going much too far
when he says:[2] 'There is no doctrine that is so valuable in life
and conduct as the *karma* theory. Whatever happens to us in
this life we have to submit in meek resignation, for it is the
result of our past doings. Yet the future is in our power, and
we can work with hope and confidence. *Karma* inspires hope
for the future and resignation to the past. It makes men feel
that the things of the world, its fortunes and failures, do not
touch the dignity of the soul.'

It lies beyond the scope of this paper to examine the effect
of the *karma* doctrine on social service. On this Cave observes:[3]
'The quiescent compassion we feel for the criminal justly
expiating his crimes is very different from the energetic help
we desire to render to the unfortunate; but, if the karmic view
be true, the leper and the cripple, the blind and the bereaved,
are all to be regarded as criminals undergoing punishment for
misdeeds done in former births'.[4] Social service is still possible,
indeed, just as social service amongst those who are expiating
crimes committed in this life is possible. But it means that all
ministry to the suffering is performed in the spirit of Job's
friends, who came to express their sympathy, but whose ministry
was destroyed for him by their inner condemnation of him.[5]

[1] Çanti Parva xxxiii (tr. of Pratāpa Chandra Rāy, i, p. 100).
[2] *Indian Philosophy*, i, p. 249 = *Philosophy of the Upaniṣads*, p. 125.
[3] *Redemption, Hindu and Christian*, 1919, p. 186.
[4] Cf. C. Humphreys, *Karma and Rebirth*, 1943, p. 28: 'He who suffers
deserves his suffering'. This statement stands in a book which is written to
commend the 'sweet reasonableness' of the law of Karma (p. 8), and which
claims that its teaching 'is not opposed to Christianity, nor even incompatible
with it' (p. 33). The sufficient answer to this is given in words written much
earlier by Mensching (*Die Bedeutung des Leidens im Buddhismus und Christentum*, 2nd ed., 1930, p. 31): 'Christi Leiden ist nicht Strafleiden, sondern ist das
notwendige Resultat des Zusammentreffens von Gott und Welt innerhalb
der Sphäre des Irdischen, es ist daher Symptom einerseits für die Gottes-
wirklichkeit in Christus—denn sonst hätte die Welt nicht so reagiert—und
andererseits für die Wesenart der Welt, die stets und notwendig so reagiert'.
[5] Cf. McKenzie, *Hindu Ethics*, 1922, p. 227: 'There can be little doubt
that it is this belief, more than any other one factor, that is responsible for
the backwardness of the people of India in the work of ministering to the

More germane to our purpose is it to consider the nature of the submission to which this doctrine leads the sufferer. In the nature of the case he cannot know what is the sin for which he is suffering, since there is no nexus of consciousness between one incarnation and another "Between one life and another there is a persisting identity', says Radhakrishnan,[1] 'though our consciousness may not testify to it. This is not a great weakness, since large portions of human life tend sometimes to be forgotten.' This cannot be denied. One of the principles on which psychoanalysis works is that long-forgotten experiences leave their mark on us, both physically and psychically. Here, however, there is an ascertainable continuum of experience connecting the forgotten experience with the self of to-day. The forgotten experience may have passed altogether out of consciousness, but it exists in the subconscious, whence it must be recalled into consciousness as the condition of healing. Moreover, there can be no doubt that there is a continuum of individuality between the self of the forgotten experience and the self of to-day. But in what sense can an ego that has no physical or psychical continuity with my ego to-day be one with me, so that I can recognize my sufferings to be the just penalty of its sins? And how can there be the sense of guilt where there is no knowledge of the sin? Great is the stress laid in the Upaniṣads on the importance of knowing, and knowledge is declared to be the key to release. Yet the sin that entails the burden from which release is to be sought is for ever unknowable, and the whole chain hangs from a link which is not.

Knowledge, then, is built on faith, but not on faith in God. It is faith in a burden of guilt which has somehow devolved upon one from a past which is not demonstrably his, a guilt whose nature he can never know though he is inexorably called upon to expiate it, a guilt of which he can never truly repent since its very character is unknown.

The believer in *karma* bears his sufferings with submission,

unfortunate.' Cf. *ibid.*, p. 224: 'The doctrine of *karma* makes our admiration of pain and suffering endured by men for the sake of others absurd. It leaves no place for what has been called vicarious suffering, such as is exemplified in ordinary life in the bearing by men of one another's burdens, and which is seen in its most sublime form in the Cross of Christ.'

[1] *Indian Philosophy*, i, p. 251 = *Philosophy of the Upaniṣads*, p. 127.

indeed, because he believes they are the just reward of his guilt.
But his belief offers him no hope save in another life, which
will be no more truly his than the life whose sins he is now
expiating is his. 'Be it happiness or be it sorrow that comes
upon creatures' we read in the Mahābhārata,[1] 'it should be
enjoyed or borne without elation or depression. There is no
method of escape from them.' He must drink to the full the
cup determined for him by the *karma* which is his inheritance,
while the future for which he can work with hope and confidence is in no demonstrable sense his, and the rigid justice
of *karma* dissolves into injustice, as complete as if John Jones
were hanged for the crime of Fred Smith on the fiction that
he was Fred Smith, though no evidence of identity was offered.
Indeed, it is much farther from justice than this. For here John
Jones is not informed of the nature of the crime he is supposed
to have committed, nor even given the name of the supposed
alias under which he is presumed to have committed it.[2] It is
merely presented as a dogma, unsupported and unsupport-
able by evidence, that there is identity. 'All that the living
agent does is to go from one body unto another. That which
is called death is only the dissolution of the body. It is thus
that the Soul, wrapped in diverse forms, migrates from form to
form, unseen and unnoticed by others.'[3] 'As a man casting off
his worn-out clothes takes other new ones, so the embodied
one, casting off its worn-out bodies, enters others that are
new.'[4]

So far from the *karma* doctrine surpassing in value all other
doctrine, it falls grievously short by its over-simplification of
the problem of suffering as due to a single cause operating in a
single manner in every case, and by the cruelty of its universal
condemnation of the wretched as wicked in proportion to their
wretchedness, making, as Cave says,[5] 'of the unhappy the

---

[1] Çanti Parva xxviii, translation of Pratāpa Chandra Rāy (i, 1890, p. 75).

[2] Cf. Streeter, *The Buddha and the Christ*, 1932, p. 281: 'It is not obvious
how a penalty can be morally justified if the individual is entirely unaware of
the actual offence for which it has been inflicted, it having been committed
in a previous existence of which he has no recollection'.

[3] Mahābhārata, Çanti Parva clxxxvii (tr. of Pratāpa Chandra Rāy, ii,
1891, p. 47).

[4] Bhagavadgītā, ii. 22 (tr. of Thomas, *The Song of the Lord*, 1931, p. 34).

[5] *Redemption, Hindu and Christian*, p. 186.

accursed'. The submission it inspires is not submission to the will of God, but submission to the harsh working of a soul-less principle of retribution, whose way is indistinguishable from arbitrary tyranny. Nevertheless its better side must not be forgotten. While any thoroughgoing belief in this doctrine would check any effort to improve one's lot, since it is already irrevocably determined, it has a fundamentally spiritual quality, since it directs attention solely to the realm of character as the determinant of the future birth. It sets less store by restless activity in the material world than is common in our western way, but it does teach that passive submission to misery and misfortune should be accompanied by the active growth of a soul.

An interesting modification of the rigidity of the determinism of *karma* is found in the teachings of the School of Philosophy founded by Nimbārka, who is assigned by Dasgupta[1] to the late eleventh and early twelfth centuries A.D. Here it was taught that the rigid working of *karma* was tempered by the mercy of God, so that while all suffering is the result of sin, not all sins are punished. God is the Lord of *karma*, which, like all else, lies under His will. 'The existence and agency of the human souls', says Dasgupta in presenting the views of this School,[2] 'ultimately depend on the will of God. Yet there is no reason to suppose that God is partial or cruel because He makes some suffer and others enjoy; for He is like the grand master and Lord who directs different men differently and awards suffering and enjoyment according to their individual deserts. The whole idea is that though God awards suffering and enjoyment to individuals and directs their actions according to their deserts, He is not ultimately bound by the law of *karma*, and may by His grace at any time free them from their

[1] *History of Indian Philosophy*, iii, 1940, p. 399.
[2] *Ibid.*, p. 412. Cf. Radhakrishnan, *Indian Philosophy*, ii, 1931, pp. 751 ff. With this view we may contrast the Jaina view that denies any interference of God with the working of *karma*, but which allows to the inheritor of *karma* initiative to modify its effect in the present life, and not merely to create a better *karma* to determine the next incarnation. 'We do not have absolute fatalism, for though *karma* decides all, our present life, which is in our power, can modify the effects of the past. It is possible for us to evade the effects of *karma* by extraordinary exertions. Nor is there any interference by God' (Radhakrishnan, *op. cit.*, i, p. 327).

bondage. The law of *karma* is a mechanical law and God as the superintendent decides each individual case. He is thus the dispenser of the laws of *karma* but is not bound by it.' This view would tend to check self-righteousness and foster humility in the fortunate, since their good fortune might be ascribed to the grace of God rather than to their own virtue, but to the miserable it would seem still to declare that there is no problem of innocent suffering in the world, but that their suffering proclaims their guilt to all. For them, therefore, while submission is submission to the will of God rather than to the blind working of a principle, it is still the submission of the guilty to the God who leaves them to bear the burden of their guilt. Submission is, however, believed to be the means of awakening the grace of God, and so the way to deliverance. 'The pure nature of the *jīva*', says Radhakrishnan,[1] 'is obscured by its *karma*, which is the result of *avidyā*, which is beginningless, yet through the grace of God can be terminated. *Prapatti*, or complete submission to God, is the way to deliverance. Those who possess this attitude of *prapannas* are favoured by God, who engenders in them *bhakti* or devotion, which eventually results in *brahmasākṣātkāra* or realization of God. . . . The grace of God is ever ready to lift up the helpless and make them see the truth of things.' Despite its implicit denial that there is innocent suffering, therefore, we must recognize the deep religious quality of this call for submission, which promises the sufferer first that profoundest deliverance, deliverance in his very suffering, and then deliverance from his suffering in the breaking of the power of *karma* and the termination of his bondage.

IV

In Buddhism, despite the charm of its founder, who so far surpassed his own teaching, the innate pessimism of the *karma* doctrine becomes yet more explicit. 'It remains a fact and the fixed and necessary constitution of being, that all its constituents are misery.'[2]

---

[1] *Indian Philosophy*, ii, 1931, p. 755.

[2] Añguttara-Nikāya iii. 134, translation of Warren (*Buddhism in Transla-tions*, 1909, p. xiv). Cf. Woodward, *The Book of the Gradual Sayings*, i (Pali

Nay, it is simply Ill that rises, Ill
That doth persist and that wanes away.
Nought beside Ill it is that comes to pass,
Nought else but Ill it is doth cease to be.[1]

The burden of life was felt to be intolerable, and the world an unendurable place to live in.[2] Hence salvation, for Buddhism as for Hinduism, consisted in breaking the round of rebirths. Buddhism differed, however, in denying that there is such a thing as an ego, or soul.[3]

Text Society's Translation Series, xxii), 1932, p. 265: 'This causal law of nature, this orderly fixing of things prevails, namely, All phenomena are misery'; Nyāṇatiloka, *Die Reden des Buddha aus dem 'Angúttara-Nikāya'*, i, 2nd ed., 1923, p. 458: 'Eine Tatsache bleibt es, eine feste und notwendige Bedingung des Daseins, dass alle Gebilde dem Leiden unterworfen sind'.

[1] Saṁyutta-Nikāya v. 10, translation of Woodward (*The Book of the Kindred Sayings*, i (Pali Text Society's Translation Series, vii), 1917, p. 170; cf. Geiger, *Samyutta-Nikāya*, i, 1930, p. 212). The same verse is quoted in Visuddhi Magga xviii; cf. Pe Maung Tin, *The Path of Purity*, iii (Pali Text Society's Translation Series, xxi), 1931, p. 716.

[2] Oldenberg, *Buddha: his Life, his Doctrine, his Order*, E. Tr., 1882, pp. 212 f.: 'All life is suffering: this is the inexhaustible theme, which, now in the strict forms of abstract philosophical discussion and now in the garment of poetical proverb, evermore comes ringing in our ears from Buddhist literature'. Dahlke (*Buddhist Essays*, E. Tr. by Sīlācāra, 1908, p. 21) observes that 'Buddhism is only adapted to such as find life to be suffering. Those only who build upon this foundation can reach the end. Nothing is to be gained by preaching Buddhism except where life is felt and understood to be suffering.'

[3] Cf. B. L. Suzuki, *Mahayana Buddhism*, 1938, p. 22: 'Mahayana, like Hinayana and Primitive Buddhism, accepts the three fundamental principles: (1) All is transitory, (2) All is suffering, (3) All is egoless'. Cf. Majjhima-Nikāya, I, i. 2 (Tr. of Sīlācāra, *The Majjhima-Nikāya*, 2nd ed., 1924, p. 12; cf. Neumann, *Die Reden Gotamo Buddhos, Mittleren Sammlung*, i, 1922, pp. 18 f.): 'With such cogitations he arrives at one or other of the following six views . . .: either the view, "I have a self", or else the view, "I have not a self", or the view, "By self I apprehend self", or the view, "By self I apprehend non-self", or else the view, "By non-self I apprehend self". Or perhaps he adopts the view: "The identical self of mine, I maintain, is veritably to be found, now here, now there, reaping the fruits of its good and of its evil deeds; and this my self is a thing permanent, constant, eternal, not subject to change, and so abides for ever." But this, monks, is a walking in mere opinion, a resorting to mere views; a barren waste of views, an empty display of views' (this passage is not in Dahlke, *Mijjhima-Nikāya*, 1923). On the other hand, however, Coomaraswamy (*Hinduism and Buddhism*, pp. 59 f.) observes that 'there are passages in which when the five constituents of our evanescent and unreal "existence" have been listed, we find, not the usual formula of negation, "That is not my Self" but the positive injunction, "Take refuge in the Self".'

It has been argued above that Hindu philosophy could establish no real continuity of self in transmigration, and that with the breach of both physical and psychical continuity, little more than a fiction could connect the two lives. In Buddhism the link became even more exiguous. In its view man consists of a transient assemblage of the five *skandhas* (Pali, *khandhas*), viz. form, sensation, perception, predisposition, consciousness. At death this complex is resolved into its elements, of which none is permanent, and still less so the combination. Man is never the same for two consecutive moments, and is without any abiding principle. Neither in this life, nor beyond it, has he any enduring soul. 'It remains a fact and the fixed and necessary constitution of being, that all its elements are lacking in an Ego'.[1]

> Misery only doth exist, none miserable.
> No doer is there; naught save the deed is found.
> Nirvana is, but not the man who seeks it.
> The Path exists, but not the traveller on it.[2]

'The words "living entity" and "Ego" are but a mode of expression for the presence of the five attachment groups (*khandhas*), but when we come to examine the elements of being one by one, we discover that in the absolute sense there is no living entity there to form a basis for such figments as

[1] Aṅguttara-Nikāya iii. 134 (Warren, *loc. cit.*). Woodward (*loc. cit.*): 'This causal law of nature this orderly fixing of things prevails, namely, All phenomena are not the self'; Nyāṇatiloka (*loc. cit.*): 'Eine Tatsache bleibt es, eine feste und notwendige Bedingung des Daseins, dass alle Erscheinungen ohne Wesenskern sind'. Cf. Saṁyutta-Nikāya xxii. 85 (Warren, *op. cit.*, pp. 138 ff., esp. pp. 144 f.; Woodward, *The Book of the Kindred Sayings*, iii (Pali Text Society's Translation Series, xiii), 1925, pp. 93 ff., esp. pp. 98 f.).

[2] Visuddhi Magga xvi, translation of Warren (*op. cit.*, p. 146); cf. Pe Maung Tin, *op. cit.*, iii, p. 609. Mrs. Rhys Davids, *Outlines of Buddhism*, 1934, pp. 67 f., quotes the lines

> Salvation is there, not the man who's saved,
> Doing is there, but not the doer,
> The Way there is, but not a goer!

and comments 'Here is no question of a permitted qualified human self or soul; here is pure nihilism. And no cult of that kind could long persist in India without dishonour and discredit. It is always possible that in a future Buddhist reformation these medieval prophets may be posthumously stoned, and a rational reform concerning the man: valuer, willer, wayfarer arise in Buddhism.'

"I am" or "I"; in other words, that in the absolute sense there is only name and form.'[1]

> 'Being'! Why dost thou harp upon that word?
> 'Mong false opinions, Māra, hast thou strayed.
> Mere bundle of conditioned factors, this!
> No 'being' can be here discerned to be.
> For just as, when the parts are rightly set,
> The word 'chariot' ariseth (in our minds),
> So doth our usage covenant to say:
> 'A being' when the aggregates (*khandhas*) are there.[2]

'For Buddhism', says Roussel,[3] 'and this is what constitutes its originality as a philosophy, there are sensations with object but no subject; there are visions of things and things seen, the seer, the spectator does not exist.'

There could, therefore, be no transmigration of souls. Coomaraswamy says:[4] 'Buddhism nowhere teaches the transmigration of souls, but only the transmigration of character, of personality without a person'. Similarly, Radhakrishnan observes:[5] 'There is no such thing in Buddhism as the migration

[1] Visuddhi Magga xviii, translation of Warren (*op. cit.*, pp. 133 f.); cf. Pe Maung Tin, *op. cit.*, iii, p. 717. Dahlke (*Buddhist Essays*, E. Tr. by Sīlācāra, p. 130) emphasizes the fundamental egoism in which Buddhism, that denies the reality of the ego, began: 'Gautama . . . does not begin his career as a saviour of the world. . . . Nothing lies farther from his mind than the welfare of others. He seeks his own salvation and that only. It is a purely egotistical impulse.' Elsewhere he commends egoism in these terms (p. 29): 'Egoism is indeed the most coldly calculating foundation for morality which this world offers, but it is also the soundest, the most solid'. He recognizes, of course, that after attaining his own salvation, Buddha was moved with sympathy for others, and sought to effect their deliverance (p. 131). It is here that the inner paradox of Buddhism lies. Neither egoism nor altruism can easily be justified, if neither the self nor others are real, but only illusion.

[2] Samyutta-Nikāya v. 10, translation of Woodward (*Book of Kindred Sayings*, i, p. 170; cf. Geiger, *loc. cit.*).

[3] *Le Bouddhisme Primitif*, 1911, pp. 203 f. Cf. Hiriyanna, *Outlines of Indian Philosophy*, 1932, pp. 138 f.: 'Buddha admitted the transient sensations and thoughts alone and denied the self . . . as an unwarranted assumption. To express the same in modern phraseology, he admitted only states of consciousness but not the mind. To him the sensations and the thoughts, together with the physical frame with which they are associated, were themselves the self.'

[4] *Buddha and the Gospel of Buddhism*, 1928, p. 106.

[5] *Indian Philosophy*, i, p. 444. Cf. Messina, *Cristianesimo, Buddhismo, Manicheismo nell' Asia antica*, 1947, p. 188: 'Non si tratta del passaggio dell'anima da un corpo all'altro. Per il buddhismo non si dà anima spirituale, duratura e independente dalla materia, che esista nel corpo o col corpo e

of the soul or the passage of an individual from life to life. When a man dies his physical organism, which is the basis of his psychical, dissolves, and so the psychical life comes to an end. It is not the dead man who comes to rebirth but another. There is no soul to migrate.' Nevertheless, in order to provide a moral cause for the suffering of men in this illusion of life, Buddhism had to connect one life with another in some way. 'Said the king: "Bhante Nāgasena, does rebirth take place without anything transmigrating?" "Yes, your majesty. Rebirth takes place without anything transmigrating." "How, bhante Nāgasena, does rebirth take place without anything transmigrating? Give an illustration." "Suppose, your majesty, a man were to light a light from another light; pray, would the one light have passed over to the other light?" "Nay, verily, bhante." "In exactly the same way, your majesty, does rebirth take place without anything transmigrating." '[1]

'Although, when a man dies', says Monier-Williams,[2] 'all the five constituents of existence are dissolved, yet by the force resulting from his actions (*karma*), combined with Upādāna, "clinging to existence", a new set of five, of which consciousness is still the dominant faculty, starts into being. The process of the new creation is so instantaneous that it is equivalent to the continuance of the same personality,[3]

raminghi da un corpo all'altro. L'io o la persona non ha alcuna realtà costante: quello che cosi suole chiamarsi è solo il prodotto di certi elementi riunitisi insieme, un intreccio, un concatenamento di facoltà e tendenze. Quando la morte dissolve quest'unione, se l'essere scomparso era attaccato alla vita, lascia il germe di una nuova vita, la quale sarà modellata secondo le azioni compiute precedentemente.'

[1] Milindapañha 71, translation of Warren (*Buddhism in Translations*; p. 234). Cf. Rhys Davids, *Sacred Books of the East*, xxxv, 1890, p. 111, Nyāṇatiloka, *Die Fragen des Milindo*, i, 1914, p. 116.

[2] *Buddhism*, 1889, pp. 109 f. Cf. Copleston, *Buddhism Primitive and Present in Magadha and in Ceylon*, 1908, pp. 71 f.: 'The death of a man is the breaking up of this combination (of faculties and characters); not the separation of soul from body, but the dissolution both of the body and of the rest of that aggregate of faculties and characters on which life depended'.

[3] Cf. Hiriyanna, *op. cit.*, p. 81: 'In its initial form, as enunciated by Yājñavalkya, there is no interval between the end of one life and beginning of the next. The belief did not, however, long remain unmodified, because it got mixed up with the earlier belief in recompense in another world. In this modified form the doctrine teaches a two-fold reward or punishment, first in the world beyond and then in a life here.' This modified form we find in

pervaded by the same consciousness; though each personality is only really connected with the previous by the force of acts done and character formed in each—such force operating through Upādāna. In short, to speak of transmigration of souls in Buddhism gives a wrong idea.'

To give a right idea, however, is more difficult, for there is much elusiveness in Buddhist thought. 'There is not', says Poussin,[1] 'a Self, a permanent substantial unity, but there is a person, to be described as "a living continuous fluid complex", which does not remain quite the same for two consecutive moments, but which continues for an endless number of existences, bridging an endless number of deaths, without becoming completely different from itself.' Similarly, Hiriyanna says,[2] 'We should be careful how we understand the Buddhistic doctrine of the denial of the soul. As a stable entity which, without itself changing, appears amidst changing conditions— bodily and mental—Buddhism does deny the self; but it recognizes instead a "fluid self" which because of its very fluidity cannot be regarded as a series of altogether distinct or dissimilar states.' It is on this fluidity that Thomas insists when he warns against the error[3] of supposing that Buddhism taught that at death the *khandhas* were destroyed, and says that the ever-changing bundle of *khandhas* may be said to be new from moment to moment, and hence from birth to birth. But from birth to birth, he declares, it remains a changing bundle. This would seem rather to overstate the element of continuity, and in view of the above-quoted denial that anything transmigrates it is difficult to see how the bundle of *khandhas*, albeit an ever-changing bundle, could remain. The bundle would seem rather to be dissolved, though its elements are not destroyed but remain to enter into new combinations of *khandhas*.

Muṇḍaka i. 2: 'Considering sacrifice and good works as the best, these fools know no higher good, and having enjoyed their reward on the height of heaven, gained by good works, they enter again this world or a lower one' (*Sacred Books of the East*, xv, p. 32; cf. Hume, *The Thirteen Principal Upanishads*, p. 369). Cf. Keith, *Religion and Philosophy of the Veda and Upanishads*, ii, 1925, pp. 574 f.

[1] *The Way to Nirvāna*, 1917, p. 35.
[2] *Op. cit.*, p. 146.
[3] *The Life of Buddha as Legend and History*, 1927, p. 205.

'The inner life of a person', says Radhakrishnan in expound-
ing the thought of Buddhism,[1] 'is only a succession of thoughts,
desires, affections, and passions, and when the corporeal bond
which holds them together falls away at death, the unseen
potencies beget a new person, psychologically if not physically
continuous with the deceased, to suffer or enjoy what his
predecessor had prepared for him by his behaviour. The
elements which constitute the empirical individual are always
changing, but they can never be totally dispersed until the
power that holds them together and impels them to rebirth,
the craving, the desire for separate existence is extinguished.'
Coomaraswamy[2] varies the favourite symbol of the flame by
that of two billiard balls, of which one transmits to the other
by its impact its momentum, its *karma*. 'Buddhist reincarna-
tion', he says, 'is the endless transmission of such an impulse
through an endless series of forms; Buddhist salvation is the
coming to understand that the forms, the billiard balls, are
compound structures subject to decay, and that nothing is
transmitted but an impulse, a *vis a tergo*, dependent on the
heaping up of the past. It is a man's character, and not himself,
that goes on.'

One life is dependent on another, and its state is the result
of another life that preceded it, whose *karma* has determined
it. Yet nothing is more elusive than the content of the term
karma. Warren tries to equate Buddhist with Christian thought,
by using 'character' as an equivalent of *karma*. 'What, indeed,
do we ordinarily mean', he says,[3] 'when we speak of personal
immortality, unless it be that the characters of our friends are
reborn in heaven? . . . It is his character, his particular set of
deeds, or *karma*, that we think of as surviving death; and this
is exactly what the Buddhists do—the only difference being
that we claim the existence of an Ego. . . . But the question
still remains: How can character that is no entity in itself be
reborn?' This question he answers by the analogy of a swallow's
egg and a lark's egg, which though outwardly alike hatch out
differently because of a difference of heredity. 'Therefore a
swallow's egg cannot hatch out a lark, because a lark is the

---

[1] *Gautama the Buddha*, 1938, pp. 16 f.
[2] *Op. cit.*, pp. 106 f.   [3] *Op. cit.*, p. 210.

result of an entirely different set of conditions; as we might say, its *karma* is different. But of course the Buddhists do not mean heredity when they use the word *karma*. *Karma* expresses, not that which a man inherits from his ancestors, but that which he inherits from himself in some previous state of existence. But with this difference the Buddhist doctrine and the scientific doctrine of heredity seem very similar.' But the analogy that is not analogous is no analogy.

Christian thought, as Warren recognizes, is of the survival of personality, and not merely of the survival of a character that does not inhere in any personality. On the other hand, Buddhist thought is not of the incarnation of *karma* in the new life. *Karma* is not passed on, for nothing is passed on. The *karma* of one life is believed to be the causal basis of another, but it is not transmitted to another. In Hinduism, on the contrary, *karma* is thought of as transmitted. Thus we find in the Mahābhārata:[1] 'The doer in his new body receives all the good and bad acts done by him in his past existence'. But of Buddhist thought all that we can say is that the *karma* of one set of *skandhas*, themselves dissolved at death, conditions the locality, nature and future of another set of *skandhas*.[2] For this reason Warren's analogy of heredity is not analogous. Between the lark and its past heredity there is a connecting link in the egg, but between a life that has no physical or psychical point of contact with another life and that other life there is no connecting link whatever, and a *karma* which is not passed on, and which nowhere touches the new life, can offer no explanation of its misery. At the best it can only conceal the complete absence of any explanation. 'Buddhism does not explain', says Coomaraswamy,[3] 'in what way a continuity of cause and effect is maintained as between one life A and a subsequent life B, which are separated by the fact of physical death; the thing is taken for granted.'

Even the comparison with the flame or the billiard ball breaks down at the vital point, for no point of contact is offered. The billiard balls are on different tables. It is this that vitiates the Buddhist comparison between the ever-changing

---

[1] Çanti Parva ccii (tr. of Pratāpa Chandra Rāy, ii, 1891, p. 107).
[2] Cf. Rhys Davids, *Buddhism*, 1910, p. 101. [3] *Op. cit.*, p. 109.

consciousness of an individual and the transition from life to life. Life is unceasing change, and the self of childhood and the self of manhood, yea, even the self of two consecutive moments, is not the same, as many Buddhist passages assert. Yet is their change held in the unity of a demonstrably single stream, and past and present may be together grasped in memory. Between life and life there is no unity that holds them together, save the wholly assumed power of *karma*. There is no accumulated knowledge and experience passed from one to the other, as there is between the successive states of consciousness, and no mere labelling of the two wholly different processes as alike can make them really so.

Yet it is claimed that this view provides a moral cause for the facts of life, and that whereas belief in fate might lead a sufferer to bow to his lot, since it was ordained for him by an inscrutable power, belief in *karma* leads him to recognize that if he suffers it must be the result of his own sin. Says Rhys Davids: 'Buddhism is convinced that if a man reaps sorrow, disappointment, pain, he himself, and no other, must at some time have sown, folly, error, sin; and if not in this life, then in some former birth'.[1] This might seem to identify the self of the former life with the self of this life. Yet that would be to fall into what Buddhism regards as heresy. For it is heresy to assert that he who experiences the fruit of a deed is the same as he who performed it, and equally heretical to say that he is different. For an ego that does not exist can hardly be equated to, or distinguished from, another non-existent ego. It would therefore be truer to Buddhist thought to say that if a man reaps trouble, then sin lies behind him, either in the stream of this life, or in the life whose *karma* conditioned his being. 'It is through a difference in their *karma* that men are not all alike, but some long-lived and some short-lived, some healthy and some sickly, some handsome and some ugly, some powerful and some weak, some rich and some poor, some of high degree and some of low degree, some wise and some foolish. Moreover, the Blessed One has said as follows: "All beings, O youth, have *karma* as their portion; they are heirs of their *karma*; they are sprung from their *karma*; their *karma*

[1] *Buddhism.* p. 103.

is their kinsman; their *Karma* is their refuge; *karma* allots beings to meanness or greatness".'[1]

The indestructibility of moral worth would therefore seem to lie at the heart of Buddhism, as its cardinal assumption, and for all its emphasis on the illusory nature of the soul, it believes that we live in a fundamentally moral universe, where absolute justice is invariably dispensed. But whereas Hinduism does postulate, though it cannot establish, some sort of identity between the self of the creator of *karma* and the self of the inheritor of *karma*, Buddhism denies the existence of both selves and denies any inheritance. To what, then, is its moral universe resolved? It is forced to speak in personal terms, though it denies the reality of personality. In the Milindapañha 46[2] we read: 'Your majesty, it is as if a man were to take away another man's mangoes, and the owner of the mangoes were to seize him, and show him to the king, and say, "Sire, this man hath taken away my mangoes"; and the other were to say, "Sire, I did not take away this man's mangoes. The mangoes which this man planted were different mangoes from those which I took away. I am not liable to punishment." Pray, your majesty, would the man be liable to punishment?' 'Assuredly, bhante, would he be liable to punishment.' 'For what reason?' 'Because, in spite of what he might say, he would be liable to punishment for the reason that the last mangoes derived from the first mangoes.' 'In exactly the same way, your majesty, with this name and form one does a deed—it may be good, it may be wicked—and by reason of this deed another name and form is born into the next existence. Therefore is one not freed from one's evil deeds.'

Here the point of the passage is the causal nexus between the mangoes that were planted and the mangoes that grew from them, as an illustration of the law of *karma*. But it is to be observed that the punishment of the act of theft falls upon a man who, however his reality as an agent may be denied,

---

[1] Milindapañha 65 (tr. of Warren, *op. cit.*, p. 215; cf. Rhys Davids, *Sacred Books of the East*, xxxv, p. 101, and Nyāṇatiloka, *Die Fragen des Milindo*, i, p. 107). Cf. also B. L. Suzuki, *Mahayana Buddhism*, 1938, p. 129.

[2] Warren, p. 235; cf. Rhys Davids, p. 72, and Nyāṇatiloka, *Die Fragen des Milindo*, i, pp. 77 f.

is treated as real for the purpose of punishment. That the doer
of a deed should be punished for his deed is just. But if only
the deed is real, and if the illusory doer has dissolved and disappeared, how can the sufferings of another illusory self be
regarded as the just penalty of the deed?[1] 'How am I responsible', asks Roussel,[2] 'if the self which performs the action is
one series of phenomena, and the self to which one attributes
it another series of phenomena, however identical they may
be?' Punishment falls not upon deeds, but upon persons, and
a theory which abandons all pretence at any real identity
between the doer and the sufferer abandons the idea of a moral
universe in which justice is wrought, and offers in place of an
explanation of the mystery of suffering the mere illusion of an
explanation.

Nevertheless the illusion has ministered to a spirit of
resignation. 'Without this explanation', says Radhakrishnan,[3]
'men would feel themselves to be the victims of an immense
injustice. It also helps to make the sufferer resigned, because
he feels that through suffering he is wiping out an old debt.'
So long as he does not reflect that the debt is not really his
he may continue to be delivered from the sense of injustice,
and to be resigned. But his resignation rests on a sense of
guilt which the principles of Buddhism cannot sustain.

Despite the great difference, therefore, between the doctrine
of *karma* as it appears in Hinduism and in Buddhism, there
is some similarity between the varieties of submission that
both induce. That Buddhist submission is deeper in its resignation than the other, despite the even greater illusoriness of the
explanation Buddhism presents, is doubtless due in no small
measure to the profounder sense that life itself is evil, and
that suffering is of the very essence of existence. It is desire
that perpetuates this misery, desire that needs to be elimin-

---

[1] Cf. Coomaraswamy, *Hinduism and Buddhism*, p. 60: 'Beings are the
heirs of acts; but it cannot be said exactly that "I" now reap the rewards
of what "I" did in a former habitation. There is causal continuity, but no *one*
consciousness (*vijñāna*), no essence (*sattva*) that now experiences the fruits
of good and evil actions, and that also recurs and reincarnates (*sandhāvati
saṁsarati*) without otherness (*ananyam*).'

[2] *Op. cit.*, p. 212. Cf. Hardy, *A Manual of Buddhism*, 1853, pp. 396 f.

[3] *Indian Philosophy*, i, p. 440.

ated,[1] yet that cannot be eliminated by desire. For even the desire for its elimination defeats its own purpose. It is eliminated in the spirit of resignation, in deep placidity of spirit, yielding perfect peace. 'Patience is the austerity supreme', we read.[2] And again: 'He who unangered bears reproach and stripes and jail, in patience strong, arrayed in strength; that man I call a brahman, man of worth';[3]

> Trained is the beast that men to concourse lead,
> Trained is the beast on which the raja rides,
> Trained is the man who is the best 'mong men,
> Who worded outrage suffers patiently.[4]

[1] See Dhamma-*K*akka-Ppavattana Sutta 5-8 (*Sacred Books of the East*, xi, 1881, pp. 148 ff.). The same recognition of desire as the fundamental cause of rebirth is found on the lips of Yājñavalkya in the Upsaniṣads. Cf. Bṛhadāraṇyaka iv. 4 (*Sacred Books of the East*, xv, pp. 176 f.; Hume, *Thirteen Principal Upanishads*, pp. 140 f.).

[2] Dhammapada 184, translation of C. A. F. Rhys Davids (*Sacred Books of the Buddhists*, vii, 1931, p. 65; cf. Müller, *Sacred Books of the East*, x, Part I, 1891, p. 50, and Radhakrishnan, *The Dhammapada*, 1950, p. 120). Dahlke, *Dhammapada*, 2nd ed., 1922, p. 40, renders: 'Geduld und Langmut höchste Busse sind'.

[3] Dhammapada 399, translation of C. A. F. Rhys Davids (*loc. cit.*, p. 131; cf. Müller, *loc. cit.*, p. 91, Dahlke, *op. cit.*, p. 79, and Radhakrishnan, *op. cit.*, p. 182). Seidenstücker, *Pāli-Buddhismus in Übersetzungen*, 1923, pp. 356 f., renders: 'Wer Schmähung, Schläge, Fesselung, von Grimm und Wut befreit, erträgt, wer da geduldig bleibt und stark, den nenn' ich einen Brahmana.' Cf. a passage from the end of the Chinese version of the Pratimôksha, cited by Beal (*Catena of Buddhist Scriptures from the Chinese*, 1871, p. 158):

> 'Patience and resignation is the one Road;
> Buddha has declared no better path exists;
> The disciple who is angry or impatient
> Cannot really be called a Shaman'.

[4] Dhammapada 321, translation of C. A. F. Rhys Davids (*loc. cit.*, p. 107; cf. Müller, *loc. cit.*, p. 77, Dahlke, *op. cit.*, p. 66, and Radhakrishnan, *op. cit.*, p. 160). A like view is found in Jainism, which, while it differs from Buddhism in its view of the mechanics of *karma*, closely resembles it in its view of the fact of *karma*, and in its response in submission. 'Not careless in his conduct, he should bear whatever pains he has to suffer. If beaten, he should not be angry; if abused, he should not fly into a passion; with a placid mind he should bear everything and not make a great noise' (Sutrakritanga I, ix. 30 f., translation of Jacobi in *Sacred Books of the East*, xlv, 1895, p. 305); 'As the lustre of a burning flame increases, so increase the austerity, wisdom and glory of a steadfast sage, who, with vanquished desires, meditates on the supreme place of virtue, though suffering pain' (Acaranga Sutra II, xvi. 5, translation of Jacobi in *Sacred Books of the East*, xxii, 1881, pp. 211 f.). On the Jaina view of *karma* cf. S. Konow and P. Tuxen, *The Religions of India*, 1949, pp. 115 f.

Submission in Buddhism, therefore, is the most profound and complete passivity. Yet in the very completeness of its passivity it attains a spirit of high exaltation and profound joy. This is finely illustrated in the poem ascribed to Kisā-gotamī, whose story of suffering and release has been made familiar by Arnold's *Light of Asia*.[1] In her bitterness at the hard blows she suffered, and especially at the death of her son, she went to the Buddha, and was sent by him to collect mustard seed from houses where none had died. Her failure to find such a house brought her to realize that suffering belongs essentially to life itself, and brought her a peace profounder than mere resignation to her loss.

> Returning home to give birth to my child
> I saw my husband in the jungle die.
> Nor could I reach my kin ere travail came.
> My baby boys I lost, my husband too.
> And when in misery I reached my home,
> Lo! where together on a scanty pyre,
> My mother, father, and my brother burn!
> O wretched, ruined woman! all this weight
> Of sorrows hast thou suffered, shed these tears
> Through weary round of many thousand lives.
> I too have seen where, in the charnel-field,
> Devourèd was my baby's tender flesh.
> Yet she, her people slain, herself outcast,
> Her husband dead, hath hither come
> Where death is not! Lo! I have gone
> Up on the Ariyan, on the Eightfold Path
> That goeth to the state ambrosial.
> Nibbana have I realized, and gazed
> Into the mirror of the holy Norm.
> I, even I, am healèd of my hurt,
> Low is my burden laid, my task is done,
> My heart is wholly set at liberty.
> I, sister Kisā-gotamī, have uttered this![2]

V

Widespread has been the view that all attempt to find a rational solution of the problem of suffering is vain, and that all we can do is to recognize that it is arbitrary in its incidence,

[1] Book V.
[2] Translation of Mrs. Rhys Davids (*Psalms of the Early Buddhists*, i, 1909, pp. 109 f.).

and accept what comes to us as our portion, against which there is no appeal. This fatalistic attitude, however, can give rise to a variety of moods of submission.

That there is innocent suffering Confucius was in no manner of doubt. Of his favourite disciple he said, 'There is Hui! He has nearly attained to perfect virtue. He is often in want';[1] and when he died at an early age Confucius lamented, 'There was Yen Hui; he loved to learn. Unfortunately his appointed time was short, and he died',[2] and also cried 'Alas! Heaven is destroying me! Heaven is destroying me!'[3] Again, it is recorded that he visited Po-niu when the latter was dying of a disease which the commentators identify with leprosy. The sage did not enter the house, but took his hand through the window and moaned, 'It is killing him! It is the appointment of Heaven, alas! That such a man should have such a sickness! That such a man should have such a sickness!'[4]

The lot of Confucius himself did not correspond to his worth, and both his contemporaries and his successors were perplexed by this. It is recorded that when he was in Ch'ên with his disciples, their provisions were exhausted and some of the disciples were so ill that they were confined to bed. Tzŭ-lu went to Confucius with evident discontent and asked, 'Must the sage also suffer in this way?' 'The sage may indeed have to endure want', replied Confucius, 'but the mean man, when he is in want, loses his self-control.'[5] The historian Ssŭ-ma Ch'ien adds that Tzŭ-lu blushed at the rebuke.[6] Mencius explained the failure of Confucius to gain the empire,

---

[1] Analects xi. 18, translation of Legge (*The Chinese Classics*, i, 1861, p. 107; 2nd ed., 1893, p. 243). Waley (*The Analects of Confucius*, 1938, p. 157) renders: 'Hui comes very near to it. He is often empty.' This literal rendering indicates the somewhat cryptic nature of the passage, but most agree with Legge, who follows Chu Hsi. So Couvreur, *Les Quatre Livres*, 1910, p. 192; Soothill, *The Analects of Confucius*, 1910, p. 533; Pauthier, *Doctrine de Confucius*, p. 138. Wilhelm (*Kung-Futse Gespräche*, 1923, p. 113) gives both the literal and an interpretative rendering agreeing with Chu Hsi's, but adds that it is not easy to interpret the passage.

[2] Analects xi. 6 (Legge, p. 103; 2nd ed., p. 239).

[3] Analects xi. 8 (Legge, p. 103; 2nd ed., p. 239).

[4] Analects vi. 8 (Legge, p. 52; 2nd ed., p. 188).

[5] Analects xv. 1 (Legge, p. 158; 2nd ed., p. 294).

[6] See *Les Mémoires historiques*, translated by E. Chavannes, v, 1905, p. 367.

despite his unique merits, by saying that he would have needed to be presented to Heaven by the preceding emperor,[1] while Hsün-tzŭ argued that the best charioteer in the world could not display his prowess without a chariot and horses, and that similarly one needed a *point d'appui* of a hundred *li* before he could achieve a unified sway.[2] In a later age Chu Hsi accounted for the fact that Confucius was poor and lowly by holding that his *ch'i*, which Bruce renders by *ether*, was attenuated, though as his *ch'i* was also clear and translucent he was a sage.[3] As this *ch'i* was the endowment he received from Heaven, the cause is thus carried outside the sage himself.

It is not surprising that Confucianism teaches that a man should accept his lot without murmuring. Yet its spirit is not just that it should be accepted because there is nothing he can do about it, but that nothing less than courageous acceptance is worthy of a man.[4] Already, before the time of Confucius, we find in the Shih Ching an expression of the view that what comes must be accepted because it cannot be helped:

> Out by the northern gate I go my way,
> Bearing a load of sorrow and of care;
> Vulgarly poor am I, and sore bestead,
> And of my hardships all are unaware.
> Ah, so indeed!
> Yet Heaven hath so decreed;
> What therefore can I say?

[1] Mencius V, i. 6. See Legge, *op. cit.*, ii, 1861, pp. 235 f.; 2nd ed., 1895, pp. 359 f.

[2] Hsün-tzŭ viii. 16. See Dubs, *The Works of Hsüntze*, 1928, pp. 108 f.

[3] See *The Philosophy of Human Nature*, translated by Bruce, 1922, p. 136.

[4] Here we may contrast a Jaina view, that nothing less than patient submission, even to undeserved sufferings, can bring a man deliverance. It should be noted that though in general Jainism accepts the usual Indian view of *karma*, it yet can recognize that there is innocent suffering. 'Those who are not given to sinful acts are, nevertheless, attacked by calamities; but then the steadfast will bear them' (Acaranga Sutra I, v. 2, translation of Jacobi in *Sacred Books of the East*, xxii, 1884, p. 44). So, too, Buddhism can say: 'Whosoever, being innocent, endures reproach, blows and bonds, the man who is strong in his endurance, and has for his army this strength, him I call a Brâhmana' (Mahâvagga ix. 30, translation of Fausböll (*Sacred Books of the East*, x, Part 2, 1881, p. 113). On the Jaina view of *karma*, cf. Tuxen, in *Illusteret Religions historie*, ed. by Johs Pedersen, 1948, p. 576.

On me devolves the business of the king,
On me official burdens fast encroach;
On me, at home, arriving from abroad,
My household all conspire to heap reproach.
    Ah, so indeed!
    Yet Heaven hath so decreed;
    What therefore can I say?

All urgent is the business of the king;
Official cares press on me more and more.
And when at home, arriving from abroad,
My household one and all thrust at me sore.
    Ah, so indeed!
    Yet Heaven hath so decreed;
    What therefore can I say?[1]

With this we may contrast the spirit of Confucius's word: 'With coarse rice to eat, with water to drink, and my bended arm for a pillow—I have still joy in the midst of these things. Riches and honours acquired by unrighteousness are to me as a floating cloud.'[2] Again, on another occasion he said, 'I do not murmur against Heaven. I do not grumble against men.'[3] Similarly, in the Doctrine of the Mean we read: 'The superior man is quiet and calm, waiting for the appointments of Heaven, while the mean man walks in dangerous paths, looking for lucky occurrences'.[4] Mencius, too, says: 'There is an appointment for everything. A man should receive submissively what

[1] Shih Ching I, iii. 15, translation of Jennings, *The Shi King*, 1891, pp. 67 f. For text and translation, cf. Legge, *The Chinese Classics*, iv, Part i, 1871, pp. 65 f., Karlgren, *The Book of Odes*, 1950, pp. 26 f., or Couvreur, *Cheu King*, 3rd ed., 1934, pp. 47 f. Waley (*The Book of Songs* 1937, p. 305) renders the closing lines of each stanza:

    'Well, it's over now.
    No doubt it was Heaven's doing,
    So what's the good of talking about it?'

[2] Analects vii. 15 (Legge, *op. cit.*, i, p. 64; 2nd ed., p. 200). Cf. Waley's rendering (*The Analects of Confucius*, p. 126): 'He who seeks only coarse food to eat, water to drink, and a bent arm for a pillow, will without looking for it find happiness to boot. Any thought of accepting wealth and rank by means that I know to be wrong is as remote from me as the clouds that float above.'

[3] Analects xiv. 37 (Legge, pp. 152 f.; 2nd ed., pp. 288 f.). The same observation is attributed to Mencius (II, ii. 13; see Legge, ii, p. 108; 2nd ed., p. 232); it also stands in the Doctrine of the Mean xiv. 3 (Legge, i, p. 260; 2nd ed., p. 396).

[4] Doctrine of the Mean xiv. 4, translation of Legge (*The Chinese Classics*, i, p. 260; 2nd ed., p. 396). On the fatalism of Confucius cf. Creel, *Confucius*, 1951, pp. 130 ff.

may be correctly ascribed thereto';[1] while Chu Hsi observes: 'When neither premature death nor long life causes a man to hesitate, but cultivating his personal character, he awaits them, whatever the issue may be—this is the way in which he establishes his destiny'.[2] With this, too, may be compared the words of Hsün-tzǔ: 'If the heart is tranquil and contented, though the colours be below the ordinary, they can nourish the eyes; though sounds be below the ordinary, they can nourish the ears; coarse food and vegetable soup can nourish the taste; coarse cotton clothes and coarse hemp sandals can nourish the body; a straw hut for a house, reed screens for doors, straw beds, ancient plain stands and mats can nourish the form. For a person may be without the goodness of all things, yet he can foster his enjoyment; he may be without a position of high rank, but he can foster his fame. If such a man were given the empire, it would mean much for the empire, but it would mean little for his contentment and joy.'[3]

Sometimes, indeed, we find a joyous acceptance of suffering. In the incident above referred to, when Confucius and his followers were so short of food that some were too ill to dress, Ssǔ-ma Ch'ien tells us that Confucius recited and sang, accompanying himself with a stringed instrument, without ceasing.[4] Chuang-tzǔ gives a garbled account of this and the following incident. 'When Confucius was travelling in K'uang, some people of Sung surrounded him several ranks deep; but he kept singing to his lute without stopping. Tzǔ-lu came in and saw him, and said, "How is it, Master, that you are so pleased?" Confucius said, "Come here, and I will tell you. I have tried to avoid being reduced to such a strait for a long time; and that I have not escaped shows that it was so appointed for me ". '[5]

This was a fatalism that could bring quiet confidence in

---

[1] Mencius VII, i. 2, translation of Legge (*op. cit.*, ii, p. 325; 2nd ed., p. 449). This rendering is to be preferred to that of Lyall (*Mencius*, 1932, p. 202): 'Nothing happens unbidden. We must obey and accept our true Bidding.'

[2] *The Philosophy of Human Nature*, translation of Bruce, pp. 149 f.

[3] Hsün-tzǔ xxii. 15, translation of Dubs (*The Works of Hsüntze*, 1928, p. 299).

[4] *Les Mémoires historiques*, translated by Chavannes, v, p. 366.

[5] Chuang-tzǔ XVII, ii. 9, translation of Legge (*Sacred Books of the East*, xxxix, 1891, pp. 385 f.). Cf. Giles, *Chuang Tzǔ*, 1926, p. 213. For text and translation see Wieger, *Taoïsme*, ii, 1913, pp. 344 f.

misfortune, and courage in difficulty. When Confucius was in peril in K'uang he said to his disciples: 'After the death of King Wên, was not the cause of truth lodged here in me? If Heaven had wished to let the cause of truth perish, then I, a future mortal'—or 'the successor of the deceased', as Chavannes renders[1]—'should not have got such a relation to that cause. While Heaven does not let the cause of truth perish, what can the people of K'uang do to me?'[2] Ssŭ-ma Ch'ien records[3] that on another occasion Confucius was passing through the state of Sung and was observing ceremonies with his disciples under a tree when Huan T'ui, an officer of the state, passed by and sought to kill the sage. Confucius withdrew, but without haste, and when his disciples sought to hurry him he replied: 'Heaven produced the virtue that is in me. Huan T'ui—what can he do to me?'[4] Confucius clearly believed that man is immortal till his work is done. So, too, did Hsin Kung, a local governor in Shensi in the sixth century A.D., of whom it is recorded that when others were deserting plague victims through fear he tended them, saying, 'Life and death are in the hands of Heaven. Why are you afraid of infection?'[5] With this may be compared the thought met with in Jewish Rabbinical sources: 'Though a plague last seven years, no one dies before his time'.[6]

The other side of fatalism is seen in another incident that is recorded of Confucius. On one occasion he was arrested by the people of P'u. His disciple Kung Liang-ju was following him with five carriages, and coming up he said: 'If I find myself again in peril here, it is fate that wills it. Since I am involved for a second time in difficulties with you, it is better that I should die fighting.'[7]

---

[1] See Ssŭ-ma Ch'ien, *Les Mémoires historiques*, translated by Chavannes, v, p. 333.

[2] Analects ix. 5 (Legge, *op. cit.*, i, pp. 81 f.; 2nd ed., pp. 217 f.).

[3] *Les Mémoires historiques*, translated by Chavannes, v, pp. 336 f.

[4] Analects vii. 12 (Legge, *op. cit.*, p. 66; 2nd ed., p. 202).

[5] See Hastings' *Encyclopædia of Religion and Ethics*, v, 1912, p. 785a.

[6] Babylonian Talmud, Sanhedrin 29a and Yebamoth 114b. See *The Baby-lonian Talmud translated into English*, Seder Nezikin v, 1935, p. 177, and Seder Nashim ii, 1936, p. 809.

[7] See Ssŭ-ma Ch'ien, *Les Mémoires historiques*, translated by Chavannes, v, p. 345.

The Chinese sages, however, did not let their fatalism carry them into foolhardiness. Said Mencius: 'He who has the true idea of what is Heaven's appointment will not stand beneath a precipitous wall. Death sustained in the discharge of one's duties may correctly be ascribed to the appointment of Heaven. Death under handcuffs and fetters cannot be correctly so ascribed.'[1] Chu Hsi, indeed, argues that while death under handcuffs and fetters is not directly due to the decree of Heaven, it is indirectly due to it, since it is the consequence of the *ch'i* with which one was originally endowed, but limits the attitude of submissiveness to the true, or direct, decree. 'If a man says he is destined to die in water or fire', he says, 'he does not, on that account, himself leap into the water, or fire, and die.'[2] This fatalism, therefore, was quite different in spirit from that of a thirteenth-century Chinese general, Chang Shih-chieh, who refused to save himself from shipwreck, saying: 'When one Emperor perished, I set up another; he also has disappeared; and now to-day I meet this great storm; surely it must be the will of Heaven that the Sung dynasty should perish'.[3] Here fatalism was a mere paralysing force, breeding helpless depression of spirit.[4]

Other Chinese schools have taught a fatalism that was not based on the decree of Heaven, but that was blind and purposeless. It was therefore different in its essence from the fatalism of Confucius, and different in the quality of the response it called forth. All that life brought was to be received with absolute passivity, and the only wise course lay in the pursuit of one's own well-being, and complete indifference to the sufferings of others.

The author of the Tao Tê Ching, the classic of Taoism,[5]

[1] Mencius VII, i. 2 (Legge, *The Chinese Classics*, ii, pp. 325 f.; 2nd ed., pp. 449 f.).

[2] *The Philosophy of Human Nature*, translated by Bruce, pp. 142 f.

[3] See Hastings' *Encyclopædia of Religion and Ethics*, v, p. 785a.

[4] Cf. Grantham, *Hills of Blue*, 1927, p. 396, for the historical setting of this incident.

[5] Y. L. Fung (*History of Chinese Philosophy*, i, 1937, pp. 170 ff.) holds that the founder of Taoism was Li Êrh, who lived after Confucius, in the period of the Warring States, and who has been confused with a legendary person, Lao Tan. He holds that the literary form of the Tao Tê Ching marks it as later than the Analects and Mencius. Cf. Waley (*The Way and its Power*,

elevated the principle of *wu wei*, or inaction, to be the highest ideal. His observation that 'it is the way of the Tao . . . to recompense injury with kindness'[1] is often quoted, without any perception that it rests on the principle of complete indifference.[2] Thus he also says: 'Heaven and earth do not act from any wish to be benevolent; they deal with all things as the dogs of grass (i.e. straw-dogs used in praying for rain and afterwards thrown aside) are dealt with. The sages do not act from any wish to be benevolent; they deal with the people as the dogs of grass are dealt with.'[3] The world therefore lies at the mercy of a hard, blind, unfeeling fate, whose quality the sage seeks to reproduce. 'Nothing of morality', says Wieger,[4] 'enters into this brutal system. It is physical, blind, immutable, eternal law.'

Similarly Têng Hsi, the father of the Fa Chia, or Law School of Chinese thinkers, whose best known exponent was Han-Fei-tzŭ, taught that fate is pitiless and blind.[5] Just as Heaven destroys by frost in a night the vegetables it has carefully

1934, pp. 86, 101 ff.), who holds that the Tao Tê Ching is an anonymous work dating from *circa* 240 B.C., and E. R. Hughes (*Chinese Philosophy in Classical Times*, 1942, p. 144), who ascribes it to the late fourth century B.C., but with some doubt. Duyvendak, in *De godsdiensten der wereld*, i, 2nd ed., 1948, pp. 500 f. says: 'Lau-tze "de Oude Meester", aan wien de *Tao-te-tsjing* wordt toegeschreven, wordt ten onrechte door de traditie tot een ouder tijdgenoot van Confucius gemaakt; van hemzelf weten wij niets, en het werk is waarschijnlijk een product van rond 300 v. Chr.'. Cf. below, pp. 108 f. n.

[1] Tao Tê Ching lxiii (translation of Legge, *Sacred Books of the East*, xxxix, 1891, p. 106). Ch'u Ta-kao (*Tao Tê Ching*, 1937, p. 92) transfers this to the beginning of chapter lxxix, and renders 'Return love for great hatred'.

[2] See below, pp. 76 ff. Wieger adopts a translation which makes this abundantly clear, and whose divergence from that given by others well indicates the cryptic and ambiguous character of the utterance for which Lao-tzŭ has received so much unmerited praise. Wieger renders: 'faire le même cas des reproches et des remerciements' (*Taoïsme*, ii, p. 54). Waley (*op. cit.*, p. 219) thinks the anonymous author of the Tao Tê Ching appropriated a pre-Confucian proverbial saying.

[3] Tao Tê Ching v (Legge, *Sacred Books of the East*, xxxix, p. 50; cf. Wieger, *Taoïsme*, ii, 1913, pp. 20 f.).

[4] *History of the Religious Beliefs and Philosophical Opinions in China*, translated by Werner, 1927, p. 150.

[5] The same view is taken by Lieh-tzŭ, who will be mentioned below. Cf. Forke, *Die Gedankenwelt des chinesischen Kulturkreises*, 1927, p. 67: 'Der Taoist Lieh-tse hat das Schicksal, welches sich noch bei Lao-tse als freie Herrschergewalt darstellt, ganz mechanisiert und zu einem blinden Naturgesetz gemacht.'

produced, so at the hour of destiny it causes all men to die. It
is foolish for men to complain that they must die prematurely
in youth, or seek to avoid evil. The law will be applied to them
without pity or consideration. The prince ought therefore to
treat his people similarly, without shadow of kindness or pity,
but with the utmost rigour.[1]

Again, Yang Chu, whose opinions and teachings Mencius
vigorously opposed, taught that men are the puppets of a blind
destiny, and made 'each one for himself' his guiding principle.[2]
Legge describes him as 'about "the least erected spirit" who
ever professed to reason concerning the life and duties of
man'.[3] He poured scorn on the sages who achieved fame by
their self-sacrificing labours for others, including Confucius and
those whom Confucius revered,[4] while he praised the wisdom
of those who won for themselves lasting execration by their
criminal selfishness,[5] and advocated that men should surrender
themselves to their lot, and disdain the accidents of life, finding
an inner peace and contentment in the recognition that everything is controlled by fate.[6] Mencius characterizes the utter
selfishness of Yang Chu by saying: 'Though he might have
benefited the whole kingdom by plucking out a single hair, he
would not have done it',[7] and this fully accords with the
account of him given by Lieh-tzŭ.[8]

Lieh-tzŭ approved of this attitude, and supported it by
the story of two voluptuous brothers, who gave utterance to
the same views with a directness much like that of Yang Chu.

[1] Cf. Wieger, *op. cit.*, p. 234.

[2] Mencius III, ii. 9 (Legge, *The Chinese Classics*, ii, p. 158; 2nd ed., p. 282).

[3] *The Chinese Classics*, ii, Prolegomena, p. 95; 2nd ed., p. 92.

[4] Wang An-shih is surely wrong when he declares that Yang Chu's teaching
was nearer to that of Confucius than was Mo Ti's (see Williamson, *Wang An
Shih*, ii, 1937, p. 383).

[5] Lieh-tzŭ vii. See text and translation in Legge, *The Chinese Classics*, ii,
Prolegomena, pp. 99 f.; 2nd ed., pp. 96 f.; or Wieger, *Taoïsme*, ii, pp. 174 f.
Cf. Forke, *Yang Chu's Garden of Pleasure*, 1912, pp. 54 ff.

[6] See Wieger, *History of the Religious Beliefs . . . in China*, p. 202. Cf.
Forke, *op. cit.*, pp. 61 f.

[7] Mencius VII, i, 26 (Legge, *op. cit.*, ii, p. 340; 2nd ed., p. 464).

[8] Lieh-tzŭ vii. See text and translation in Legge, *The Chinese Classics*,
ii, Prolegomena, pp. 98 f.; 2nd ed., pp. 95 f.; or Wieger, *Taoïsme*, ii, pp. 172 f.
Y. L. Fung (*op. cit.*, i, pp. 133 ff.). distinguishes between the views of Yang
Chu and the complete hedonism attributed to him by Lieh-tzŭ.

'All we desire', they said, 'is to get as much happiness as a single existence can give, to extract from each year as it passes the utmost pleasure that it can afford. Our only trouble is that the belly can hold no more while the mouth is still greedy, that the powers of the body give out while lust is still strong. We have no time to worry about such questions as to whether our conduct is injurious to our worldly reputations or dangerous to our constitutions. . . . He who is bent on putting the world around him in order cannot be certain that the world will accept his rule, but may be sure that his own life will be disagreeable. He who is bent only upon enjoying life cannot be certain that the world will therefore be disordered, but he may be sure that he himself will be a great deal more comfortable.'[1] That these views were approved by Lieh-tzŭ is to be inferred from his ascription of approval to the sage Têng Hsi.

Similar views are ascribed to the Indian materialistic school of the Lokāyatikas in the Sarva-Darśana-Saṁgraha,[2] where they are said to have taught that 'the only end of man is enjoyment produced by sensual pleasures'.[3] Of their views Radhakrishnan says:[4] 'On this theory pleasure and pain are the central facts of life. An unqualified hedonism is the ethical ideal of the materialist school. Eat, drink, and be merry, for death comes to all, closing our lives.

> "While life is yours, live joyously:
> None can escape Death's searching eye;
> When once this frame of ours they burn,
> How shall it e'er again return?"[5]

Virtue is a delusion and enjoyment is the only reality. Life is the end of life. There was a distrust of everything good, high, pure and compassionate. The theory stands for sensation and selfishness and the gross affirmation of the loud will.'

[1] Lieh-tzŭ vii, translation of Waley (*Three Ways of Thought in Ancient China*, 1939, pp. 49 f.). For text and translation, see Wieger, *op. cit.*, ii, pp. 168 f. Cf. Forke, *Yang Chu's Garden of Pleasure*, p. 48.

[2] Cf. Cowell and Gough, *Sarva-Darśana-Saṁgraha*, 1882, chapter i, pp. 2 ff. See also Rhys Davids, *Dialogues of the Buddha*, i, 1899, pp. 166 ff.

[3] See Cowell and Gough, *op. cit.*, p. 3.

[4] *Indian Philosophy*, i, pp. 281 f. On this school cf. Belvalkar and Ranade, *History of Indian Philosophy*, ii, 1927, pp. 458 f.

[5] See Cowell and Gough, *op. cit.*, p. 2.

Returning to Chinese teachers, we find that Chuang-tzŭ, again, inculcates an attitude of passive indifference to the blind workings of fate. Waley describes his attitude as being one not merely of resignation, or acquiescence, but a lyrical, almost ecstatic acceptance.[1] 'When Chuang-tzŭ's wife died, Hui-tzŭ went to condole with him, and finding him squatted on the ground, drumming on the basin and singing, said to him: "When a wife has lived with her husband and brought up children, and then dies in her old age, not to wail for her is enough. When you go on to drum on this basin and sing, is it not an excessive demonstration?" Chuang-tzŭ replied: "It is not so. When she first died, was it possible for me to be singular and not be affected by the event? But I reflected on the commencement of her being. She had not yet been born to life; not only had she no life, but she had no bodily form; not only had she no bodily form, but she had no breath. During the intermingling of the waste and dark chaos, there ensued a change, and there was breath; another change, and there was the bodily form; another change, and there came birth and life. There is now a change again, and she is dead. . . . There now she lies with her face up . . .; and if I were to fall sobbing and going on to wail for her, I should think that I did not understand what was appointed for all." '[2]

So again, in writing of the death of Lao-tzŭ, he says 'When the Master came, it was at the proper time; when he went away, it was the simple sequence of his coming. Quiet acquiescence in what happens at its proper time, and quietly submitting to it ceasing afford no occasion for grief or joy.'[3]

Another writer, Wang Ch'ung, who is said by Wieger to

[1] *Three Ways of Thought in Ancient China*, p. 51.

[2] Chuang-tzŭ XVIII, ii. 11, translation of Legge (*Sacred Books of the East*, xl, 1891, pp. 4 f.). Cf. Giles, *Chuang Tzŭ*, pp. 223 f., Wieger, *Taoïsme*, ii, pp. 350 f. (for text and translation).

[3] Chuang-tzŭ III, i. 3, translation of Legge (*Sacred Books of the East*, xxxix, p. 201). Cf. Giles, *op. cit.*, pp. 36 f. Wieger (*Taoïsme*, ii, pp. 228 f.) gives the text and renders: 'The law, forgotten by the vulgar herd, but which the Sage remembers, is that every one comes into the world at his time, and leaves it at his time. The Sage does not therefore rejoice at births, or trouble himself at deaths.'

be the greatest genius of all Chinese writers,[1] believed that all things were governed by their own inner law. All that is has its own inner force, by which it irresistibly follows its course, and neither destiny nor merit can affect its way. When in its course its path crosses the path of another, and there is a collision, the stronger force destroys the weaker. By this means both individual and collective tragedies and catastrophies are to be explained. To regard them as ordained of Heaven is foolish; to regard them as punishments of evil is incredible. They are but to be accepted as inevitable collisions of helpers and blind forces.[2]

A closely similar view is found in the teaching of the Indian ascetic Gosāla, founder of the Ājīvikas,[3] and contemporary of the Buddha. We learn from Buddhist texts, where his teaching was criticized, that he taught: 'There is no cause for the sufferings of beings; they therefore all suffer without any cause; there is no cause for the purity of beings; they all become pure without any cause; there is no efficiency in one's deeds or in the deeds of others or in one's free efforts; there is no power, no energy, no human strength or heroic endeavours. All vertebrates, all animals with one or more senses, all lives emanating from eggs or ovaries, all vegetable lives, are without any power or efficiency. They become transformed in various forms by their inherent destiny, by their manifestation in

---

[1] *History of the Religious Beliefs . . . in China*, p. 318. Cf. Forke, *Lun-Hêng*, i, 1907, p. 3, and *Geschichte der mittelalterlichen chinesischen Philosophie*, 1934, p. 114, where is cited the view expressed in 1874 that Wang Ch'ung was 'a philosopher, perhaps the most original and judicious among all the metaphysicians China has produced'. R. Wilhelm (*A Short History of Chinese Civilization*, E. Tr, 1929, p. 178) calls him 'that sceptical eccentric'.

[2] See Wieger, *op. cit.*, pp. 318 ff. Cf. Forke, *op. cit.*, i, p. 27: 'The destiny, says Wang Ch'ung, which fixes the duration of human life, is the heavenly fluid, i.e. the vital force, with which man is imbued at his birth'; p. 28: 'Wang Ch'ung's Fate is not the inexorable decree of Heaven, the εἱμαρμένη of the Greeks, the *dira necessitas*, or the patristic predestination, being partly natural (vital fluid), partly supernatural (starry fluid) and partly chance'. For the translation of the passages in which these views are expressed, see Forke, *Lun-Hêng*, i, pp. 136 ff.; ii, 1911, pp. 1 ff. Cf. too, Giles, *Confucianism and its Rivals*, 1915, pp. 156 ff.

[3] Hoernle (in Hastings' *Encyclopædia of Religion and Ethics*, i, 1908, p. 268a) identifies the Ājīvikas with the Digambara Jains, but Dasgupta (*History of Indian Philosophy*, iii, 1940, pp. 523 f.) disputes this view. Cf. Farquhar, *An Outline of the Religious Literature of India*, 1920, p. 77 n.

various life-forms, and by their different natures, and it is in accordance with their six kinds of life-states that they suffer pains and enjoy pleasures.'[1]

All such fatalism, of whatever type, was strongly opposed by the Chinese sage Mo-tzŭ, who founded a rival philosophy to Confucianism, and who repudiated fatalism as tending to produce idleness. 'In ancient times', he said, 'the miserable people indulged in drinking and eating and were lazy in their work. Thereupon their food and clothing became insufficient, and the danger of hunger and cold was approaching. They did not acknowledge: "I was stupid and insolent, and was not diligent at work". But they would say: "It is but my lot to be poor".'[2] Again, 'Fatalism was an invention of the wicked kings and the practice of miserable men';[3] 'To hold there is fate is the great disaster of the world';[4] 'Fatalism is not helpful to Heaven above, nor to the spirits in the middle sphere, nor to man below. The eccentric belief in this doctrine is responsible for pernicious ideas and is the way of the wicked.'[5] Mo-tzŭ

---

[1] Dīgha-Nikāya ii. 20, translation of Dasgupta (*op. cit.*, iii, p. 524). Cf. Rhys Davids, *Dialogues of the Buddha*, i, 1899, p. 71 ; Grimblot, *Sept Suttas Pâlis*, 1876, pp. 170, 197 f. The passage is cited by Jacobi in *Sacred Books of the East*, xlv, 1895, pp. xxv f., and by Hoernle in Hastings' *Encyclopædia of Religion and Ethics*, i, p. 261a. Buddhaghosa's commentary on it is translated by Hoernle in *The Uvāsagadasāo*, 1885, Appendix II, pp. 15 ff. Cf. also Keith, *Buddhist Philosophy in India and Ceylon*, 1923, p. 136. The Jaina account of Gosāla's teaching credits him with the view that 'there is no such thing as exertion or labour or power or vigour or manly strength, but all things are unalterably fixed' (Uvāsagadasāo, 166, translation of Hoernle, *op. cit.*, pp. 109 f.). Cf. Mrs. Sinclair Stevenson, *The Heart of Jainism*, 1915, pp. 58-60. On Gosāla and his teaching, cf. Shah, *Jainism in North India*, 1932, pp. 58 ff.

[2] Mo-tzŭ xxxv, translation of Mei (*The Works of Motse*, 1929, p. 187). Mo-tzŭ is the same as the Mo Ti referred to above.

[3] Mo-tzŭ xxxvii (Mei, p. 199). Tomkinson (*The Social Teachings of Meh Tse*, 1927, p. 122) renders: 'these were the inventions of tyrants, imitated by the lowest classes'. Cf. Forke, *Mê Ti*, 1922, p. 395: 'Dagegen ist zu sagen, dass das Schicksal eine Erfindung der verbrecherischen Herrscher ist. Das elende Volk folgt ihnen nach.'

[4] Mo-tzŭ xxxvi (Mei, p. 193).

[5] Mo-tzŭ xxxv (Mei, p. 188). Cf. Forke, *op. cit.*, p. 382: 'Also nützt das Schicksal in der oberen Sphäre nicht dem Himmel, in der mittleren nicht den Geistern und in der unteren nicht den Menschen. Das hartnäckige Festhalten an dieser Ansicht hat die verwerflichsten Äusserungen hervorgerufen, denn es ist eine Lehre für Frevler.' Tomkinson (*op. cit.*, p. 114) has: 'Wherefore belief in fate benefits neither Heaven, nor the spirits, nor men. From clinging to this idea, springs all manner of evil teaching, and it is injurious to men.'

was much less specific, however, in defining his own positive view. He was interested in overthrowing fatalism on pragmatic grounds, because of its effects on men, and he taught that rulers should, like Heaven, reward the virtuous. 'He who obeys the will of Heaven, loving universally and benefiting others, will obtain rewards. He who opposes the will of Heaven, by being partial and unfriendly and harming others, will incur punishment.'[1] Yet it is not to be supposed that Mo-tzŭ really believed that justice is universally done in the affairs of men. Wang Ch'ung declared that he did, and said that on his principles it would be necessary to suppose that all the inhabitants of Li-yang, which was engulfed in a night in a subterranean lake, deserved this fate, and, similarly, that the four hundred thousand men whom Pai-ch'i put to the sword in a single day were justly slain.[2] In truth, however, Mo-tzŭ propounded no consistent principle. Like those teachers at whose utterances we first looked, he was only concerned to inculcate virtue by promising it reward, and to eliminate vice by promising it punishment. 'For the murder of an innocent individual there will be a calamity', he said,[3] recognizing the possibility of innocent suffering, while the earnestness with which he advocated the exaltation of the virtuous and the discharge of the vicious from the service of the state[4] sufficiently shows that he recognized that virtue and vice did not invariably and necessarily ensure their own due recompense. To Mo-tzŭ we shall have to return below. Here it is only necessary to notice him as a strenuous, but unsuccessful, critic of the fatalistic strain in Chinese teaching. He does not distinguish between the nobler fatalism of Confucius and the meaner view of other teachers, since whatever the inner quality of the submission to which they lead, both lead to an attitude of submission. And Mo-tzŭ favoured no tame resignation to circumstances.

---

[1] Mo-tzŭ xxvi (Mei, p. 137).

[2] See Wieger, *op. cit.*, p. 319. The passage is translated by Forke in *Lun Hêng*, i, pp. 136 f. Cf. also Wang Ch'ung's essays *On Reprimands* (in Forke, *op. cit.*, i, pp. 119 ff.) and *Wrong Notions on Unhappiness* (*ibid.*, pp. 164 ff.).

[3] Mo-tzŭ xxvi (Mei, p. 139).

[4] Mo-tzŭ viii-x (Mei, pp. 30 ff.).

VI

Islamic fatalism is associated in western minds with the word *qismat*. 'In Turkish', says the *Encyclopædia of Islam*,[1] '*kismet* is not so much an expression of theological doctrines concerning predestination as of a practical fatalism which accepts with resignation the blows and vicissitudes of fate. The same sentiment is often expressed among Persian and Turkish poets by the words *falak* and *čarkh* to express the irrational and inevitable influence exercised by the spheres.'

The word *qismat* does not occur in the Qur'ān in this sense, though it is found in a different sense, and Muḥammad 'Ali[2] denies that there is any fatalism in the Qur'ān, though he recognizes that it has been found amongst the Islamic schools. The discussion of Islamic fatalism, however, is commonly linked with that of the wider question of predestination, and it is of this that Muḥammad 'Ali is really thinking. It would carry us far beyond the scope of this paper to consider how far Islam teaches that the character and eternal destiny of men are fixed beforehand by divine decree, *qadar* or *taqdir*.[3] We are only concerned to see how it accounts for the sufferings of men, and what response it seeks to evoke.

Margoliouth says: 'There is little reason for thinking that Moslems interpret what happens by the unalterable will of God to a much greater extent than others. Resentment at injury, impatience, querulousness, which this doctrine should restrain, are probably less controlled in the East than in the West.'[4] This again is somewhat beside the point so far as our present purpose is concerned, since we are examining the teaching of some eastern religions, rather than the extent to which that teaching is followed by their adherents.

In the Jāhaliyyah, or 'time of ignorance', prior to the time of Muḥammad, blind and irresistible fate was believed to cause misfortunes, and the path of wisdom accordingly to lie in a

---

[1] *Encyclopædia of Islām*, ii, 1927, p. 1041*b*.

[2] *The Religion of Islām*, 1936, p. 324 n.

[3] On this cf. Sweetman, *Islam and Christian Theology*, Part I, ii, 1947, pp. 157 ff., and Watt, *Free Will and Predestination in Early Islam*, 1948.

[4] *Mohammedanism* (Home University Library), p. 150.

stoical acceptance of trouble. Thus, in the third of the Seven Mu'allaqāt, ascribed to Zuhair bin 'Abu Sulmâ 'al-Muzanî, we read:[1]

> Fate, to me, is like a stumbling, eyeless camel—
> Whom it hits it kills, and whom it misses lives and grows old;

while Waddâk bin Thumail 'al-Mâzanî says:[2]

> Meet them, and ye will know how patient
> They are in bearing the injustice of fortune.

To Muḥammad, with his strong sense of the divine sovereignty, any such idea of blind and impersonal fate was quite impossible. To him all the sorrows of life were to be attributed to the will of God, whether they were the punishment for human sin and rebellion or not. The submission to which he called men, therefore, was quite different from the helpless submission to an irresistible fate; it was the submission of will to will, the recognition that God is not only powerful but wise, and that though His way is inscrutable to man, it is to be trusted. The submission to which he called men was thus a submission touched with faith.[3]

'No one can die', he said, 'except by God's permission, according to the Book that fixeth the term of life';[4] or again

---

[1] Verse 49. The text and translation of this passage, and of several other Islamic passages referred to below, may be found in an important article by E. E. Salisbury, 'Muhammadan Predestination and Free Will', in *Journal of the American Oriental Society*, viii, 1866, pp. 101-182. Zuhair's verse stands on p. 106. Cf. Johnson, *The Seven Poems*, 1894, p. 84, or, for Arabic text only, Arnold, *Septem Mo'allakât*, 1850, p. 85. Lyall's fine rendering of this verse (*Translations of Ancient Arabian Poetry*, 1885, p. 114) is:

'I have seen the Dooms trample men as a blind beast at random treads—
Whom they smote, he died; whom they missed, he lived to strengthless eld'.

[2] Salisbury's rendering, *loc. cit.*, p. 107. Cf. Freytag, *Hamasæ Carmina*, i, 1828, p. 57; ii, 1847, p. 108.

[3] Ringgren (*Islam, 'aslama and muslim*, 1949) has argued that *'islām* means more than mere submission, and should be understood to mean *total submission*, while the frequent linking of *'īmān, faith*, with *'islām*, and the apparent equivalence of the verbs *'amana* and *'aslama*, lead him to conclude that 'total surrender is total confidence'.

[4] Qur'ān iii. 139, Rodwell's translation (*The Koran*, Everyman's Library, p. 399). Bell (*The Qur'ān Translated*, i, 1937, pp. 58 f.) has 'except by permission of Allah written and dated', and Montet (*Le Coran*, 1949, p. 146) 'écrite pour un temps déterminé.'

'Nothing will afflict us save what Allah has ordained for us';[1] similarly, 'No misfortune has befallen either the land or yourselves, but it was in a book before We brought it to be';[2] and 'No misfortune has happened but by the permission of Allah'.[3]

In Jewish sources we find a similar view that all the misfortunes of men are predetermined by God. 'Good things and evil', said Ben Sira,[4] 'life and death, Poverty and riches, are from the Lord'. Again we are told that 'Rabbi Eleazar ben Pedath was greatly distressed by poverty. One day he was bled, and after the operation had nothing to eat. He found some garlic and swallowed it, whereupon he fainted. Some of the Rabbis went to visit him and noticed that he was weeping and laughing, and that a ray of light proceeded from his forehead. When he awoke, they asked him, "Why did you weep and laugh, and why did a ray of light proceed from your forehead?" "I saw the Shekinah", he replied, "and complained before her, saying, 'How long shall I continue to live in this poverty?' and the Shekinah replied to me: 'Would it be acceptable to thee that I should destroy the world and create it anew?' " '[5]

Sir Mohammad Iqbal, quoting the text 'God created all things and assigned to each its destiny',[6] maintains that this destiny is the working out of an inner law rather than an external control. 'The destiny of a thing', he says,[7] 'is not an unrelenting fate working from without like a task master; it is the inward reach of a thing, its realizable possibilities which lie within the depths of its nature, and serially actualize themselves without any feeling of external compulsion. Thus the organic wholeness of duration does not mean that full-fledged

[1] Qur'ān ix. 51, translation of Muhammad 'Ali (*The Holy Qur-án containing the Arabic Text with English Translation and Commentary*, 2nd ed., 1920, p. 409).

[2] Qur'ān lvii. 22, Bell's translation (*op. cit.*, ii, 1939, p. 561).

[3] Qur'ān lxiv. 11, Bell's translation (*ibid.*, p. 584).

[4] Ecclus. xi. 14.

[5] Babylonian Talmud, Ta'anith 25a, translation of Malter (*The Treatise Ta'anit of the Babylonian Talmud*, 1928, p. 189). Cf. Rabbinowitz, *The Babylonian Talmud translated into English*, Seder Mo'ed, vii, 1938, Ta'anith, p. 130.

[6] Cf. Qur'ān liv. 49, lxxxvii. 2 f.

[7] *The Reconstruction of Religious Thought in Islam*, 1934, pp. 47 f.

events are lying, as it were, in the womb of Reality, and drop one by one like the grains of sand from the hour-glass.'

The founder of Islam was less concerned with the mechanics of the divine control than with the fact of that control, and clearly wished men to regard the vicissitudes of fortune as the will of God for them. 'If good falls to their lot', he said,[1] 'they say: "This is from Allah", but if evil befalls them, they say: "This is from thee". Say: "Everything is from Allah".'

These quotations from the Qur'ān can be reinforced by some of the traditions containing the Prophet's sayings, found in the collections of Ḥadīth. 'If any ill befalls thee, say not: "Had it been my doing, it would not have been so and so", but say: "It is God's decree, and whatever He wills He does".'[2] 'Said 'Umar: "Permit me, and I will sever his neck". The Prophet replied: "Let alone! If that is to be, the power to do it is not in thee; and if not to be, in vain would'st thou kill him." '[3] 'Whenever God is pleased to determine the nature of the new being, the angel inquires: "O my Lord, a male or a female? miserable or blessed?" and so: "What is the allotment of good? and what is the term of life?" and it is written down accordingly in the womb of the mother.'[4] With this last passage we may compare a Jewish passage found in the Talmud,[5] which says that the angel who presides over conception cries, 'Lord

---

[1] Qur'ān iv. 80, Bell's translation (*op. cit.*, i, p. 79).

[2] See Salisbury, *Journal of the American Oriental Society*, viii, p. 142, for the text of the passage, and translation. This tradition is taken from Muslim's collection. See Muslim, *Jami' 'al-Ṣaḥīḥ, with a commentary by Nawawi*, ii, 1885, p. 338.

[3] See Salisbury, *loc. cit.*, p. 143, for text and translation. For text also, *Recueil des traditions mahométanes par el-Bokhâri*, ed. Krehl and Juynboll, iv, 1908, p. 256. For the phrase 'if that is to be' Houdas renders 'if it is he—i.e. the Antichrist' (Houdas and Marçais, *El-Bokhâri: Les Traditions islamiques*, iv, 1914, p. 326), and Guillaume, similarly, 'if it is he (the Dajjal)' (*Traditions of Islam*, 1924, p. 177=*Journal of the Royal Asiatic Society*, 1924, p. 60).

[4] See Salisbury, *ibid.*, p. 124, for text and translation. For text, ed. Krehl and Juynboll, iv, p. 251; for translation, Guillaume, *Traditions of Islam*, p. 172 (=*J.R.A.S.*, 1924, pp. 51 f.), or Houdas, *op. cit.*, iv, p. 319. Cf. Goldziher, *Le dogme et la loi de l'Islam*, 1920, p. 76: 'Chaque embryon a toute sa destinée vitale tracée par un ange spécialement désigné à cet effet, . . . et, entre autres choses, il est destiné au salut ou à la damnation.' Cf. also Watt, *Free Will and Predestination in Early Islam*, 1948, p. 18.

[5] Niddah 16*b* (cf. Slotki, *The Babylonian Talmud translated into English*, Seder Ṭohoroth, i, 1948, Niddah, p. 111).

of the world! what shall this child be, strong or weak, wise or ignorant, rich or poor?'

Sir Mohammad Iqbal distinguishes the original principle of Islam from the later degrading type of fatalism prevalent in the world of Islam. He says:[1] 'But is it not true that a most degrading type of Fatalism has prevailed in the world of Islam for many centuries? This is true, and has a history behind it which requires separate treatment. It is sufficient here to indicate that the kind of Fatalism which the European critics of Islam sum up in the word "Qismat" was due partly to philosophical thought, partly to political expediency, and partly to the gradually diminishing force of the life-impulse which Islam originally imparted to its followers. Philosophy, searching for the meaning of cause as applied to God, and taking time as the essence of the relation between cause and effect, could not but reach the notion of a transcendent God, prior to the universe, and operating upon it from without. God was thus conceived as the last link in the chain of causation, and consequently the real author of all that happens in the universe. Now the practical materialism of the opportunist Omayyad rulers of Damascus needed a peg on which to hang their misdeeds. . . . Thus arose . . . a morally degrading Fatalism, and the constitutional theory known as the "accomplished fact" in order to support vested interests.'

It should not be forgotten that some support for this view can be found in the Qur'ān, and that it is not merely a later degenerate view that God is the real author of all that happens. Of the battle of Badr we read: 'Ye did not kill them but Allah killed them, and when thou didst throw, it was not thou but Allah who threw'.[2] With this we may compare Gen. xlv. 8: 'So now it was not you that sent me hither, but God'. But whether or no God is the author of man's *actions*, the Qur'ān and the Ḥadīth would seem to establish that the Prophet held Him to be the determiner of men's *fortunes*. But this is not necessarily a degrading type of fatalism, and in Muḥammad's view it was elevated by the spirit he called forth from men. In a world where good and evil alike come by the ordinance of

---

[1] *Op. cit.*, pp. 104 f.
[2] Qur'ān viii. 17, Bell's translation (*op. cit.*, i, p. 163).

God, patient submission is the wise response, and to this he called men. 'Allah loves the patient', he said. [1]

There are many passages in the Qur'ān where the patient endurance of suffering, and especially of persecution, is enjoined. In a passage referring to Joseph, we read: 'Truly if one shows piety and endures patiently—Allah alloweth not to perish the reward of those who do well'.[2] Again we find: 'Peace be upon you, for the patient endurance ye have shown';[3] 'Good is the reward of those who labour, who have endured and upon their Lord have set their trust.'[4] It will be observed that here endurance is accompanied with trust. It is not merely helpless and uncomplaining acceptance of suffering that is enjoined, but a quiet confidence in God. With this we may compare: 'Why should we not set our trust upon Allah, seeing He hath guided us in our ways? Surely, we shall endure patiently under the injuries ye inflict upon us';[5] and 'We shall surely try you with some experience of fear and hunger and defect of property and persons and fruits; so give good tidings to those who patiently endure, who when misfortune falls upon them say: "Verily we are Allah's, and to Him do we return" '.[6]

Similarly, in the Ḥadīth we find that when Muḥammad's grandchild was at the point of death, the Prophet sent to the child's Mother the message: 'To God belongs both what he takes away and what he grants; every one has a fixed term of life; be thou, then, patient, and consider'.[7] Elsewhere we find:

[1] Qur'ān iii. 140, Muḥammad 'Ali's translation (*op. cit.*, p. 182, where it is numbered 145). Cf. Rodwell's rendering: 'God loves those who endure with steadfastness' (*op. cit.*, p. 399).

[2] Qur'ān xii. 90, Bell's translation (*op. cit.*, i, p. 226).

[3] Qur'ān xiii. 24, Bell's translation (*ibid.*, p. 232).

[4] Qur'ān xxix. 58 f., Bell's translation (*ibid.*, ii, pp. 389 f.).

[5] Qur'ān xiv. 15, Bell's translation (*ibid.*, i, p. 238).

[6] Qur'ān ii. 150 f., Bell's translation (*ibid.*, pp. 21 f.); Montet (*Le Coran*, 1949, p. 99 n.) comments 'Pensée religieuse profonde; elle rapelle les paroles célèbres de Job frappé par le malheur: Job 1 v. 21 et 2 v. 10.'

[7] See Salisbury, *Journal of American Oriental Society*, viii, p. 133, for text of the passage and translation. For text, see ed. Krehl and Juynboll, iv, p. 252; for translation, see Guillaume, *Traditions of Islam*, p. 173 (=*J.R.A.S.*, 1924, p. 53), and Houdas, *op. cit.*, iv, p. 321. Guillaume renders the last sentence: 'Let her therefore be patient under bereavement and earn the reward of patience'.

'Take ye refuge with God from the pressure of calamity, the vexation of misfortune, the ills of destiny, and the malice of enemies';[1] 'No mortal, being in a city where there is pestilence, who waits in the midst of it, not leaving the city, patient and collected, knowing that no evil will befall him but that which God foreordained for him—shall he not have a like reward with the martyr?';[2] 'Do Thou then inspire us with a tranquil mind, and make firm our feet, that we may bear the onset of the idolaters who have defied us'.[3]

Sometimes this attitude has led to an actual glorying in suffering. Thus Margoliouth records that 'a saint who had been bedridden with dropsy thirty years repudiated sympathy, because he liked best what God liked best'.[4] With this we may compare Paul's 'Most gladly therefore will I rather glory in my infirmities, that the power of Christ may rest upon me. Therefore I take pleasure in infirmities, in reproaches, in necessities, in persecutions, in distresses for Christ's sake; for when I am weak, then am I strong.'[5]

Some ascetics have gone beyond this, and courted suffering and shame for its own sake,[6] but the Khalīf Omar expressed a more balanced point of view when he said: 'He who is in the fire should resign himself to the will of God; but he who is not yet in the fire need not throw himself into it'[7]—with which observation we may compare utterances of Mencius and Chu Hsi quoted above.

If is clear that this Islamic submission is other than that of the Indian and Chinese thinkers at whose words we have looked above. It is not based on philosophical or practical considerations, but on fundamentally religious grounds. It is still in essence a passive resignation. But it believes in a sovereign

[1] See Salisbury, *loc. cit.*, p. 142; Krehl and Juynboll, iv, p. 256; Guillaume, p. 177 (=*J.R.A.S.*, p. 59); Houdas, iv, p. 326.
[2] See Salisbury, *loc. cit.*, p. 144; Krehl and Juynboll, iv, p. 257; Guillaume, p. 178 (=*J.R.A.S.*, p. 60); Houdas, iv, pp. 326 f.
[3] See Salisbury, *loc. cit.*; Krehl and Juynboll, *loc. cit.*; Guaillume, p. 178 (=*J.R.A.S.*, p. 61); Houdas, iv, p. 327.
[4] *Early Development of Mohammedanism* (Hibbert Lectures), 1914, p. 172.
[5] 2 Cor. xii. 9 f.
[6] Cf. Margoliouth, *op. cit.*, pp. 167 ff.
[7] Quoted by Baron Carra de Vaux in Hastings' *Encyclopædia of Religion and Ethics*, v, p. 796a.

Lord of the universe, and it believes not only that His will cannot be resisted, but that it would be folly to resist it, even though it could be successfully resisted. His will is not alone bound to triumph, but is worthy to triumph, even when its triumph brings sorrow and pain. 'This is the true expression of a Muslim's resignation under trials', says Muḥammad 'Ali, ' "We come from Allah, and Allah is our goal". Therefore no trial or misfortune can disturb the course of our life, which has a much higher goal before it than mere comfort. These words are uttered by a Muslim when any misfortune befalls him. Come what may, the contentment of his mind is never disturbed.'[1] The same point of view is found not infrequently in the Bible. A single instance will here suffice. 'My life is spent with sorrow', cried the Psalmist,[2] 'and my years with sighing: My strength faileth because of mine affliction, and my bones are wasted away. Because of all mine adversaries I am become a reproach. . . . But I trusted in thee, O Lord; I said, Thou art my God. My times are in thy hand.'

A Babylonian text presenting a similar point of view is now known.[3] It is in the form of a dialogue between a dire sufferer, who impugns the justice of the gods, and a pious man who preaches humble resignation to the will of the gods, and who finally converts the sufferer to his point of view. 'A slave,[4] wise and submissive, am I', says the sufferer in the last surviving strophe of the text; 'Help and encouragement I have at no moment experienced. Through the square of my city I go

---

[1] *The Holy Qur-án*, p. 71. Cf. Mirza Ghulam Ahmad (*The Teachings of Islam*, 1921, p. 69): 'Everyone has, after much sorrowing and suffering, to make his peace with the misfortunes that befall him. But such contentment is by no means a noble moral quality. It is a natural consequence of the continuance of affliction that weariness at last brings about conciliation. . . . It is only when the loss is received with total resignation to the will of God and in complete submission to His pleasure that the deed deserves to be called virtuous.'

[2] Psalm xxxi. 10 ff. In verse 10 (Hebrew 11) the rendering 'mine affliction' follows the Greek and Syriac, instead of the Hebrew 'mine iniquity'.

[3] See Landsberger, 'Die babylonische Theodizee,' *Zeitschrift für Assyriologie*, xliii (N. F. ix), 1936, pp. 32-76; Pritchard, *Ancient Near Eastern Texts relating to the Old Testament*, 1950, pp. 439 f. Cf. also Dhorme, 'Ecclésiaste ou Job?', *Revue biblique*, xxxii, 1923, pp. 1-27.

[4] Dhorme (*loc. cit.*, p. 26) does not read quite so much into *rêšu=head* here, and takes it to mean individual, rather than *slave*, but equally finds the passage to breathe the spirit of deep humility.

5

with quiet steps, My voice never loud and my speech subdued.
My head I raised not, but looked on the ground. As a slave I
was not extolled in the assembly of my companions. May
Ninurta, who has cast me off, grant me help! May Ishtar, who
(was angry with me), pity me! May the shepherd Shamash as a
god (be gracious to me)![1] 'Here', says Albright,[2] 'is stressed the
inscrutability of divine justice and the need of the most complete
humility and abnegation of self in one's relation to the gods.'

VII

Not infrequently suffering is teleologically explained, in
terms of an educative or purifying purpose. This may be found
combined with various conceptions of the causation of suffering
in terms of the past. It appears, therefore, in the utterances of
several of the teachers already considered.

Thus Mencius, who, as we have seen, regarded misfortune
as self-entailed or as brought about by the decree of Heaven,
can speak of it as a divine discipline for the development of
character. 'When Heaven is about to confer a great office on
any man', he says, 'it first exercises his mind with suffering,
and his sinews and bones with toil. It exposes his body to
hunger, and subjects him to extreme poverty. It confounds
his undertakings. By all these methods it stimulates his mind,
hardens his nature, and supplies his incompetencies. Men for
the most part err, and are afterwards able to reform. They are
distressed in mind and perplexed in their thoughts, and then
they arise to vigorous reformation. When things have been
evidenced in men's looks, and set forth in their words, then
they understand them. If a prince have not about his court
families attached to the laws and worthy counsellors, and if
abroad there are not hostile states or other external calamities,
his kingdom will generally come to ruin. From these things
we see how life springs from sorrow and calamity, and death
from ease and pleasure.'[3]

[1] Strophe xxvii, lines 289-297. The translation follows that of Landsberger
(*loc. cit.*, p. 73).

[2] *From the Stone Age to Christianity*, 1940, p. 253.

[3] Mencius VI. ii. 15, translation of Legge (*The Chinese Classics*, ii, p. 323;
2nd ed., p. 447).

There is no suggestion here that the pains and calamities one has to face are the fruit of sin, or the ordinance of a fate that must be passively accepted. They are for the development of character and resource, and to equip a man to achieve greater things in the world. He should find in them, therefore, a challenge and an opportunity.

Again, in the Upaniṣads the doctrine of *karma* is combined with a sense of the educative value of suffering. 'The discipline of suffering has also its use in the education of the spirit', says Radhakrishnan; 'resistance drives the soul to put forth its whole strength, and thus compels it to grow.'[1] In the Upaniṣads we read: 'The good is one thing, the pleasant another; these two, having different objects, chain a man. It is well with him who clings to the good; he who chooses the pleasant misses his end.'[2] Or again, 'The sharp edge of a razor is difficult to pass over; thus the wise say the path to the Self is hard'.[3] The unpleasant and difficult experiences of life are here regarded as the way of growth and progress. 'Morality', says Radhakrishnan again,[4] 'implies a wrestling with the lower tendency, the pursuit of which appears pleasant. . . . Suffering is the condition of progress. . . . Suffering is the ransom the son of man has to pay if he would attain his crown. . . . Suffering is the messenger of God revealing to us the imperfection of the world, the episodic nature of earthly life'; and again,[5] 'The progress to perfection is through pain and suffering. The hard flints must come into violent conflict before they can produce the sparks of fire. The chick has to undergo the pain of separation from the shell before it can reach the intangible light and air.'

In the Qur'ān, also, we find the thought of suffering as a means of testing men and of bringing them gain. 'Think men that when they say, "We believe", they shall be let alone and

[1] *Indian Philosophy*, i, p. 244 = *The Philosophy of the Upaniṣads*, p. 120.

[2] Kaṭha ii. 1, translation of Müller (*Sacred Books of the East*, xv, p. 8). Cf. Hume, *The Thirteen Principal Upanishads*, p. 346, Rawson, *The Kaṭha Upaniṣad*, p. 81, and Otto, *Die Kaṭha-Upanishad*, 1936, p. 16.

[3] Kaṭha iii. 14 (Müller, *op. cit.*, p. 14). Cf. Hume, *op. cit.*, p. 353, Rawson, *op. cit.*, p. 145, and Otto, *op. cit.*, p. 20.

[4] *Indian Philosophy*, i, pp. 243 f. = *The Philosophy of the Upaniṣads*, pp. 119 f.

[5] *Indian Philosophy*, i, p. 243 = *The Philosophy of the Upaniṣads*, p. 119.

not put to the proof? We put to the proof those who lived
before them; for God will surely take knowledge of those who
are sincere, and will surely take knowledge of liars. . . .
Whoso maketh efforts for the faith, maketh them for his own
good only. Verily God is rich enough to dispense with all
creatures. . . . But some men say, "We believe in God", yet
when they meet with sufferings in the cause of God, they regard
trouble from man as chastisement from God'.[1] 'We shall surely
try you with some experience of fear and hunger and defect
of property and persons and fruits; so give thou good tidings
to those who patiently endure, who when misfortune falls
upon them say: "Verily we are Allah's, and to Him do we
return". Upon such are blessings and mercy from their Lord.'[2]
'The principle is laid down here', comments Muḥammad 'Ali,[3]
'that the faithful are brought to perfection through adversities
and trials, because we are told that Allah intends to try the
believers by means of various kinds of afflictions, and through
patience in suffering, they make themselves deserving of
Divine blessings and mercy.'

Sometimes the affliction is thought of as the instrument of
the divine reclamation. 'When some evil toucheth men, they
turn to their Lord and call upon him. . . . Destruction hath
appeared by land and sea on account of what men's hands have
wrought, that it might make them taste somewhat of the fruit of
their doings, that haply they might turn to God.'[4] This thought
is found also in the Bible. Psalm cvii narrates at length how
through adversity and sorrow men ever turn to God, and find
in Him a deliverance that should call forth their glad thanks-
giving and praise, and the Deuteronomic pragmatism which
dominates the framework of so much of the Old Testament
historical books regards calamity as not alone the divine
punishment for apostasy, but the gracious instrument of the
divine reclamation.

There are not a few passages in the Bible which declare
that suffering is sent to chasten, and through chastening to

---

[1] Qur'ān xxix. 1 ff., Rodwell's translation (*op. cit.*, pp. 261 f.).
[2] Qur'ān ii. 150 ff., Bell's translation (*op. cit.*, i, pp. 21 f.).
[3] *The Religion of Islām*, pp. 327 f.
[4] Qur'ān xxx. 32, 40, Rodwell's translation (*op. cit.*, p. 213).

purify and strengthen men. 'My son, despise not the chastening of the Lord; neither be weary of his reproof. For whom the Lord loveth he reproveth; even as a father the son in whom he delighteth.'[1] 'If ye endure chastening, God dealeth with you as with sons; for what son is he whom the father chasteneth not? . . . Furthermore, we have had fathers of our flesh which corrected us, and we gave them reverence: shall we not much rather be in subjection unto the Father of spirits, and live? For they verily for a few days chastened us after their own pleasure; but he for our profit, that we might be partakers of his holiness. Now no chastening for the present seemeth to be joyous but grievous: nevertheless afterward it yieldeth the peaceable fruit of righteousness unto them which are exercised thereby.'[2]

The Elihu speeches in the book of Job offer this as the solution of the problem of suffering. Suffering is sent 'that he may turn man aside from his purpose, And cut away pride from man.[3] . . . He is chastened also with pain upon his bed, And with continual strife[4] in his bones, So that his life abhorreth food, And his soul dainty meat. . . . If there be for him an angel, An interpreter, one of a thousand, To declare unto man what is right for him, And to render unto man his just reward;[5] And if he be gracious unto him and say, Deliver him from going down to the pit, I have found a ransom for his life.[6] . . . He prayeth unto God and he is favourable unto him, So that he seeth his face with joy. He singeth before men and saith, I have sinned and perverted that which was right, And he requited me not according to my iniquity.[7] . . . Lo, all these

---

[1] Prov. iii, 11 f.   [2] Heb. xii. 7 ff.

[3] For the justification of this rendering, cf. Driver and Gray, *Critical and Exegetical Commentary on the Book of Job*, 1921, Part 2, pp. 243 f. Dhorme (*Le Livre de Job*, 1926, pp. 451 f.) prefers to transpose two words and to render: 'Pour détourner l'homme de l'orgueil, il cache à l'homme son action'.

[4] Dhorme (*op. cit.*, p. 454) prefers here to render 'tremblement,' giving to the Hebrew word a rare meaning for which he adduces support in Assyrian usage.

[5] Dhorme (*op. cit.*, p. 457) transposes here from verse 26 this line, and interprets the terms forensically, instead of rendering with R.V. 'he restoreth unto man his righteousness'.

[6] A word is here added to the Hebrew, following Duhm (*Das Buch Hiob*, 1897, p. 161).

[7] The text followed here is that proposed by Duhm, on the basis of the Greek (*op. cit.*, p. 162).

things doth God work, Twice, yea thrice, with a man, To
bring back his soul from the pit, That he may be enlightened [1]
with the light of the living.'[2] 'If they be bound in fetters, And
be taken in the cords of affliction, Then he showeth them their
work, and their transgressions, That they behave themselves
proudly. And he uncovereth their ear to instruction, And
commandeth that they return from iniquity. If they hearken
to his voice[3] and serve him, They shall spend their days in
prosperity.'[4]

In all this there is implied a penal as well as an educative
purpose, and it is precisely here that its setting in the book of
Job exposes its insufficiency. That suffering may be effective
in reclaiming to piety men who have forgotten God in prosperity is undoubtedly true. But the tacit assumption that
suffering, educative as it may be, is evidence of some sin it is
sent to purge away, ranges Elihu with the other friends of Job
as one who does not believe that suffering can be innocent
suffering. He therefore denies the very existence of the fundamental problem to which the book of Job so magnificently
directs attention. He assumes that what may be one of the
effects of suffering is its only purpose, and that the principle
of retribution for sin is the invariable explanation of the
incidence of suffering. This is undoubtedly less profound than
the view of the Upaniṣads, as Radhakrishnan interprets it.
It is also less profound than some other passages in the Bible,
which find in suffering that which can minister to the soul's
growth, without any implication that penalty is necessarily
involved, such as the Psalmist's cry: 'It is good for me that I
have been afflicted; that I might learn thy statutes'.[5]

The Epistle to the Hebrews speaks of Christ, Who 'though
he was a Son, yet learned obedience by the things which he
suffered'.[6] Here there is clearly no idea of penalty for His
misdeeds, but solely of the educative value of the discipline
of suffering. In the Epistle to the Romans we find Paul saying:

---

[1] Driver and Gray (*op. cit.*, Part 1, p. 294) render: 'that he might see his
fill of the light of life'.

[2] Job xxxiii. 17 ff.

[3] A word is here added to the Hebrew text, following Driver and Gray
(*op. cit.*, Part 2, p. 275).

[4] Job xxxvi. 8 ff.   [5] Psalm cxix. 71.   [6] Heb. v. 8.

'For I reckon that the sufferings of this present time are not worthy to be compared with the glory which shall be revealed in us. For the earnest expectation of the creature waiteth for the manifestation of the sons of God. . . . For we know that the whole creation groaneth and travaileth in pain together until now. And not only so, but ourselves also, which have the firstfruits of the spirit, even we ourselves groan within ourselves. . . . And we know that all things work together for good to them that love God.'[1] Here again, there is no suggestion of penal suffering, but only the thought that every experience can contribute something to the enrichment of those who face it in the love of God. With this we may contrast Ecc. vii. 3 f.: 'Sorrow is better than laughter: for by the sadness of the countenance the heart is made better. The heart of the wise is in the house of mourning; but the heart of fools is in the house of mirth.' Here the thought is of the enriching power of sorrow in itself, rather than of the grace of God to turn it to the enrichment of His own.

Ben Sira regarded suffering as a crucible for the testing and refining of the spirit of the godly. 'My son, when thou comest to serve the Lord, Prepare thy soul for testing. Set thy heart aright and constantly endure, And be not dismayed[2] in time of calamity. . . . Accept whatsoever is brought upon thee, And be patient in disease and poverty.[3] For gold is tried in the fire, And acceptable men in the furnace of affliction. Put thy trust in God,[4] and he will help thee.'[5] A similar thought is found in The Wisdom of Solomon, combined with what is closely akin to the Pauline thought quoted above. 'The souls of the righteous are in the hand of God, And no torment shall touch them. . . . For even if in the sight of men they be punished, Their hope is full of immortality; And having borne a little chastening, they shall receive great good; Because God made trial of them, and found them worthy of himself.

[1] Rom. viii. 18 ff.
[2] Following the conjecture of Smend (*Die Weisheit des Jesus Sirach erklärt*, 1906, p. 18) that the Greek 'hasten not' rests on a misunderstanding of Hebrew *tibbāhēl*, which means *hasten* and also *be dismayed*.
[3] Following the reading of the Syriac.
[4] Following the reading of the Latin and the Syriac.
[5] Ecclus. ii. 1 f., 4 ff.

As gold in the furnace he proved them, And as a whole burnt offering he accepted them.'[1]

So, too, in Jewish Rabbinical writings we find the same view. 'To him who gives thanks for his afflictions and rejoices in them, life is granted in this world, and in the world to come, without end';[2] 'Those are to be considered chastenings of love which do not involve neglect of *Tōrāh*. . . . Those are to be considered chastenings of love which do not involve neglect of prayer. . . . The word *bᵉrīt* "covenant" is mentioned in connection with salt and also with chastenings. . . . As with the "covenant" mentioned in connection with salt, it is salt which sweetens meat, so with the "covenant" mentioned in connection with chastenings, they are chastenings which purge all the iniquities of man';[3] 'Not merely should we be ready to receive the evil as well as the good from God, but a man should rejoice over sufferings more than over good, for if a man is in prosperity all his life, his sins will not be forgiven him. But they are forgiven him through sufferings.'[4]

This view of suffering, whether deserved or innocent, as charged with power to bless, inevitably affects the quality of the submissiveness with which it is borne. It is received with an activity of spirit, that seeks to learn its lessons and to appropriate its profit, and not merely with resignation. Muḥammad 'Ali observes that, in contrast to the passivity of the popular *qismat*, 'Muslims are taught to remain absolutely contented when they have to meet adversity or death in fulfilment of their duties. If a Muslim meets adversity or even death, he must believe that it is by God's order, that being the real meaning of *kitāba* in such cases. That faith upholds a Muslim in adversity because he knows that out of an adversity which is by the order of the good God, will undoubtedly come good.'[5] On such a view, suffering calls forth not prostration of

---

[1] Wisd. iii. 1, 4 ff.

[2] Seder Eliyyahu Rabbah 4, end (see M. Friedmann, *Seder Eliahu rabba und Seder Eliahu zuta*, 1902, p. 17).

[3] Babylonian Talmud, Berachoth 5*a*, translation of Cohen (*op. cit.*, pp. 21 f.).

[4] Sifre on Deuteronomy, § 32 (ed. Friedmann, 1864, p. 73*b*, or ed. Horovitz and Finkelstein, 1935, p. 56), quoted in Montefiore and Loewe, *Rabbinic Anthology*, pp. 544 f., and in Moore, *Judaism*, ii, 1927, p. 253.

[5] *The Religion of Islām*, p. 328.

spirit before an arbitrary God or a relentless fate, but a joyous confidence of spirit, and a profound trust that God is through the anguish of suffering fashioning a spirit more choice, and more after His Heart. 'Most gladly therefore', cried Paul,[1] 'will I rather glory in my infirmities, that the power of Christ may rest upon me. Similarly, Jewish Rabbis regarded suffering as the proof of the divine favour. In the Talmud we read:[2] 'Him in whom the Holy One, blessed be He, delighteth He crusheth with sufferings'; and in the Midrash:[3] 'A flax-beater does not beat his flax very vigorously when it is hard, for fear it should split, but if it is good flax, the more he beats it the better it becomes. So the Holy One, blessed be He, does not try the wicked, because they could not stand the trial, but He does try the righteous. . . . When a potter tests his furnace, he does not test it with cracked jars, because a single blow would break them, but he tests it with sound jars, which can withstand many knocks.' 'No feelings rooted themselves more deeply in Judaism', says Montefiore,[4] 'than those of absolute faith in God and unconditional resignation to His will.'

VIII

Innocent suffering may yet again be conceived of as a form of service, either of man or of God, and here once more the quality of the submission with which it is faced will be affected by this view. Further, it may be brought on one by circumstances wholly beyond his own control, or it may be voluntarily endured. The lines cannot be hardly drawn, however, since the service of man may be the service of God, and the suffering that is voluntarily endured may be equally the suffering that is cruelly inflicted.

The author of the book of Job is not primarily concerned with offering an intellectual solution of the mystery of innocent suffering. He wishes to insist that there is innocent suffering,

---

[1] 2 Cor. xii. 9.

[2] Berachoth 5*a*, translation of Cohen (*op. cit.*, p. 21).

[3] Cant. Rabba II, 16, § 2, translation of Simon (*The Midrash Rabbah Translated*, ix, 1939, Song of Songs, p. 141). Text in *Midrash Rabbah*, Warsaw ed., 1877, p. 35*b* (where it is numbered ii. 35).

[4] *Lectures on the Religion of the Ancient Hebrews*, 1893, pp. 451 f.

and so presents Job as a man 'perfect and upright, one that feared God and eschewed evil,'[1] acknowledged as such by God himself,[2] and a man against whom the Satan can make no complaint, so that he is reduced to impugning the motives of Job's piety. The cause of Job's suffering must be given to the reader, to show that it is innocent suffering, and so far from its cause being traced to any sin it is due to his very innocence. It is a test, but not in the sense considered in the preceding section of this paper. For there suffering was conceived as a divine test for the revealing and purifying of character. But here the test is carried out by the Satan, and not by God, and its object is to vindicate God's trust in Job. God has staked Himself on Job's integrity, and in his suffering the sufferer is not alone approving himself, but vindicating God's judgment. He is serving God in his very agony. Nevertheless he can never know this, and the author keeps him in ignorance of the cause of his sufferings to the very end. For the book is written to bring a message to sufferers rather than to explain their sufferings, and to men who must suffer in ignorance of the cause of their sufferings a Job who was given the explanation of his pain could bring no wholly relevant message. It was essential to the author's purpose, therefore, to open to the reader the source and explanation of Job's sufferings, while keeping it closed to Job himself. It could never be deduced from the suffering; and it was not unfolded to Job in the speeches of God from heaven. The book thus expresses the author's profound conviction that though we are completely in the dark as to the cause of any particular innocent suffering, it serves a purpose known to God, and worthy of God. So far from its being ever the relentless working out of the principle of retributory *karma*, it may be in itself a form of divine service, and the sufferer, instead of being deserted by God, may be supremely honoured of God, as Job was in his sufferings.

This means that his pain should be borne in something richer than the spirit of patient resignation, or even the submission of his will to the inscrutable will of God. It means that there may be an inner peace, and even elation of spirit, in the very depths of his suffering, in the faith that the suffering instead

[1] Job i. 1.   [2] Job i. 8.

of interrupting his service of God may be its very avenue. It is a submission charged with the activity of service in its very passivity. 'Who best bear His mild yoke, they serve Him best', sang Milton, when he through suffering had learned the greatness of the message of Job. And because they serve God, His fellowship may be their joy through all their agony—the more deeply theirs because it becomes theirs through suffering. And when the book of Job reaches its climax in Job's response to the utterance of God, he says: 'I had heard of thee with the hearing of the ear; But now mine eye seeth thee'.[1] In the service of his suffering he had gained a new intimacy of knowledge of God, compared with which his former knowledge was but as a second-hand story compared with the immediacy of sight.

This is not alone the message of the book of Job, able therefore to be discounted as based on nothing more substantial than the author's creative imagination, or an old folk-story. It is found elsewhere in the Bible, where it rests on the solid basis of experience. In the tragedy of his home, and the faithfulness of a wife he dearly loved, Hosea found a spiritual agony no easier to be borne than the physical agony of Job. Yet to him that bitter pain became the avenue of service, leading him to a deeper understanding of the love of God that he might make that love the burden of his message to men. God's revelation of Himself came to him in his sorrow, and it was because of the anguish he endured that he was serviceable unto God for the utterance of this message.

In the figure of the Suffering Servant of the book of Isaiah, we have another form of suffering service presented. This time it is vicariously endured for the blessing of men. It is again the avenue of service, but its service lies in its vicarious character. 'My back to the lash I gave, My cheeks to be plucked; My face I did not hide, From insult and spitting';[2] He was despised and forsaken of men, A man of pains, and familiar with suffering; As one from whom men turned shuddering away, He was despised, and we heeded him not. But it was our sufferings that he endured, And ours were the pains that he bore; Yet

---

[1] Job xlii. 5.
[2] Isa. l. 6. The translation here followed is that given in the present writer's *Israel's Mission to the World*, 1939, p. 19.

we looked on him as stricken, Smitten of God and afflicted.
Whereas he by our sins was pierced, Crushed by the guilt that
was ours; The discipline of our welfare fell upon him, And by
his stripes there came healing for us'.[1] That his sufferings were
in no degree the reward of his own misdeeds we are left in no
doubt, 'Although he had wrought no violence, And there was
no deceit in his mouth'.[2]

His sufferings were at once voluntarily endured and
brought on him by the will of God, for in his service of those
for whom he gave his life he was furthering the will of God.
'But Yahweh chose to crush him with pain, Truly he gave
himself an offering for sin;[3] He shall see his offspring, he shall
prolong his days, The will of Yahweh through him shall
triumph'.[4] It is therefore not surprising that they were borne
with patience. ' Though ill-treated, submissive was he, Nor
opened his mouth in complaint'.[5]

Into the question of the identify of the Suffering Servant
it is unnecessary to enter here. It suffices for our purpose to
recognize the concept of vicarious suffering as the organ of
service of God and man. It is deserved, but not by him upon
whom it falls, who enters into the depths of its anguish with
patience, indeed, but also with purpose. In his eager desire to
serve those over whom he yearns he identifies himself with
them, and complaint against the anguish is swallowed up in
his love for those whose pains he bears.

It is inevitable that Christian thought should pass from
the Suffering Servant to the Cross of Christ. For whatever was
in the mind of the author of the Servant Songs, they profoundly influenced our Lord, and in Him we find a vicarious
suffering that fully exemplifies their thought. Before we turn
to Him, however, we may turn again to Mo-tzŭ, to find in
him an example of vicarious suffering cheerfully borne for

[1] Isa. liii. 3 ff. (*ibid.*, pp. 21 f.).
[2] Isa. liii. 9 (*ibid.*, p. 22).
[3] The rendering 'with pain' follows the Vulgate, and involves no change
of the Hebrew consonantal text (cf. Torrey, *The Second Isaiah*, 1928, p. 421),
while 'truly he gave' follows Levy (*Deutero-Isaiah*, 1925, p. 266) in re-dividing
the Hebrew consonants to read '*ᵉmeth šām*, instead of '*im tāśîm*='if thou
shalt make'.
[4] Isa. liii. 10 (*Israel's Mission*, pp. 22 f.).
[5] Isa. liii. 7 (*ibid.*, p. 22).

others, producing an activity of spirit that is not content with gathering into itself enrichment and strength from the pain, but that expresses its activity in the very service of the suffering.

Of him Mencius, who bitterly opposed his teaching, said: 'The philosopher Mo loves all equally. If by rubbing smooth his whole body from the crown to the heel, he could have benefited the kingdom, he would have done it.'[1] Similarly, Chuang-tzŭ says, 'The idea of Mo Ti and Ch'in Hua-li was good, but their practice was wrong. They would have made the Mohists of future ages feel it necessary to toil themselves, till there was not a hair on their legs, and still be urging one another on; thus producing a condition superior indeed to disorder, but inferior to the result of good government.[2] Nevertheless, Mo-tzŭ was indeed one of the best men in the world, which you may search without finding his equal. Decayed and worn his person might be, but he is not to be rejected—a scholar of ability indeed.'[3]

In these passages Mo-tzŭ's practice of his own principle of service through sacrifice is referred to. Frequently he referred with admiration to the great Yü, whose heroic conquest of the floods was so treasured in national memory. Chuang-tzŭ says: 'Mo-tzŭ in praise of his views said, "Anciently, when Yü was draining off the waters of the flood, he set free the channels of the Chiang and the Ho, and opened communications with them from the regions of the four Î and the nine provinces. . . . With his own hands he carried the sack and wielded the spade, till he had united all the streams of the country conducting them to the sea. There was no hair left on his legs from the knee to the ankle. He bathed his hair in the violent wind,

---

[1] Mencius VII, i. 26, translation of Legge (*The Chinese Classics*, ii, p. 340 ; 2nd ed., pp. 464 f.).

[2] Giles (*Chuang Tzŭ*, p. 443) renders this sentence, 'The evil of that system would have predominated over the good'.

[3] Chuang-tzŭ XXXIII, iii. 11, translation of Legge (*Sacred Books of the East*, xl, p. 221). L. T. Chen, the translator of Liang Ch'i-ch'ao's *History of Chinese Political Thought* (1930, p. 105), translates the closing sentences: 'Mo-tzŭ is truly the epitome of goodness; it is impossible to find one like him. Although in many respects he is like a withering tree, one cannot leave him unnoticed. He is a genius.' Cf. Wieger, *Taoïsme*, ii, pp. 500 ff., for text and translation.

and combed it in the pelting rain, thus marking out the myriad states. Yü was a great sage, and thus he toiled in the service of the world.'' The effect of this is that in this later time most of the Mohists wear skins and dolychos cloth, with shoes of wood or twisted hemp, not stopping day or night, but considering such toiling on their part as their highest achievement.'[1]

This is supported by a passage in the Preface to Ssŭ-ma Ch'ien's *Historical Records* : 'Mo Tzŭ lived in a small house built of rough unworked timbers, and with a thatched roof. He used none but earthenware utensils, and partook of the coarsest food. His clothing was of the simplest, of skin or grass according to the season. He was buried in a plain coffin of thin boards.'[2]

'The following story told in numerous sources', says Hu Shih,[3] 'best portrays the spirit of Mohism and the character of its founder. Kung Shu Pan, the State Engineer of Chu, had just completed his new invention of a "cloud ladder" for besieging walled cities, and the King of Chu was planning an invasion into the State of Sung. When Mo Ti learned of this, he started out from his native state and travelled ten days and ten nights all on foot, arriving at the capital city with sunburnt face and battered feet. There he secured an interview with the State Engineer, whom he succeeded in convincing that his cause was wrong and condemnable.'[4]

It is clear that Mo-tzŭ, whose principal teaching was of the love of all men, practised his own teaching, and gave evidence

---

[1] Chuang-tzŭ XXXIII, iii. 11 (Legge, *op. cit.*, pp. 219 f.). Cf. Giles, *op. cit.*, pp. 441 f., and Wieger, *op. cit.*, pp. 500 f. With Mo-tzŭ's high regard for Yü we may contrast the contempt shown for him and other sages by Yang Chu, who after narrating their arduous and self-sacrificing labours, and the sorrows they brought on themselves, expresses his scorn for the fame they thus achieved. See Lieh-tzŭ vii (text and translation in Legge, *The Chinese Classics*, ii, Prolegomena, pp. 99 f.; 2nd ed., 96 f.; and in Wieger, *op. cit.*, 172 ff.).

[2] See Williamson, *Mo Ti: a Chinese Heretic*, 1927, p. 3. Cf. Chavannes, *Les Mémoires historiques de Se-ma Ts'ien*, i, 1895, p. xiv.

[3] *The Development of the Logical Method in Ancient China*, 1928, p. 57. Cf. Mo-tzŭ, Kung Shu (Mei, *The Ethical and Political Works of Motse*, 1929, p. 257); also Liang Ch'i-ch'ao, *History of Chinese Political Thought*, pp. 178 ff. Liang Ch'i-ch'ao adds the further detail that Mo-tzŭ was forced to tear up his clothes to bandage his blistered feet.

[4] It should perhaps be added that more effective than Mo-tzŭ's condemnation of the cause of Chu was his demonstration of its futility against his science of defensive warfare, which would be at the disposal of Sung. See Mo-tzŭ, Kung Shu (Mei, *op. cit.*, 257 ff.) and Liang Ch'i-ch'ao, *op. cit.*, pp. 178 ff.

of his love in his self-forgetting service and sacrifice. 'For depth of sympathy, for vigour of altruism, and for the richness of the spirit of self-sacrifice there is none like him, save Christ, in the whole world', says Liang Ch'i-ch'ao.[1] He held up to men as an example the Sage-King T'ang, who in time of drought called down on himself the wrath of Heaven, and pleaded that the people might escape. 'That is to say that though having the honour of being an emperor and the wealth of possessing the whole world, T'ang did not shrink from offering himself as sacrifice to implore God and the spirits. This is universal love on the part of T'ang and what Mo-tzŭ has been talking about is really derived from the example of T'ang.'[2] Of his exaltation, both by precept and example, of the spirit of service and sacrifice there can be no doubt. Unfortunately, he seems to have inculcated an ascetic severity of life for its own sake, as the above quotation from Chuang-tzŭ indicates.[3] It was this that exposed him to criticism, and destroyed the effect of his high principles. Thus Chuang-tzŭ says again: 'Is it reasonable to prohibit singing, weeping, and rejoicing in due season? According to Mo-tzŭ one ought to toil through life and die in poverty. Such an unattractive picture of life would bring men to sorrow and lamentation. It is so unpractical that it cannot be regarded as the Tao of the true Sage; it is so opposed to human passions that the world could not bear its consequences. Even if Mo-tzŭ could endure it himself, that does not prove it to be generally practical. To develop one's life isolated in the world is far from the true way of the Sage.'[4] Similarly, Hsün-tzŭ says: 'Mo-tzŭ's one-sided doctrine of utility made him ignore the significance of culture and refinement'.[5]

[1] *Op. cit.*, p. 105.

[2] Mo-tzŭ xvi, translation of Mei (*op. cit.*, p. 94). Cf. Legge, *The Chinese Classics*, ii (Prolegomena, p. 117; 2nd ed., p. 114), where the Chinese text and a translation are given.

[3] It lies outside our purpose to consider the self-imposed sufferings of ascetics in the cause of self-discipline. The ascetic strain in Mo-tzŭ was an asceticism for service and not for self-development.

[4] Chuang-tzŭ XXXIII, iii. 11, translation of Chen in Liang Ch'i-ch'ao, *op. cit.*, pp. 103 f. Cf. Legge, *Sacred Books of the East*, xl, p. 219, and Giles, *Chuang Tzŭ*, p. 441. Cf. Wieger, *Taoïsme*, ii, pp. 500 f.

[5] Hsün-tzŭ xxi. 5, translation quoted, without acknowledgement of source, by Kennedy (*Chinese Recorder*, lxii, 1931, p. 696) and Holth (*Micius*, 1935, p. 2). Cf. Dubs, *The Works of Hsüntze*, 1928, pp. 263 f.

In spite of this, however, we are bound to recognize the fineness of Mo-tzŭ's spirit of service. His self-denial and sacrifice, his toil and suffering were but the organ of the service whereby he proved his love for all men. By them, too, he equally proved his submission to the will of God. For to Mo-tzŭ God was real and personal,[1] and His will supreme for men. In all his teaching he believed he was unfolding the will of God, in obedience to which man's welfare lay. Mo-tzŭ's submission in suffering, therefore, was the submission of will to will, the submission of his will to the will of God. But it was not merely the submission of his will to accept the lot ordained for him by the will of God; it was the dedication of his will to be the organ of God's will, to be actively infused with God's will that it might effect His purpose.[2]

This is closely similar to the quality of submission we find in some passages in the New Testament. In the Garden of Gethsemane, on the eve of the Crucifixion, Jesus prayed, 'Father, if thou be willing, remove this cup from me: nevertheless not my will, but thine, be done'.[3] He was under no illusions as to what the cup was. When He was in the way going up to Jerusalem He had already begun to tell the disciples what things should happen to Him, saying, 'Behold, we go to Jerusalem; and the Son of Man shall be delivered unto the chief priests, and unto the scribes; and they shall condemn him to death, and shall deliver him to the Gentiles: And they shall mock him, and shall scourge him, and shall spit upon him, and shall kill him'.[4] It might therefore seem that when He stood under the immediate shadow of the Cross, the flesh shrank from the physical pain of it, and that though in the hour of suffering He manifested a calm and unflinching dignity, His sensitive spirit could not bear its contemplation in advance, but that nevertheless the spirit of resignation triumphed, and He patiently submitted Himself to accept whatever the will of God ordained for Him. It is very

---

[1] Many writers believe that Mo-tzŭ's God was merely a lay figure, but the present writer is unable to accept this view. Cf. below, pp. 102 ff., 139 ff.

[2] Forke (*Mê Ti*, 1922, p. 41) observes that Mo-tzŭ is much nearer to Christianity than Confucius. So far as the subject of the present study is concerned, this could be stated with more emphasis.

[3] Luke xxii. 42.   [4] Mark x. 33 f.

improbable that this has any relation to the real meaning of
the Gethsemane scene. He Who had ever thought of others
did not begin to think of Himself now. When He was being
led out to Golgotha after the bitter mocking and scourging,
and was followed by those who wept for Him, He did not
think of Himself, but said, 'Weep not for me, but weep for
yourselves, and for your children',[1] and when the nails were
being driven through His hands and feet, He still thought in
pity of those who did the cruel deed. 'Father, forgive them',
He cried, 'for they know not what they do'.[2] It can only be in
the light of what we know from these and other passages of
His character that the Gethsemane scene can be understood,
and in that light we can be certain that He was not obsessed
with His own suffering, but with human sin. 'The Son of
Man came not to be ministered unto, but to minister', He had
said to his disciples, 'and to give His life a ransom for many.'[3]
To fulfil the mission of the Suffering Servant, and to give His
life vicariously for the sin that was not His own, was not what
he shrank from; rather was it the climax of human sin manifested in the Crucifixion. When He had approached Jerusalem
but a few days earlier, He had wept over it. But His tears had
flowed for the city, and not for Himself. 'Oh that thou hadst
known, even thou, in this thy day, the things which belong
unto thy peace!'[4] He had cried, in a great compassion for the
city where His mission was about to be fulfilled in His death.
To save men was His mission; to die for men held no terrors
for Him. But with a yearning born of the very love which
brought Him to the Cross He yearned for a way of saving
them that would spare them the guilt of this crowning rejection
of God in Him. And when He added, 'Nevertheless not my will,
but thine be done', He did not mean that He was prepared to
put up with the Cross if it must be. He meant that in this
supreme moment, His supreme desire was still to be the
instrument of the divine will for the redemption of men. Not
'Thy will be done upon me', but 'Thy will be done in me, and
through me' was the burden of His cry. It was not a cry of
resignation to suffering, but a cry of consecration to service,

---

[1] Luke xxiii. 28. [2] *Ibid.*, 34.
[3] Mark x. 45. [4] Luke xix. 42.

6

the yielding of His will to be the organ of God's will and the
yielding of Himself to be the instrument of man's salvation.
And God's will was done, not in the mere experience of Christ's
sufferings, but through the instrumentality of those sufferings.
In the passivity of His sufferings there was the activity of His
redemption.

In the New Testament the sufferings of Christ are frequently
held up to men, not merely as an example but as something
into which they may enter. 'We are the children of God: And
if children, then heirs; heirs of God, and joint-heirs with
Christ; if so be that we suffer with him, that we may be glorified
together.'[1] 'That I may know Him . . . and the fellowship
of his sufferings, being made conformable unto his death.'[2]
'Rejoice, inasmuch as ye are partakers of Christ's sufferings.'[3]
Paul could even declare that he filled up that which was
lacking of the afflictions of Christ in his flesh.[4] In all this
thought suffering is conceived of as an active force of service,
potent to bless not the sufferer alone, but others. Nor is this
thought alien to Judaism. For we read that Rabbi Joshua ben
Levi said: 'He who accepts gladly the sufferings of this world,
brings salvation to the world'.[5] And again, when Eleazar was
being martyred, we read that he cried: 'Thou, O God, knowest
that though I might save myself I am dying by fiery torments
for thy Law. Be merciful unto thy people, and let our punishment be a satisfaction in their behalf. Make my blood their
purification, and take my soul to ransom their souls.'[6]

The submission to which such a view leads is the deepest
and richest of all its varieties. It does not ask to understand
the cause of the suffering.[7] It is content to believe that by the
mystery of the divine power the suffering may become an
instrument of blessing, and to consecrate the very agony to
the service of God and man.

---

[1] Rom. viii. 17.   [2] Phil. iii. 10.
[3] I Pet. iv. 13.   [4] Col. i. 24.
[5] Babylonian Talmud, Ta'anith 8*a*, translation of Malter (*op. cit.*, p. 54).
Cf. Rabbinowitz, *op. cit.*, pp. 33 f.
[6] 4 Macc. vi. 28 f., translation of Townshend (Charles's *Apocrypha and
Pseudepigrapha of the Old Testament*, ii, 1913, p. 674).
[7] Cf. Pirqe Aboth iv. 15 (Danby, *The Mishnah*, p. 454): 'It is not in our
power to explain the well-being of the wicked or the sorrows of the righteous'.

It was said at the outset that the problem of suffering was complex, and it is not pretended that we have probed its complexity. The causes of suffering are undoubtedly many and varied. There is suffering which is brought on oneself by folly and sin : there is suffering brought on the community by collective folly and sin, sweeping into its net of agony individuals who have little or no share in the folly and sin, but who as parts of the one whole society partake alike of the good and ill of its life. There is suffering, both individual and social, which is the entail of the acts of those who have gone before, who leave in countless ways a heritage of woe as well as of achievement for those who follow them. There is suffering brought on one by the wickedness and selfishness of another; there is also suffering that is brought out of the inscrutable play of circumstance, which is beyond all human explanation, though faith can yet believe that it is not without explanation in the will of God, and can trust that will. There is suffering which is vicariously borne for others, freely accepted in the service of men. But whatever the cause of the suffering, it can be met in a spirit which yields not alone resignation to that which, whether justly or unjustly, whether voluntarily or involuntarily, is now inescapably ours. It can be met in the spirit which finds God in the suffering, sometimes to chasten, always to instruct, and which, because it finds God is able to gather from the bitterness of the anguish fruits that are sweet. It can be met in the spirit of consecration that converts the pain into a channel of service, either service in itself, or service in the creation of a new fineness of character that shall be serviceable to God here or hereafter. Ringing through all the resignation, whatever else its character, and whatever the cause of the anguish, may be the cry, 'Thy will be done' in the sense that we have found in our Lord's cry—'Thy will be done in me, and through me'. It is that supreme consecration of spirit that can dignify every experience, and that can turn all life into a high adventure in the service of God.

THE CHINESE SAGES AND
THE GOLDEN RULE

DISCUSSIONS of the Golden Rule, as it occurs in the Gospels and as it is found elsewhere, have commonly been concerned primarily with the form of the wording, whether positive, as in the Gospels, or negative, as generally elsewhere. Parallels are widely found, indeed, and have been copiously collected from Classical, Jewish, Indian and Chinese sources. It lies beyond the scope of the present paper to examine them all, but for the collections of parallels and discussions of them reference may be made to the works of Poole,[1] Taylor,[2] Tasker,[3] Spooner,[4] Abrahams,[5] and G. B. King.[6]

Most of the parallels which have been adduced stand in the negative form, of which Tobit iv. 15 (Vulgate 16) may serve as an example: 'What thou thyself hatest, do to no man'. It is generally argued that this is inferior to the positive form found in Matt. vii. 12: 'All things therefore whatsoever ye would that men should do unto you, even so do ye also unto them', or in Luke vi. 31: 'As ye would that men should do to you, do ye also to them likewise'. The negative form, it is maintained, belongs to the realm of law, and means no more than 'Refrain from injuring another', whereas the Gospel maxim means 'Do thy neighbour good'. The latter is therefore correctly described by Jesus as expressing 'the law and the prophets'.

G. B. King, in the papers already referred to, collects a whole series of writers who have thus exalted the positive form above the negative, including both English and German writers. His list might be largely augmented, but since it includes no

[1] *Synopsis Criticorum*, iv, 1686, col. 240.
[2] *Sayings of the Jewish Fathers*, 2nd ed., 1897, pp. 142 f. Cf. also Strack-Billerbeck, *Kommentar zum Neuen Testament aus Talmud und Midrasch*, i, 1922, pp. 459 f.
[3] In Hastings' *Dictionary of Christ and the Gospels*, i, 1906, pp. 653 f.
[4] In Hastings' *Encyclopædia of Religion and Ethics*, vi, 1913, pp. 310-312.
[5] *Studies in Pharisaism and the Gospels*, 1st series, 1917, pp. 18-29.
[6] 'The Negative Golden Rule', in *Journal of Religion*, viii, 1928, pp. 268-279; xv, 1935, pp. 59-62.

French writer, the addition of a single distinguished French scholar may be permitted. Lagrange[1] says: 'Le chef des Pharisiens avant le temps de Jésus, Hillel, disait seulement: "Ce qui ne te plaît pas, ne le fais à aucun autre : c'est toute la Loi, dont tout le reste n'est que l'explication". Telle est bien en effet la règle de la justice . . . Mais cette abstention négative ne lui suffit pas.'

This view, however, is contested by King, as it has also been contested by others. Thus Abrahams[2] says: 'The contrasts between the negative and positive forms of the Golden Rule are not well founded'. It is to be noted that in the addition to the Western text of Acts xv. 29 we find the negative form, as also in the *Teaching of the Twelve Apostles*, i. 2, and in other early Christian writings. This would suggest that the early Church did not distinguish between the negative and the positive forms. As little did Calmet, who closed his comment[3] on Luke vi. 31 with the words: 'Voyez Tobie, iv. 16, la même sentence en d'autres termes'.

Hirsch and Abrahams go much farther than this, and argue that the negative form is definitely superior to the positive form. Thus Hirsch says:[4] 'The negative form of the Golden Rule marks if anything a higher outlook than the positive statement in which it is cast in Matthew'; and Abrahams:[5] 'The negative form is the more fundamental of the two, though the positive form is the fuller expression of practical morality'. This view rests on the consideration that our power of evil is so much greater than our power of good, and hence the negative precept goes deeper into the heart of the problem.

It is clear that the distinction between the two forms of the maxim is not very secure, and with the loss of this distinction it is sometimes supposed that the originality of Jesus in this connection disappears. Thus Reinach, in treating of Confucius, says:[6] ' "Do unto others as ye would men should do unto you" was a precept Confucius had no need to borrow from our Scriptures'. It is tacitly assumed that the equation

---

[1] *L'Évangile de Jésus-Christ*, 1936, p. 148. Cf. his *Évangile selon Saint Matthieu*, 8th ed., 1948, p. 149.   [2] *Op. cit.*, p. 21.

[3] *Commentaire littéral sur tous les livres de l'A. et du N.T.*, vii, 1726, p. 483.

[4] In *Jewish Encyclopedia*, vi, 1904, p. 22*b*.

[5] *Op. cit.*, p. 22.   [6] *Orpheus*, revised ed., 1930, p. 159.

of the terms of the precepts involves the equation of their content. Were this really so, then we should be forced to the conclusion that this saying of Jesus, so often regarded as the climax of His ethical teaching, is a mere commonplace of the world's moralists.

Actually it seems futile to discuss the sayings merely as isolated maxims, unrelated to the rest of the teaching of those who uttered them, since it can only be in the context of that other teaching that the real meaning of the words on the lips of any teacher can be discerned.[1] Moreover, before the relative worth of the precepts can be appraised, it is important to consider how far they embody the penetrating observation of the philosopher, or how far the inspiring call of the leader. Yet again, it is essential to ask what was the motive power to which the teacher looked for the realization of his teaching.

To cover in this manner the whole field of the parallels that have been discovered would be impossible in a single paper, and we must therefore limit the present consideration to the Far Eastern corner of the field. Here it is common to adduce the parallel in the recorded sayings of Confucius, and less frequently an utterance of Lao-tzŭ. A third sage also calls for attention, though he is generally completely overlooked in all discussion of the subject, despite the fact that he seems to come much nearer to the level of the New Testament than either of the others. This is Mo-tzŭ, the long neglected sage, who is attracting increasing attention both in China and in the West.

I

The date of Lao-tzŭ is uncertain, but he has been traditionally believed to have been an older contemporary of Confucius. The date of his birth is commonly given as 604 B.C.,[2] but Wieger[3] puts it somewhat later, and says that his

---

[1] Cf. Maclagan, *Chinese Religious Ideas*, 1926, p. 73: 'Sayings get their meaning from their context as colours get their value from the light that falls on them. What by daylight is pink may in gaslight seem grey; and a maxim legitimate or even admirable in the light of the Cross may be something less praiseworthy in the light of Tao.'

[2] So Legge, *Sacred Books of the East*, xxxix, 1891, p. 2. So also, most recently, Schoeps, *Gottheit und Menschheit*, 1950, p. 170.

[3] *Histoire des croyances religieuses et des opinions philosophiques en Chine*, 2nd ed., 1922, p. 145.

life falls between 570 B.C. and 490 B.C.[1] H. A. Giles, while allowing that Lao-tzŭ is a historical person, is completely sceptical of the reasons for connecting him with the age of Confucius,[2] and leaves his *floruit* entirely undefined. He believes that the Tao Tê Ching is a forgery of the second century B.C.[3] This scepticism is declared by Maclagan[4] to rest on a somewhat crude criticism, and its arguments, which had first appeared in the *China Review* in 1886, had already been rejected by Legge,[5] who concluded his discussion of the subject by saying: 'I do not know of any other book of so ancient a date as the Tâo Teh *K*ing, of which the authenticity of the origin and genuineness of the text can claim to be so well substantiated'.[6] More recently, however, the tendency is to doubt the tradition that Lao-tzŭ was an older contemporary of Confucius, and to date the work in the post-Confucian age.[7] For our present purpose these questions are of little importance, since our concern is with the teachings of the book, and Lao-tzŭ merely stands for the author of the book, whoever he was and whenever he lived.

Amongst the recorded teachings of Lao-tzŭ there is none that formally parallels the Golden Rule, but there is one oft-quoted saying that parallels other related New Testament teaching, which stands beside the Golden Rule in its Lucan setting. This is the famous maxim: 'Recompense injury with kindness', which stands in the Tao Tê Ching, chap. lxiii.[8] The

[1] Cf. Hu Shih, who places the birth of Lao-tzŭ *circa* 590 B.C. (*The Development of the Logical Method in Ancient China*, 1928, p. 13).

[2] *Confucianism and its Rivals*, 1915, p. 130.

[3] *Ibid.*, p. 147.

[4] In Hastings' *Encyclopædia of Religion and Ethics*, xii, 1921, p. 197b. Cf. also Maclagan, *Chinese Religious Ideas*, 1926, pp. 70 f., where the criticism is said to be too arbitrary and subjective to be convincing.

[5] *Sacred Books of the East*, xxxix, 1891, pp. 4 ff.

[6] *Ibid.*, p. 9.

[7] Cf. below, pp. 108 f. note. E. R. and K. Hughes, *Religion in China*, 1950, p. 25, say: 'To-day . . . the Lao Tan of the Taoists has become a much more legendary figure than Confucius. . . . The stories about Lao-tzŭ have become so overlaid with legend that it is impossible to say even whether such a person really existed, and certainly modern scholars do not recognize him as the author of the *Tao Tê Ching*.' Hackmann, *Chinesische Philosophie*, 1927, p. 54, observes: 'es wäre übertriebene Skepsis, an der Geschichtlichkeit des Mannes zweifeln zu wollen.' Cf. H. Maspero, *Le Taoïsme*, 1950, p. 229.

[8] *Sacred Books of the East, loc. cit.*, p. 106.

word which is here translated *kindness* normally means *virtue* or *moral excellence*, and it is identical with the second word of the title of the Tao Tê Ching, which Julien translated 'Le livre de la Voie et de *la Vertu*'.

The maxim is referred to in the *Confucian Analects*, xiv. 36, where the comment of Chu Hsi is that *tê* here means *ên hui*=*kindness*. This view has been followed by Legge and other translators. Maclagan, however, holds [1] that it is a mistake so to translate it. He says that in the Taoist sense *tê* is 'activity devoid of self-determination, the expression of the spontaneity of the immanent *Tao*'. Hence he declares that the maxim 'is no more than a precept of indifferent self-possession', and that it simply means 'Be a Taoist, even though provoked'. This view is borne out by a study of the context, and of the whole teaching of Lao-tzŭ, though I am not persuaded that it is necessary to disagree with the rendering of Legge.

When the maxim was submitted to Confucius, he replied:[2] 'With what, then, will you recompense *tê*? Recompense injury with justice, but recompense *tê* with *tê*.' Here the meaning would seem quite clearly to be 'Do good to them that do good to you', and it would appear to be certain that Confucius did not understand the word *tê* in the sense Maclagan attaches to it, but in the sense Chu Hsi assigns it. While this does not prove that it had the same sense for Lao-tzŭ, the presumption that it does may be allowed, and that he did mean 'Recompense injury with kindness'. But even so, the maxim cannot be understood in a Christian sense without more ado. Legge's translation of the context is as follows: '(It is the way of the Tâo) to act without (thinking of) acting; to conduct affairs without (feeling the) trouble of them; to taste without discerning any flavour; to consider what is small as great, and a few as many; and to recompense injury with kindness'. From this it is manifest that the principle does not spring from any root of love for the injurer, but rather from complete indifference to him. On the Taoist view, it is the part of the superior man to be completely unmoved by the vicissitudes and experiences of life, to taste without discerning any flavour,

---

[1] *Loc. cit.*, p. 199*a*.
[2] Legge, *The Chinese Classics*, 2nd ed., i, 1893, p. 288.

to be uninfluenced by what he suffers, to let the initiative of his life be wholly from within, without relation to circumstances. The maxim springs, therefore, from a radical selfishness of spirit, from the view that the superior man must guard his own superiority.

This is in accordance with the general principles of Taoism. Soothill says[1] that Lao-tzŭ 'advocates the policy of inaction, that is, non-interference or quietism. It naturally follows from this quietist spirit that the doctrine of requiting injury with kindness, for which Confucius had no use, finds clear expression.' Similarly Moore observes:[2] 'The Taoist cultivates inaction; he is silent even about the Tao; he teaches without words; he renounces learning and wisdom, he has an air of indecision and irresoluteness, a vacant and stupid look'.

It is true that Lao-tzŭ inculcates the principles of gentleness and humility and frugality, but all from a purely self-regarding point of view. It is in these things that a man's true well-being lies, and in deserting them for the fret and fuss of life, he forfeits his own greatness of spirit. In Lao-tzŭ's view, weakness is stronger than strength, and strength weaker than weakness. The way of yielding is therefore the victorious way. In all this there is no concern for the transforming of the world, or for helping others, but only the idea that in the way of the Tao a man may realize his own truest well-being.[3]

There is one frequently quoted passage, however, which might seem to support a different view. In *Tao Tê Ching*, xlix. 2, we read:[4] 'To those who are good (to me), I am good; —and to those who are not good (to me), I am also good;—and thus (all) get to be good. To those who are sincere (with me) I am sincere; and to those who are not sincere (with me), I am sincere;—and thus (all) get to be sincere.' This would certainly seem to imply that the power of the example of the

---

[1] *Three Religions of China*, 3rd ed., 1929, p. 49.

[2] *History of Religions*, i, 1931, p. 52.

[3] Cf. Krause, *Ju-Tao-Fo*, 1924, p. 152: 'So ist der Rat des Lao-tse die Abkehr von der Welt der realen Dinge, die widersprechende Eigenschaften zeigen, und die Versenkung in das eine, wahre, ewige Tao. Der Weise zieht sich zurück aus einer Welt der scheinbaren Gegensätze, die für ihn bedeutungslos sind, auf ein Gebiet, wo es keine Gegensätzlichkeit giebt. Im Tao erkennt er sein eignes Wesen.'

[4] Legge, *Sacred Books of the East*, xxxix, 1891, p. 91.

superior man may be expected to transform others, and that his triumph will consist not alone in maintaining his own superior spirit, but in communicating it. It has to be observed, however, that in Legge's rendering the crucial word *get* rests on a conjectural emendation of the text, and certain other important words, enclosed in brackets above, are unexpressed in the text, and have to be supplied by the translator.[1] On so obscure a passage, it is therefore difficult to build with confidence. But even though the translation could be unreservedly accepted, it would still be far from established that it taught any genuine altruism. For it continues: 'The sage has in the world an appearance of indecision, and keeps his mind in a state of indifference'. Whatever this may mean, it is surely back at once in the realm of detachment. If the Taoist sage believed that the force of his example would influence others, that was to him rather the effect of his example than its motive and inspiration.

I am therefore far from sharing the common view that Lao-tzŭ rose to a greater height than Confucius. Thus Moore says:[2] ' "To recompense injury with kindness" is the way of the Tao. This principle, which rises as high above the Confucian "reciprocity" as Matt. 5, 44-48, does above the "Golden Rule", is not an *obiter dictum* of Lao-tse, but is the logical consequence of his fundamental axioms.' Confucius was eager to promote the principles of righteousness in all the relationships of life, because he was fundamentally interested in human well-being and happiness. Lao-tzŭ believed that the sage should be interested in his own well-being and happiness alone, and that they were best secured by the limitation of

[1] Cf. Wells Williams' rendering: 'He who is good, I would meet with goodness; and he who is not good, I would still also meet with goodness; (for) *teh* (i.e. virtue) is goodness. He who is sincere I would meet with sincerity; and he who is insincere, I would still also meet with sincerity; (for) *teh* is sincerity' (*The Middle Kingdom*, ii, 1883, p. 210). Cf. also the renderings of Wilhelm and Waley. The former (*Laotse Tao Te King : Das Buch des Alten vom Sinn und Leben*, 1923, p. 54) has : 'Zu den Guten bin ich gut, und zu den Nichtguten bin ich auch gut ; denn das LEBEN ist die Güte. Zu den Treuen bin ich treu, und zu den Nichttreuen bin ich auch treue ; denn das LEBEN ist die Treue '; while the latter (*The Way and its Power*, p. 202) has : ' Of the good man I approve, but of the bad I also approve, and thus he gets goodness. The truthful man I believe, but the liar I also believe, and thus he gets truthfulness.'   [2] *Op. cit.*, p. 53.

desire, and not by the enlargement of achievement. For all the formal beauty of the maxim, therefore, the hollowness of its spirit is a sufficient explanation of its failure to exercise any profound influence on China.

Nor is this all. It is equally important to observe that the maxim is entirely unrelated to any religious thought or teaching. It is disputed whether Lao-tzŭ uttered any specifically religious teaching at all. Giles attributes to him a genuine theism, by rendering the term *T'ien=Heaven* by *God*. But Legge objects[1] to the rendering, and says that 'neither Lâo nor *K*wang (i.e. Chuang-tzŭ, the great interpreter of Taoism) ever attached anything like our idea of God to it; and when one, in working on books of early Tâoist literature, translates *thien* by God, such a rendering must fail to produce in an English reader a correct apprehension of the meaning'. Similarly Maclagan says:[2] 'In some instances of its use a near approach is made to what we mean by Heaven when we use it as equivalent to Providence. In this, its highest, use it is not merely the physical sky, but a power supreme in the world of visible things obscurely connected with the sky, which is the supreme exemplar of *Tao*, but, even so, posterior and subordinate to it. *Tao* is to Lao-tse the ultimate and determining fact.' A vague belief in Providence is quite other than a real belief in a personal God, with whom men can come into living relationship, and whose resources are available to enable them to fulfil His revealed will.

There is one passage, and one passage only, in the Tao Tê Ching, where another term for God, this time the definitely personal term *Ti*, is used. This is in iv. 3:[3] 'I do not know whose son it (i.e. Tao) is. It might appear to have been before God (*Ti*).' It is impossible to build on such a reference any proof that Lao-tzŭ cherished any true Theism. For the mere belief that there is a God, expressed in so casual a way, is insufficient to make Lao-tzŭ a religious teacher, or to give his teaching the value of a religion. So far as we know, he was not in the least interested in any of the forms of religion, or in leading men to seek and to know God.

[1] *Sacred Books of the East*, xxxix, pp. 17 ff.
[2] In Hastings' *Encyclopædia of Religion and Ethics*, xii, 1921, p. 198*b*.
[3] *Sacred Books of the East*, xxxix, p. 50.

'Of a personal God', says Douglas,[1] 'Laou-tsze knew nothing, as far as we may judge from the *Taou-tih king*; and indeed a belief in such a being would be in opposition to the whole tenour of his philosophy. There is no room for a supreme God in his system.' Similarly Moore observes:[2] 'Of religion in the common acceptance of the word Lao-tse says nothing. Forms of worship, to the correctness of which Confucius attached so much importance, in so far as they were an effort to influence the course of nature in man's favour, were, upon Taoist principles, like the efforts of the practical statesman and reformer, vain and impertinent.' It is true that Taoism has become a religion, but that religion is quite other than the Taoism of Lao-tzŭ. It is true also that the mystic identification of the follower of Lao-tzŭ with the Tao, the ultimate principle of the universe, was not unassociated with the religious instinct. It offered beatific peace, not strength for service, and therefore at the best it sought to maintain one element only, though an important element, of the full religious life; and even this element it sought to maintain without a God. Of a genuinely religious motive and power for the returning of good for evil, or for any altruistic service, Lao-tzŭ, is silent.

II

When we turn to Confucius, we find a specific repudiation of the principle 'Recompense injury with kindness', but more than one utterance which is akin in form to the Golden Rule.

In *Analects*, xiv. 36, a passage to which reference has already been made, we read:[3] 'Some one said, "What do you say concerning the principle that injury should be recompensed with kindness?" The Master said, "With what then will you recompense kindness? Recompense injury with justice, and recompense kindness with kindness".' Legge comments that Confucius here falls below the standard of Lao-tzŭ, but it has been maintained above that this is not really so. Confucius's stiff insistence on a correct attitude, marked by the strictest justice, aimed doubtless to preserve moral standards which

---

[1] *Confucianism and Taoism*, 1879, p. 211.
[2] *Op. cit.*, p. 55.   [3] Legge, *Chinese Classics*, i, 1893, p. 288.

might seem to be menaced by Lao-tzŭ's lack of differentiation. Had Lao-tzŭ's teaching been based on love, it would have transcended justice, but as it was based rather on indifference to others and a fundamental selfishness, it fell far short of justice. There is some evidence, indeed, that Confucius understood the saying to be based on nothing higher than selfishness, and grounded his rejection of it on this. For in the *Li Chi*, xxix. 12, where the same subject is dealt with, we read:[1] 'The Master said, "They who return kindness for injury are such as have a regard for their own persons" ', i.e. people who are thinking only of their own interests and security.

There is another story of Confucius, preserved by Han Ying, which Legge translates:[2] 'Tsze-lû said, "When men are good to me, I will also be good to them; when they are not good to me, I will also be not good to them". Tsze-kung said, "When men are good to me, I will also be good to them; when they are not good to me, I will simply lead them on, forwards it may be or backwards". Yen Hui said, "When men are good to me, I will also be good to them; when they are not good to me, I will still be good to them". The views of the three disciples being thus different, they referred the point to the Master, who said, "The words of Tsze-lû are such as might be expected among the (wild tribes of the) Man and the Mo; those of Tsze-kung, such as might be expected among friends; those of Hui, such as might be expected among relatives and near connexions".' Whether this story is apocryphal or genuine cannot be known, but if it be genuine, Legge's comment that 'the Master was still far from Lâo-tsze's standpoint, and that of his own favourite disciple, Yen Hui' seems hardly justified.

Other similar pronouncements of Confucius on the opinions of these three disciples are recorded, in which Hui comes off with the Master's approval, and it seems probable that the Master was here expressing his approval. For it is far less likely that Confucius meant that all these three principles would be equally appropriate in different circumstances, than that he was appraising the relative worth of the principles, and placing

---

[1] Legge, *Sacred Books of the East*, xxviii, 1885, p. 332. Cf. Couvreur, *Li Ki*, ii, 1899, p. 484. [2] *Op. cit.*, xxxix, p. 92.

Yen Hui's above the others, since it was a carrying into all life of the spirit which belonged to life at its highest.

But whether the approval of Confucius be assumed or not, the incident, if genuine, would show that Yen Hui was not behind Lao-tzŭ in the form of his utterance, and definitely before him in its substance. For the stories that are recorded of Yen Hui reveal a spirit gentle and unselfish, modest and self-effacing, filled with the Master's own desire to spread the principles whereby men and nations might live indeed. Tzŭ-lu was ever impetuous and ambitious for glory and ostentation, while Yen Hui was quite indifferent to these considerations, uncomplaining in adversity, and only eager to be of service to men.

A single story will illustrate the superiority of his spirit to anything Lao-tzŭ ever attained. It is recorded that Confucius once asked these three disciples to define their ambitions. Tzŭ-lu at once craved for military glory, and Tzŭ-kung for oratorical distinction, but Yen Hui said, 'I should like to find an intelligent king and sage ruler whom I might assist. I would diffuse among the people instructions on the five great points, and lead them on by the rules of propriety and music, so that they should not care to fortify their cities by walls and moats, but would fuse their swords and spears into implements of agriculture. They should send forth their flocks without fear into the plains and forests. There should be no sundering of families, no widows or widowers. For a thousand years there would be no calamity of war. Yû (i.e. Tzŭ-lu) would have no opportunity to display his bravery, or Ts'ze (i.e. Tzŭ-kung) to display his oratory.' It is not surprising that we read that Confucius pronounced this virtue admirable.[1] In the context of this character, the above recorded utterance of Yen Hui goes far beyond that for which Lao-tzŭ has received much unmerited praise.

In *Analects*, v. 11, we read:[2] 'Tsze-kung said, "What I do not wish men to do to me, I also wish not to do to men". The Master said, "Ts'ze, you have not attained to that".'

---

[1] Legge, *Chinese Classics*, i, 1893, pp. 112 f. Cf. Kramers, *K'ung Tzŭ Chia Yü*, 1950, pp. 230 f.

[2] Legge, *op. cit.*, p. 177.

In *Analects*, xii. 2:[1] 'Chung-kung asked about perfect virtue
(*jên*).[2] The Master said, "It is, when you go abroad, to behave
to every one as if you were receiving a great guest; to employ
the people as if you were assisting at a great sacrifice; not to
do to others as you would not wish done to yourself; to have
no murmuring against you in the country, and none in the
family".' In *Analects*, xv. 23 again:[3] 'Tsze-kung asked, saying,
"Is there one word which may serve as a rule of practice
for all one's life?" The Master said, "Is not reciprocity (*shu*)
such a word? What you do not want done to yourself, do not
do to others".' Again in the *Doctrine of the Mean*, xiii. 3,
we have:[4] 'When one cultivates to the utmost the principles
of his nature, and exercises them on the principle of reciprocity
(*shu*), he is not far from the path. What you do not like when
done to yourself, do not do to others.' Finally, in the *Great
Learning*, Commentary x. 2, we find:[5] 'What a man dislikes
in his superiors, let him not display in the treatment of his
inferiors; what he dislikes in inferiors, let him not display in
the service of his superiors; what he hates in those who are
before him, let him not therewith precede those who are behind
him; what he hates in those who are behind him, let him not
therewith follow those who are before him; what he hates to
receive on the right, let him not bestow on the left; what he
hates to receive on the left, let him not bestow on the right;
this is what is called "The principle with which, as with a
measuring-square, to regulate one's conduct" '.

[1] Legge, *op. cit.*, p. 251.

[2] Z. K. Zia (*The Confucian Civilization*, 1925, pp. 30 ff.) collects a number
of texts from the *Analects* where the word *jên* is used, and complains that
Legge renders by a variety of terms. Yet he admits (p. 34) that no one term
can represent the whole meaning of *jên*, which is said to include charity,
sincerity, grace, loyalty and self-denial. It was, however, a quality with a
human reference only, and did not include any relation to God. Granet (*La
pensée chinoise*, 1934, p. 486) also discusses the meaning of this term, and
observes: 'La conception confucéenne du *jen* ou de l'homme accompli, et qui
mérite seul le nom d'homme, s'inspire d'un sentiment de l'humanisme qui peut
déplaire, mais qu'on n'a point le droit de céler . . . L'idée maîtresse de Confucius et de ses premiers disciples . . . fut de rejeter toute spéculation sur
l'Univers et de *faire de l'homme l'objet propre du savoir*.' In the *Chia Yü*
Confucius is credited with the observation : ' In goodness (*jên*) nothing is
greater than to love others ' (cf. Kramers, *K'ung Tzŭ Chia Yü*, 1950, p. 211).

[3] *Ibid.*, p. 301.   [4] *Ibid.*, p. 394.   [5] *Ibid.*, pp. 373 f.

There are two other passages containing the word *shu*, which deserve to be noted, though there Legge translates it differently. The first[1] is *Analects*, iv. 15: 'The Master said, "Shăn, my doctrine is that of an all-pervading unity". The disciple Tsăng replied, "Yes". The Master went out, and the other disciples asked, saying, "What do his words mean?" Tsăng said, "The doctrine of our master is to be true to the principles of our nature (*chung*) and the benevolent exercise of them to others (*shu*),—this and nothing more".' Here it would be equally possible to translate by the words which Legge elsewhere uses for *chung* and *shu*: 'The Master's teaching is wholly summed up in faithfulness (*chung*) and reciprocity (*shu*)'.[2]

The other is in the *Great Learning*, Commentary ix. 4, where Legge renders:[3] 'On this account, the ruler must himself be possessed of the good qualities, and then he may require them in the people. He must not have the bad qualities in himself, and then he may require that they shall not be in the people. Never has there been a man, who, not having reference to his own character and wishes in dealing with others, was able effectually to instruct them.' Here once more the presence of *shu* is disguised. It is well brought out by Couvreur:[4] 'Un prince sage, avant d'exiger une chose des autres, la pratique d'abord lui-même; avant de reprendre un défaut dans les autres, il a soin de l'éviter lui-même. Un homme qui ne sait pas mesurer et traiter les autres avec la même mesure que lui-même, ne peut pas les instruire.'

It should, however, be noted that Soothill objects to Legge's rendering of *shu* by *reciprocity*, and maintains [5] that it 'seems

---

[1] Legge, *Chinese Classics*, i, 1893, pp. 169 f.

[2] Couvreur (*Les Quatre Livres*, 2nd ed., 1910, pp. 104 f.) renders: 'Toute la sagesse de notre maître consiste à se perfectionner soi-même et à aimer les autres comme soi-meme.'

[3] *Chinese Classics*, i, p. 371.   [4] *Op. cit.*, p. 17.

[5] *Three Religions of China*, p. 34. Cf. his *Analects of Confucius*, 1910, pp. 746, 748. In *Analects*, xv. 23 he uses the word *sympathy* instead of *reciprocity* to represent *shu*. This is unsatisfactory, since it misses the mutual element of the word. Wilhelm (*Kung-Futse Gespräche*, 1923, p. 176) uses *Die Nächsten-liebe*, but Hackmann complains that this imports too much into the word. He says: 'Dem Begriff, der Gegenseitigkeit fehlt die Gemütswärme, die mit 'Nächstenliebe" verbunden ist, es ist ein kühlerer, mehr rationaler Begriff,

to mean more than this, for reciprocity means, Do as you are done by, whereas "shu" suggests the idea of following one's better nature, that is, Be generous'. As against this, however, we may observe that Legge does not understand reciprocity to mean 'Do as you are done by', but 'Do as you would be done by', and this interpretation is not really Legge's, but is explicitly stated in the above quoted passage from the *Doctrine of the Mean*. It must therefore be accepted as the authoritative Confucian interpretation of the term.[1]

It will be observed that the Golden Rule, in its negative form, is not merely a casual utterance of the Sage's, but a fundamental principle. This is quite clear from its repeated enunciation. In the first of the above-quoted instances, it is found on the lips of a disciple, but all of the other cases are in sayings attributed to Confucius himself, except that from the *Great Learning*. This work is of doubtful authorship, but it is believed to reflect the teachings of Confucius faithfully.[2] In any case its evidence is here only confirmatory of what is so well evidenced in other passages.

Giles equates[3] the Golden Rule of Confucius with that of Christ, and will have none of the common distinction on the ground of its negative form. Legge, on the other hand, emphasizes[4] the negative character of the Confucian maxim, as against the positive character of the New Testament form. Elsewhere, however, he notes[5] that its occurrence in the *Doctrine of the Mean* is immediately followed by the rule virtually in its positive form. This passage is therefore worth quoting:[6] 'In the way of the superior man there are four things, to not one of which I have as yet attained.—To serve

eine logische Ableitung aus dem Verhältnis des Menschen als eines Gemeinschaftswesens' (*Chinesische Philosophie*, 1927, p. 86). Couvreur also reads too much into the word by translating 'le précepte d'aimer tous les hommes comme soi-même' (*Les Quatre Livres*, 2nd ed., 1910, p. 244), while Waley reads too little by rendering *consideration* (*The Analects of Confucius*, 1938, p. 198). Kramers (*K'ung Tzŭ Chia Yü*, 1950, p. 338) finds *reciprocity* to represent best the meaning of this word.

[1] Granet (*La pensée chinoise*, 1934, p. 485) renders *shu* by *réversibilité*, and observes: 'Ce haut sentiment de la réciprocité . . . a un double aspect: le respect d'autrui, le respect de soi-même'.

[2] Legge, *Chinese Classics*, i, p. 27.　　　[3] *Op. cit.*, p. 85.
[4] *Op. cit.*, p. 109.　　　[5] *Ibid.*, p. 49.
[6] *Ibid.*, p. 394. Cf. Wilhelm, *Li Gi*, 1930, pp. 6 f.

7

my father, as I would require my son to serve me: to this I have not attained; to serve my prince, as I would require my minister to serve me: to this I have not attained; to serve my elder brother, as I would require my younger brother to serve me: to this I have not attained; to set the example in behaving to a friend, as I would require him to behave to me: to this I have not attained'. In view of this passage, it would seem to be unfair to lay any emphasis on the negative form of the Golden Rule in the Confucian Classics, and it should be understood to mean 'Treat others as you would like to be treated by them if your positions were reversed'. And surely this is exactly what Jesus meant by the Golden Rule.

It has been already said, however, that the equation of the form does not necessarily involve the equation of the content, and Legge draws a further distinction[1] on the ground that whereas 'the rule of Christ is for man as man, having to do with other men, all with himself on the same platform', Confucius 'did not think of the reciprocity coming into action beyond the circle of his five relations of society'. This, I believe, is a sound distinction, though Legge immediately undermines it by adding:[2] 'Possibly, he might have required its observance in dealings even with the rude tribes, which were the only specimens of mankind besides his own countrymen of which he knew anything'. Surely no man can be expected to legislate for hypothetical relationships that lie beyond the world of his experience, and if he lays down a principle which he declares is to be applied to every relationship of life of which he has cognizance, and which is equally capable of being applied to wider relationships which lie beyond his horizon, it may fairly be treated as an inherently universal principle. It is, however, doubtful if Confucius gave it universal application within the world he knew. The only passage to which Legge appeals to justify his suggestion that Confucius might have applied the principle of reciprocity to dealings with the rude tribes, does not seem to bear out the suggestion. This passage is *Analects*, xiii. 19:[3] 'Fan Ch'ih asked about perfect virtue

---

[1] Legge, *Chinese Classics*, i, pp. 109 f.   [2] *Ibid.*, p. 110.
[3] *Ibid.*, p. 271. Soothill here renders: 'Once when Fan Ch'ih asked about Virtue the Master said: "In private life be courteous, in handling public

(*jên*). The Master said, "It is, in retirement, to be sedately grave; in the management of business, to be reverently attentive; in intercourse with others, to be strictly sincere (*chung*). Though a man go among rude, uncultivated tribes, these qualities may not be neglected".'

That Confucius contemplated *chung*, which is here rendered by *sincerity*, but which is normally rendered by *faithfulness*, being applied in relationships with the rude tribes does not necessarily imply that *shu* was of like application. Elsewhere the virtues of faithfulness (*chung*) and sincerity (*hsin*) are frequently inculcated, and in *Analects*, xv. 5, it is clearly indicated that these are of universal application:[1] 'The Master said, "Let his (i.e. a man's) words be sincere (*chung*) and truthful (*hsin*) and his actions honourable and careful;—such conduct may be practised among the rude tribes of the South or the North. If his words be not sincere and truthful, and his actions not honourable and careful, will he, with such conduct, be appreciated, even in his neighbourhood?" ' Again, in *Analects*, xiv. 13[2] the virtue of the complete man (*ch'êng jên*) is defined in terms of righteousness, courage and faithfulness, as exemplified in the loyal observance of a long-standing agreement: 'The man, who in the view of gain thinks of righteousness; who in the view of danger is prepared to give up his life; and who does not forget an old agreement however far back it extends:—such a man may be reckoned a complete man'.

Shu, or *reciprocity*, however, would seem to be limited in the Confucian view to the five relations of society. These are defined most clearly in the *Doctrine of the Mean*, which is believed to have been written by the grandson of Confucius,[3] and which may be accepted as of reliable authority. The passage is in xx. 8:[4] 'The duties of universal obligation are five, and the

business be serious, with all men be conscientious. Even though you go among barbarians you may not relinquish these" ' (*The Analects of Confucius*, 1910, p. 633). Cf. also the renderings of Couvreur (*Les Quatre Livres*, 2nd ed., 1910, p. 217) and Wilhelm (*Kung-Futse Gespräche*, 1923, p. 142).

[1] Legge, *Chinese Classics*, i, pp. 295 f.

[2] *Ibid.*, pp. 279 f.

[3] E. R. Hughes (*The Great Learning and the Mean-in-Action*, 1942, pp. 86 ff.) denies the unity of this work, but accepts the authorship of Confucius's grandson, Tzŭ Ssŭ, for the section that contains this saying.

[4] Legge, *op. cit.*, pp. 406 f.

virtues wherewith they are practised are three. The duties are
those between sovereign and minister, between father and son,
between husband and wife, between elder brother and younger,
and those belonging to the intercourse of friends. Those five
are the duties of universal obligation.' Within the limits of
these relationships a man has special ties, and reciprocity is to
prevail. But beyond these relationships, which far from cover
all the relationships within a single community, and which therefore were well within the experience of Confucius, there is, as
Legge observes, nothing to indicate that the principle of reciprocity had any validity for the sage. Certainly there is nowhere in
the records of the teaching of Confucius any suggestion that its
validity could extend even to enemies. Its range is therefore
more limited than the range of Christ's principle, and despite
the formal equation of the words of Confucius and of Christ,
their sayings cannot really be equated.

The superiority of Confucius to Lao-tzŭ, however, can be
illustrated at every turn. He had a far greater interest in his
fellow-men, and his whole conception of virtue was of an active
force of beneficence in the world. Thus, in *Analects*, vi. 28,
we read:[1] "Now the man of perfect virtue (*jên*), wishing to
be established himself, seeks also to establish others; wishing
to be enlarged himself, he seeks also to enlarge others"; in
Analects, xii. 16:[2] 'The Master said, "The superior man seeks
to perfect the admirable qualities of men, and does not seek to
perfect their bad qualities" '. Moreover, as against Lao-tzŭ's
fundamental indifference to men, Confucius inculcates love
for men. To this, however, we shall return below, in the discussion of Mo-tzŭ.

Again, that Confucius held a truly altruistic view of virtue
is illustrated in his interest in the principles of good government. He is ever eager to promote the principles which he
believed would entail peace, prosperity and happiness for
mankind in general.

As to the power on which he relied for the carrying out
of his principles, Confucius again shows a definite advance on
Lao-tzŭ, but falls far short of Christ. He relied to an extrav-
agant extent on the force of example. Thus, in *Analects*

[1] Legge, *Chinese Classics*, p. 194.   [2] *Ibid.*, p. 258.

iv. 25, we find:[1] 'The Master said, "Virtue is not left to stand
alone. He who practises it will have neighbours" '; in *Analects*,
xii. 1:[2] 'Chî K'ang, distressed about the number of thieves
in the State, inquired of Confucius how to do away with them.
Confucius said, "If you, sir, were not covetous, although you
should reward them to do it, they would not steal" '; and in
the *Great Learning*, Commentary x. 21:[3] 'Never has there been
a case of the sovereign loving benevolence, and the people
not loving righteousness. Never has there been a case where
the people have loved righteousness, and the affairs of the
sovereign have not been carried to completion. And never has
there been a case where the wealth in such a State, collected
in the treasuries and arsenals, did not continue in the sovereign's
possession.'

That the force of example is real may readily be allowed,
but it is a lamentably inadequate view of human nature which
supposes that men have only to see the good to desire it and to
achieve it, and that they are inherently prone to follow a noble
example.[4] Ovid showed a deeper understanding of the fundamental problem when he wrote *Metamorphoses*, vii. 20 f.: Video
meliora proboque, deteriora sequor. Paul, too, recognized
the need for some greater resources of power than a man can
find in himself, or in the ideal that is set before him, when he
wrote Rom. vii. 19: 'The good that I would I do not; but
the evil that I would not, that I do'. Of any spiritual source
of strength, Confucius knew nothing.

Though the more personal name for God, *Shang Ti*, or *Ti*,
is not found on the lips of Confucius anywhere in the *Analects*,
where it stands only in an utterance attributed to T'ang in xx. 1,
and stands in the *Great Learning* only in a single quotation
from the *Book of the Odes* in Commentary x. 5, it is found
once on the Master's lips in the *Doctrine of the Mean*, xix. 6.

---

[1] Legge, *Chinese Classics*, p. 172.

[2] *Ibid.*, p. 258.   [3] *Ibid.*, p. 359.

[4] Cf. Shang Yang, chap. iv, § 18 (translation of Duyvendak, *The Book of
Lord Shang*, 1928, pp. 293 f.): 'The benevolent may be benevolent towards
others, but cannot cause others to be benevolent; the righteous may love
others, but cannot cause others to love. From this I know that benevolence
and righteousness are not sufficient for governing the empire.' The word
benevolent here renders the Chinese *jên* (cf. above, p. 85 n.) and *righteous* renders
i (cf. above, p. 5 n.) See Duyvendak, *op. cit.*, p. 111.

Ordinarily, however, he preferred to use the term *T'ien*. On the lips of Confucius this seems to have meant something more than the impersonal force behind the universe, or even Providence, and to have denoted a conscious and purposive Power that was cognizant of human affairs. Thus he says in *Analects*, xiv. 37:[1] 'Is it not Heaven that knows me?'; and in *Analects*, iii. 13:[2] 'He who offends against Heaven has none to whom he can pray'; while in *Analects*, ix. 5, we read:[3] 'The Master was put in fear in K'wang. He said, "After the death of King Wăn, was not the cause of truth lodged here in me? If Heaven had wished to let this cause of truth perish, then I, a future mortal, should not have got such a relation to that cause. While Heaven does not let the cause of truth perish, what can the people of K'wang do to me?" '; and again in *Analects*, vii. 22:[4] 'The Master said, "Heaven produced the virtue that is in me. Huan T'ûi (from whom the sage stood in some danger)—what can he do to me?" '

In addition to this recognition of Heaven, Confucius recognized the existence of other spiritual beings, as well as the continued existence of ancestors, and their worship has a definite place in his practice and teaching. But it rested, as will be seen, on no truly religious interest.[5] Confucius had no interest in the character of God, and Legge describes him[6] as 'unreligious', while Moore well observes[7] that it is 'the absence of any teaching about the nature of these "spiritual beings" and their relations to men that is significant '. Nor

---

[1] Legge, *Chinese Classics*, p. 289. The translation is not here, as normally above, that of Legge, but follows the more literal rendering he gives in his note. So Couvreur (*op. cit.*, p. 233): 'Celui qui me connaît, n'est-ce pas le Ciel?' Cf. Pauthier, *Doctrine de Confucius*, p. 167, has 'Si quelqu'un me connaît c'est le ciel!' Waley robs the saying of its implication of personality by rendering (*The Analects of Confucius*, 1938, p. 189): 'perhaps after all I am known; not here, but in heaven'.

[2] Legge, *op. cit.*, p. 159.　　　[3] *Ibid.*, pp. 217 f.　　　[4] *Ibid.*, p. 202.

[5] Zia (*The Confucian Civilization*, 1925, p. 21) says 'No one in Chinese history has ever had a clear conception of God'. Nevertheless, he holds that there was a personal element in Confucius' thought of God. He says: 'After most careful examination, we concede that the concept of God in Confucianism has a personal element, even though it does not give us distinctly a personal deity.'　　　[6] Legge, *op. cit.*, p. 99.

[7] *Op. cit.*, p. 34. Cf. H. G. Creel, *Confucius*, 1951, p. 124: ' He refrained from raising fundamental issues.'

is the evidence merely negative. We are told, indeed, in *Analects*, vii. 20[1] that 'the subjects on which the Master did not talk were—extraordinary things, feats of strength, disorder, and spiritual beings'. But beyond this we are told that he positively warned his followers to keep aloof from spiritual beings. For *Analects*, vi. 20, says:[2] 'The Master said, "To give one's self earnestly to the duties due to men, and, while respecting spiritual beings, to keep aloof from them, may be called wisdom" '.

It is true, as has been noted, that Confucius was deeply interested in the performance of religious ceremonies, but his interest lay solely in the forms of worship as ancient ceremonies that should be maintained to preserve the proprieties of life, and not as spiritual means of grace. In the one passage in the *Doctrine of the Mean* where he himself mentions God, it is not God, but religious ceremony, that holds the centre of his interest, and that but as the expression of filial piety and the key to effective government. Speaking of King Wu and the Duke of Chou, whose filial piety was shown in their repair of ancestral temples and the offering of due sacrifices, he says in xix. 6:[3] 'By the ceremonies of the sacrifices to Heaven and Earth they serve God (*Ti*), and by the ceremonies of the ancestral temples they sacrificed to their ancestors. He who understands the ceremonies of the sacrifices to Heaven and Earth, and the meaning of the several sacrifices to ancestors, would find the government of a kingdom as easy as to look into his palm.'

Once more, therefore, we fail to find any genuinely religious motive or power for the practice of the principle of reciprocity. Soothill says:[4] 'The whole code of Confucius resembles the wintry silver of the moon rather than the golden glow and warmth of the sun'; and again:[5] 'His own writings, as well as those of his disciples, lack that throbbing pulse of divinity which has made the history, poetry, and soul-inspiring prophecy of the Old Testament live with perennial vitality'; while Wieger sums up[6] the demand of Confucius on the superior

[1] Legge, *op. cit.*, p. 201.   [2] *Ibid.*, p. 191.
[3] *Ibid.*, p. 404.   [4] *Op. cit.*, p. 33.
[5] *Ibid.*, p. 36.   [6] *Op. cit.*, p. 135.

man as being a demand for 'la neutralité de l'esprit et la froideur de cœur'. In such a context the Golden Rule becomes quite other than the Golden Rule of Jesus.

III

The precise date of Mo-tzŭ cannot be determined, but it is certain that he falls somewhere between Confucius and Mencius. Legge places him[1] very little before the time of Mencius, while Wieger is of the opinion[2] that he probably died before 400 B.C. This is in accordance with the view of Hu Shih,[3] who assigns him the years 500-420 B.C. Z. L. Yih follows this and says[4] that he lived 'somewhere between 500-416 B.C.', while Forke[5] puts him but slightly later at 480-400 B.C. Liang Ch'i-ch'ao goes somewhat later still,[6] from 466-459 B.C. to 390-382 B.C., and is followed substantially by Williamson[7] and Holth,[8] who assign him the years 468-382 B.C., while Y. P. Mei, after a careful re-examination of the evidence, arrives at the same conclusion,[9] but 'for convenience of memory' uses the dates 470-391 B.C.

Mo-tzŭ was a strong critic of Confucianism, and he in turn was criticized by Mencius, who condemned him in the same breath with the egoist Yang Chu, whose teachings were the very antithesis of Mo-tzŭ's. For centuries Mo-tzŭ suffered neglect, and his works, though in part preserved, underwent much disorder of text. In modern times they have attracted much attention in China, and they are now attracting increasing

---

[1] *Chinese Classics*, 2nd ed., ii, 1895, p. 100.

[2] *Op. cit.*, p. 207.

[3] *The Development of the Logical Method in Ancient China*, 1928, p. 56.

[4] 'Introduction to Mo-tzu' in *Hirth Anniversary Volume*, 1923, pp. 612-619.

[5] *Mê Ti*, 1922, p. 27.

[6] Cf. Mei, *Motse : the Neglected Rival of Confucius*, 1934, p. 31.

[7] *Mo Ti : a Chinese Heretic*, 1927, p. 1.

[8] *Micius*, 1935, p. 10. The form Micius, for Mo-tzŭ, is used by some writers, on the analogy of Confucius, for K'ung-tzŭ. Others prefer to use his name Mo Ti, instead of Mo-tzŭ, which means 'the philosopher Mo'. The great variety of romanizations of these words may at first puzzle the reader. I have throughout the paper employed the standard romanization of Wade, employed by modern English lexicographers, except in quotations.

[9] *Op. cit.*, pp. 31 ff.

attention in the West.[1] Legge translated the chapters on Universal Love (*chien ai*, or *chien hsiang ai*) into English,[2] but it is only in recent years that fuller translations have been available to western readers. A French translation of some passages, based on Legge so far as the chapters on Universal Love are concerned, was published in 1907 by Alexandra David,[3] and a complete translation in German by Forke appeared in 1922.[4] Two translations in English, one by Tomkinson,[5] and the other by Mei,[6] have since appeared. Of these the second contains a larger selection of the chapters of the work, though it is still less complete than Forke's German work. The translations of extracts that stand below, instead of being normally Legge's, as in the case of extracts from the Confucian classics above, will be based on these various renderings, but will not exactly follow any.

There is no precise verbal parallel to the Golden Rule in the teachings of Mo-tzŭ. Nevertheless, he approaches much nearer to the spirit of that Rule than either Lao-tzŭ or Confucius.[7] Williamson says:[8] 'It has often been said that Chinese ethical philosophy affords no instance of the Golden Rule, except perhaps the negative form in which that Rule is enunciated by Confucius, but it would seem that Mo-tzŭ's words mean much the same as Christ's'. Similarly Mei says[9] of his teaching on Universal Love: 'It may also be regarded as a concrete expression of the Christian Golden Rule'.

Mo-tzŭ traced the ills of society to the want of mutual love amongst men, and he advocated a love that should embrace all alike. In chapter xiv (Universal Love, I), he says:[10] 'If universal mutual love (*chien hsiang ai*) prevailed throughout the

---

[1] For a fuller study of the teaching of Mo-tzŭ, and the attention given to his work in modern times, see below, pp. 108 ff.

[2] *Chinese Classics*, ii, pp. 101-116.

[3] *Le philosophe Meh-ti et l'idée de Solidarité.*

[4] *Mê Ti, des Sozialethikers und seiner Schüler philosophische Werke.*

[5] *The Social Teachings of Meh Tse*, 1927.

[6] *The Ethical and Political Works of Motse*, 1929.

[7] Cf. Forke (*op. cit.*, p. 41): 'Jedenfalls steht er dem Christentum sehr viel näher als Konfuzius'.

[8] *Op. cit.*, p. 21.   [9] *Motse: the Neglected Rival*, p. 92.

[10] Cf. Legge, *Chinese Classics*, ii, p. 102; Mei, *Works of Motse*, pp. 79 f.; David, *op. cit.*, pp. 32 f.; Forke, *op. cit.*, pp. 242 f.

world, if men loved others as themselves, would anyone be unfilial? When every one regarded his father, elder brother, and emperor as himself, towards whom could he be unfilial? . . . Would there be any thieves or robbers? When every man regarded the homes of others as his own home, who would steal? When every man regarded the persons of others as his own person, who would rob? . . . Would there be mutual discord among the families of the great, or mutual aggression amongst states of the princes? When every man regarded the families of others as his own, who would create discord? When every man regarded the states of others as his own, who would initiate aggression?'

This is one of the principal, fundamental doctrines of Mo-tzŭ, to which three parallel chapters, with a considerable element of repetition, are devoted. In one of its developments we have an interesting reminder of the parable of Matt. xxv. 31-46. This is in chapter xvi (Universal Love, III), where we read:[1] 'Suppose there are two men, one of whom adopts the principle of making distinctions (*pieh*), and the other of whom adopts the principle of universality (*chien*). The advocate of distinctions will say, "How can I be for my friend's person as for my own, how for my friend's parents as for my own?" Hence, if he sees his friend in hunger, he will not feed him; if he sees him cold, he will not clothe him; if he finds him sick, he will not minister to him; if dead, he will not bury him. Such is the language, and such the conduct of the advocate of the principle of distinctions. Quite other will be the language and the conduct of the advocate of universality. He will say, "I have heard that he who would be great amongst men should be for his friend as for himself, for his friend's parents as for his own, and only so can he become great amongst men". Hence, if he sees his friend in hunger, he will feed him; if he sees him cold, he will clothe him; if he finds him sick, he will minister to him; if dead, he will bury him. Such is the language, and such the conduct of the advocate of universality.'

It might seem at first sight that this illustration is narrower in its range than the New Testament parable referred to, since

[1] Cf. Legge, *op. cit.*, p. 110; Mei, *op. cit.*, pp. 89 f.; David, *op. cit.*, pp. 45 f.; Forke, *op. cit.*, pp. 255 f.

it deals merely with one's friend. A closer view shows that this is not really so. When Mencius criticized the teaching of Mo-tzŭ, it was precisely on the ground that the universalizing of love abolished all the distinctions of the five relationships, on which Confucianism laid such emphasis, and that it threatened the carefully regulated affections due to those who are especially near to us. In *Mencius*, III, ii. 9, we read:[1] 'Mo's principle is —"to love all equally (*chien ai*)", which does not acknowledge the peculiar affection due to a father. But to acknowledge neither king nor father is to be in the state of a beast. . . . If the principles of . . . Mo be not stopped, and the principles of Confucius not set forth, then those perverse speakings will delude the people, and stop up the path of benevolence and righteousness.'

Actually, Mo-tzŭ was replying in advance to this criticism in the passage above-quoted. What he is arguing is that a love which is all-embracing will include those who are near, and will express itself in relation to them as fully as Confucian principles would demand. Mo-tzŭ teaches that love for all should be levelled up to the highest level required by Confucianism for those who have the greatest claim upon us. It does not fall below Confucianism, therefore, but goes far beyond it in universalizing its most exacting demands. While, therefore, Mo-tzŭ does not formulate any principle verbally similar to the Golden Rule, he does formulate a principle verbally similar to the maxim 'Thou shalt love thy neighbour as thyself', where 'neighbour' is given the universal sense of the New Testament parable of the Good Samaritan.

It is sometimes said, as by Bullock,[2] that Confucius taught that one should love all men, and Rawlinson quotes[3] from a Chinese writer of the eight century A.D., Han Yü, who says: 'When Confucius speaks of "overflowing in love" to all and cultivating the friendship of the good, and of how the extensive conferring of benefits constituted a sage, does he not teach universal love?' It is therefore necessary to ask wherein

[1] Legge, *op. cit.*, pp. 282 f.
[2] In Hastings' *Encyclopædia of Religion and Ethics*, v, 1912, p. 466a.
[3] *Chinese Recorder*, lxiii, 1932, p. 94, in an article on 'The Ethical Values of Micius'. Cf. Forke, *op. cit.*, p. 62.

Mo-tzŭ's doctrine differed from that of Confucius. The first passage to which appeal may be made for the teaching of Confucius on this subject is that to which Han Yü refers, *Analects*, i. 6:[1] 'The Master said, "A youth, when at home, should be filial, and abroad, respectful to his elders. He should be earnest and truthful. He should overflow in love to all (*fan ai chung*), and cultivate the friendship of the good." ' Again, in *Analects*, xii. 22, we read:[2] 'Fan Ch'ih asked about benevolence (*jên*). The Master said, "It is to love all men".'

It is interesting to observe that Mencius declared in the above-quoted passage that Mo-tzŭ's doctrine of universal love (*chien ai*) threatened the foundations of benevolence (*jên*). Clearly, therefore, he did not regard the Master as having taught any comparable doctrine as the very expression of benevolence. In truth, however, the crucial word *all*, which Legge has imported into his rendering of *Analects*, xii, 22, does not stand in the Chinese text, and what Confucius said to Fan Ch'ih was simply 'It is to love men'. What he had in mind was certainly a love governed by the relationships of the fivefold duty, as he quite explicitly shows elsewhere.

Before we turn to that passage, however, we may observe that *Analects*, i. 6, to which Han Yü appeals, is a lesson to the young in manners, and that it contemplates something quite other than Mo-tzŭ's principle of love. It is rather an injunction to a young man to bear himself agreeably towards all men, as becomes his youth.

There is another important passage in the opening sentence of the text of the *Great Learning*, which we may also examine before turning to the crucial passage in the *Doctrine of the Mean*, though the orthodox interpretation does not associate it with our present subject. Here Legge, following the orthodox Chinese view, renders:[3] 'What the Great Learning teaches is—to illustrate illustrious virtue (*ming ming tê*); to renovate the people (*hsin min*); and to rest in the highest excellence (*chih yü chih shan*)'. The Chinese text, however, has *ch'in min*=*to love the people*, for which *hsin min* is substituted by the orthodox in reading and interpreting the passage. Legge, in

---

[1] Legge, *Chinese Classics*, i, p. 140.
[2] *Ibid.*, p. 260.   [3] *Ibid.*, p. 356.

his note, rejects the substitution as unsatisfactory, and has no doubt that what the passage really taught was love for the people. This view has not been unknown amongst Chinese commentators, who have not all followed the orthodox path.[1] It appears in a modern commentary in the spoken language, *Ssŭ Shu Pai Hua Chieh Shuo*, whose fourteen volumes, exhibiting considerable acquaintance with foreign thought as well as Chinese, are said to have been written by a nine year old boy, Chiang Hsi-chang, who is in consequence called *Shên-t'ung*=the divine, or prodigious, child.[2] Even if we follow the reading *ch'in*, however, this passage is of little importance for our present purpose, since it is clear, as Legge says,[3] that the *Great Learning* was designed to give instruction to a ruler. While it contains some instruction of general application, this particular teaching is manifestly intended for the ruler, and it inculcates beneficent care for his people, rather than such a love as Mo-tzŭ had in mind.

We may now turn to the most important passage for the understanding of the Confucian conception of love's range and control. This stands in the *Doctrine of the Mean*, xx. 5:[4] 'Benevolence (*jên*) is the characteristic element of humanity, and the great exercise of it is in loving relatives[5] (*ch'in ch'in wei ta*). Righteousness is the accordance of actions with what is right, and the great exercise of it is in honouring the worthy. The decreasing measures of the love due to relatives, and the steps in the honour due to the worthy, are produced by the principle of propriety.' It has already been said that the *Doctrine of the Mean* may be accepted as the work of the grandson of Confucius, and as giving an authoritative account of his principles. From this passage it is abundantly clear that Confucianism contemplated only a love which was severely controlled by the rules of propriety, and that its objects and its

---

[1] So Wang Yang-ming, who strongly argues for the meaning *to love the people*. Cf. Henke, *The Philosophy of Wang Yang-Ming*, 1916, pp. 48 ff.

[2] My copy of this work was given to me by the boy's father.

[3] *Chinese Classics*, i, p. 29.   [4] *Ibid.*, pp. 405 f.

[5] The character *ch'in* may mean *parents* or *relatives*. In the second quotation from Mo-tzŭ given above, it is rendered *parents*, where it might equally have been given the wider reference. The sequel here demands the wider reference.

measure were to be strictly determined. It was precisely on this ground that Mo-tzŭ, who was a contemporary of the author of this work, opposed the Confucian teaching, and Mencius did not misunderstand the Master in contending for it.

The surviving recension of the chapter of Mo-tzŭ devoted to a polemic against Confucianism, chapter xxxix, begins:[1] 'The Confucianist says, "Love among relatives should depend on the degree of kinship, and the honour due to the worthy should be graded". This is to advocate distinctions between the near and the distant relations, and between the exalted and the humble.' It is clear that Mo-tzŭ did, and Confucius did not, teach a genuinely universal love.

Moreover, it was no merely academic teaching. Mo-tzŭ practised the love he preached. His critic Mencius, in VII, i. 26, said of him:[2] 'The philosopher Mo loves all equally (*chien ai*). If by rubbing smooth his whole body from the crown to the heel, he could have benefited the whole kingdom, he would have done it.' It is recorded that on one occasion, on hearing that a war was about to break out between two of the small states of China, Mo-tzŭ travelled from his home to the scene, journeying for ten days and nights without rest, with his feet blistered and his clothes torn to shreds to provide bandages for them, and then interviewed the aggressor and persuaded him to abandon the enterprise—not indeed by moral suasion alone, but by convincing him that his own science of defence was more than a match for the aggressor's science of offence, and that his skill would be freely offered to the attacked.[3]

Clearly, Mo-tzŭ exemplified in himself the spirit of service through sacrifice. He also demanded it of his disciples. Nor did he demand it in vain. Williamson says:[4] 'Their self-denial and sacrifice were such as to lead such an authority as Liang Ch'i-ch'ao to say, "Their self-sacrifice is equal to that of Christ and His disciples" '. The same Chinese authority says of Mo-tzŭ:[5] 'In his willingness to endure hardship he is truly like Christ. If men had nailed him to a cross, he would

---

[1] Cf. Mei, *Works of Motse*, p. 200; Forke, *op. cit.*, p. 395.
[2] Legge, *Chinese Classics*, ii, pp. 464 f.
[3] Williamson, *op. cit.*, p. 24.   [4] *Ibid.*, p. 31.
[5] Cf. Holth, *op. cit.*, p. 3.

certainly not have regretted it, but would have endured it with a smile.' An ancient Chinese writer, the Taoist Chuang-tzǔ, paid equally high tribute to Mo-tzǔ and his followers in these words:[1] 'The idea of Mo Tî and *Kh*in Hwa-lî was good, but their practice was wrong. They would have made the Mohists of future ages feel it necessary to toil themselves, till there was not a hair on their legs, and still be urging one another on; (thus producing a condition) superior indeed to disorder, but inferior to the result of good government. Nevertheless, Mo-tsze was indeed one of the best men in the world, which you may search without finding his equal. Decayed and worn (his person) might be, but he is not to be rejected—a scholar of ability indeed!'

It is when we turn to examine the motive power to which Mo-tzǔ looks to bring in the age of universal mutual love that we find once more the real differences between him and Christ. Mo-tzǔ believed that men had but to see this universal love in practice to desire it. If a ruler would but display it, even men who objected to the principle would flock to him. In chapter xvi (Universal Love, III), he says:[2] 'I consider that there is no man on earth so foolish, even though he condemns the principle of universal love, as not to prefer a ruler who embraces it'; and again in chapter xv (Universal Love, II):[3] 'When a man loves others, they love him in return; when a man profits others, they profit him in return'. This, as Legge observes,[4] shows real ignorance of human nature. Nor did he really understand the nature of love. For in chapter xvi (Universal Love, III), he says:[5] 'If superiors delighted in it, and promoted it by rewards and praise, and discouraged its opposite by punishments and fines, I believe people would move towards universal mutual love and the mutual sharing of benefits, as fire rises upwards and water flows downwards'.

[1] Legge, *Sacred Books of the East*, xl, 1891, p. 221.
[2] Cf. Legge, *Chinese Classics*, ii, p. 112; Mei, *Works of Motse*, p. 92; David, *op. cit.*, p. 48; Forke, *op. cit.*, p. 258.
[3] Cf. Legge, *op. cit.*, p. 106; Mei, *op. cit.*, p. 84; David, *op. cit.*, p. 37; Forke, *op. cit.*, p. 246.
[4] *Op. cit.*, p. 117.
[5] Cf. Legge, *op. cit.*, p. 116; Mei, *op. cit.*, p. 97; David, *op. cit.*, p. 56; Forke, *op. cit.*, p. 265.

But love is not created by punishments, and cannot be compelled by a monarch.

The third constraint to which Mo-tzŭ looked was self-interest. It was because he rightly saw that the way of mutual love would be the way of mutual profit that he hoped to be able to persuade men to adopt it. *Chiao hsiang li*, or the mutual sharing of profit, is as fundamental a concept of his philosophy as *chien hsiang ai*, or universal mutual love. The very love that he inculcated rested therefore on a basis of selfishness. And selfishness is the antithesis and denial of love. This was clearly perceived by Mencius's younger contemporary Hsün-tzŭ, who observed:[1] 'Micius was prejudiced towards utility and did not know the elegancies of life. . . . For if we consider life from the standpoint of utility, it will merely be seeking for profit.' It is by a strange irony that desire for gain should have been a cardinal element of the philosophy of one who practised sacrifice for others to a rare degree with a fine disregard for any gain he might himself receive.

Mo-tzŭ is notably distinguished from both Lao-tzŭ and Confucius in that his principle is associated with his religion. Confucius was interested in ethics and politics, and in so far as he was religious, his religion was a thing separate and apart, and not the spring and fount of his teaching. But with Mo-tzŭ it is different. Wieger describes him[2] as 'le seul écrivain chinois dont on puisse penser qu'il crut en Dieu', and Hu Shih is of the opinion[3] that 'he was the only Chinese who can truly be said to have founded a religion'. His God was not the impersonal, or semi-personal, Power of the earlier sages we have dealt with, though he still used the term *T'ien*, but a beneficent Power, whose will for men was the ultimate basis of the love Mo-tzŭ taught. Williamson says:[4] 'The "will of Heaven" was to him the ultimate and universal standard, by which everything was to be judged. His interpretation of the will of Heaven is of peculiar interest, in that, according to

---

[1] Hsün-tzŭ xxi, 5; translation of Dubs, *The Works of Hsüntze*, 1928, pp. 263 f. Kennedy (*Chinese Recorder*, lxii, 1931, p. 696) quotes a better rendering, but does not indicate its source: 'Mo-tze's one-sided doctrine of utility made him ignore the significance of culture and refinement. When utilitarianism prevails, the Tao is lost in commercialism'.

[2] *Op. cit.*, p. 207.   [3] *Op. cit.*, p. 57.   [4] *Op. cit.*, p. 35.

modern critics like Liang Ch'i-ch'ao and Hu Shih, it permits of a personal interpretation. In fact, it would seem that the personal interpretation is the only one which meets the case.' Similarly Hackmann insists firmly on the personal character of Mo-tzǔ's 'Heaven'.[1]

Others, however, give a rather different complexion to the matter. Thus Mei believes[2] that Mo-tzǔ's Heaven is just the deification of the principles he teaches, a deification that is intended to secure an added motive for their practice. He says:[3] 'Motse personified social values for their preservation and enhancement. He threw a religious halo around his fundamental ethical convictions, and lifted his doctrines to the commanding position of creeds, so that man could feel a closer tie with his fellow and that in loving men he was also doing the will of God.'

A similar view has been taken by several other students of Mo-tzǔ. Thus Suzuki says:[4] 'The difference between the Christian God and Mu Ti's Heaven is that while the former made the conception of God foremost and its worship the paramount issue of the religious life, the latter conceded the first place to utilitarianism, for the execution of which the God idea became necessary to him'. Similarly Holth says:[5] 'Micius, it must be admitted, was decidedly religious, but he can hardly claim to be considered as a founder of religion. . . . His religious convictions were made to support his main interest in the ethical and social relations of life.' So, too, Wallace:[6] 'Motse's argument is always a utilitarianism, and the thing is then given an additional reference to Heaven, which is so nominal that the argument is not strengthened by it'. And finally Kennedy:[7] 'He was interested in man's relationship with man, and he appealed to religious ideas to support his social suggestions'.

---

[1] Cf. *Chinesische Philosophie*, 1927, p. 111: 'Mê Ti ist eine stark religiös angelegte Natur . . . Er nennt die höchste Gottheit "Himmel" (*T'ien*) und sieht in dem atmosphärischen Himmel über unsern Häuptern eine Art sinnenfälligen Beweises ihrer Existenz. Doch fasst er den "Himmel" als ein persönlich geistiges Wesen nach Menschenart, aber ins Grosse und Rein-Gute gesteigert.'   [2] *Motse : the Neglected Rival*, pp. 149 ff.

[3] *Ibid.*, p. 158. Cf. also Forke, *op. cit.*, pp. 40 f.

[4] *Brief History of Early Chinese Philosophy*, 1914, p. 100.

[5] *Op. cit.*, p. 48.

[6] *Chinese Recorder*, lxii, 1931, p. 560.   [7] *Ibid.*, p. 695.

8

Despite his apparent religious interest, therefore, these writers charge him with a fundamental irreligion, since, in their view, his religion is merely his own creation to be a buttress to his precepts. The same charge was made by Alexandra David:[1] 'Jamais le philosophe n'invoque, pour nous convaincre, que des motifs purement matérials et humains: le bon ordre social et, surtout, notre propre intérêt. C'eût été pourtant le cas, pour un esprit religieux, ou supplément quelque peu porté aux rêveries métaphysiques, de faire intervenir, dans un semblable sujet, des arguments extra-terrestres, tels que ceux sur lesquels s'appuie, par exemple, l'Épître de Paul aux Corinthiens. Mais non, génies, mânes ou l'empereur suprême (Chang-ti) ne jouent aucun rôle dans ces discours. Si l'on nous y propose l'imitation du Ciel "dont les dons généreux se répandent sur tous" c'est uniquement pour nous donner un haut exemple, celui de la nature et nous ne pourrions, quelque désir que nous en ayons, rien y trouver qui ressemble au commandement d'une Puissance supérieure.'

In spite of this heavy array, it seems to me more appropriate to err on the side of charity in discussing one whose fundamental doctrine was of love, and reasonable to credit him with a genuine belief in God, and a genuine belief that He is a God of love, who loves men, and desires that they should love one another, and a real conviction that in being an apostle of love he was serving as an apostle of God. But even so, as a religious teacher he is quite inadequate. For while the will of God might be revealed to men through the Sage, he does not call men into any direct relationship with God.[2] He neither calls forth their love to God, nor offers them any spring of divine power for the fulfilment of the demands he makes on them. 'He presents no direct teaching as to the person or character of God, his attributes or how he is to be conceived. The whereabouts of God, his spirituality, the problem of his goodness, and other problems with which we are accustomed to wrestle in the more

---

[1] *Op. cit.*, pp. 141 f.

[2] Forke (*op. cit.*, p. 65) quotes a Japanese scholar, Koyanagi, who finds in Mo-tzǔ's teaching the twin weaknesses that his religion is negative, since his God was merely to be feared, and his universal love mere egoism, since it had ever one's own profit in mind.

highly developed doctrinal discussions of our Christian faith are not found here.'[1]

It is clear, therefore, that among China's sages there is none who can offer a true parallel to the Golden Rule of the Gospels, and that when the content, motive and strength for the execution of the maxim or its supposed equivalents are examined, the widest differences at once appear.

IV

It would carry us too far to examine the Golden Rule of the Gospels fully in relation to the other teaching of Jesus, or to consider at length the motive for its acceptance as a way of life in the thought of Jesus, or the source of the power for its achievement to which He directed men. That it was a rule intimately and essentially associated with His specifically religious teaching no student of the New Testament will deny.

When Jesus taught that evil should be recompensed with good, He did it in the words 'Love your enemies, bless them that curse you, do good to them that hate you, and pray for them which despitefully use you, and persecute you; that ye may be the children of your Father which is in heaven. . . . Be ye therefore perfect'—or, as Torrey renders it,[2] 'all including (in your good will)' —'even as your Father which is in heaven is perfect' (Matt. v. 44 f., 48).

Again, the Lucan form of the Golden Rule is associated with similar inculcations of love that shall embrace enemies, and it leads up to the promise of the reward of a God-like character: 'Ye shall be the children of the Highest; for he is kind unto the unthankful and the evil' (Luke vi. 35). Neither here nor in Matthew is it regarded as an isolated thing, an end in itself.

Commenting on the verse in Matthew, Durand observes:[3] 'La maxime de la "réciprocité" en matière de service a sans doute un étroit rapport avec le précepte de la charité chrétienne,

---

[1] Wallace, *Chinese Recorder*, lxii, 1931, p. 557.

[2] *The Four Gospels: a new translation*, 1933, p. 12; *Our Translated Gospels*, 1935, p. 92.

[3] *Évangile selon Saint Matthieu* (Verbum Salutis), 1938, p. 130.

mais sans se confondre avec lui. Ici, nous n'avons qu'une règle d'ordre pratique, "une mesure", comme il est dit dans le texte; ou, tout au plus, un critère psychologique pour reconnaître l'étendue de nos devoirs envers autrui. On aurait tort d'y chercher le but ou même le mobile de notre dévouement, qui dès lors se ramènerait à l'egoïsme. En définitive, "la règle d'or" n'est qu'une expression concrète du commandement: "Tu aimeras ton prochain, comme toi-même". Pourquoi et avec quelles dispositions intérieures un chrétien doit aimer, c'est ce que Notre-Seigneur a dit ailleurs (Matt. v, 43-48; xix, 19; xxii, 39; Lc. x, 29-37; Jn. xiii, 35).'

When Jesus teaches men to love their neighbours as themselves, He does more than lift a word out of the Old Testament and make it His own. He fills it with a content which is plainly surprising to His hearers, by interpreting it to include even the hated enemy (Luke x. 25 ff.). But more than that. He makes it the corollary of a deeper love. In this passage His questioner is represented as culling from the Old Testament the two great commands 'Thou shalt love the Lord thy God', and 'Thou shalt love thy neighbour as thyself'. Elsewhere, Jesus Himself is represented as selecting these as the supreme commands (Mark xii. 29 ff.). In both passages Jesus sets His approval upon the choice, and it is significant that He demands first of all a love for God that shall claim a man's whole being, his mind, his emotions, his will, his entire service. His love for his neighbour is the corollary of that love.

Wallace compares Mo-tzŭ with Jesus in this. He says:[1] Mo-tzŭ's 'most complete phrase on worship seems to be the one where he says that men of the highest order "revere Heaven, worship the spirits and serve their fellowmen". It reminds us of the great commmandent given by Jesus: love God with all thy heart, and thy neighbour as thyself.' This is once more to equate words rather than their significance, and is especially surprising in one who, as above indicated, denies to Mo-tzŭ's religion any vital reality.

None could suppose that with Jesus God is a pale, impersonal or semi-personal, Power, or could imagine that He might be a mere deification of the principles Jesus propounded. To

---

[1] *Chinese Recorder*, lxii, 1931, p. 156.

Him God was intensely real and personal, a God whose lofty character was the inspiration and strength offered to men. He called men into relations of intimacy with this God, taught them to think of Him as Father, made His worship to mean for them not a mere matter of forms and ceremonies, but a rich fellowship of heart that should bring divine strength into their lives. It is in such a context that the Golden Rule of the New Testament, and its kindred teachings, are lifted far from any of the sayings of the Chinese sages, and the mere attention to verbal similarity misses the spirit in the letter.

THE CHINESE PHILOSOPHER
MO TI [1]

THE names of Confucius and his great exponent Mencius and
of Lao-tzŭ, the founder of Taoism[2], are familiar in the West

[1] A lecture delivered in the John Rylands Library on Wednesday, the
10th of December, 1947.

[2] Whether the Lao-tzŭ, who founded Taoism, was contemporary with
Confucius, as has been traditionally supposed, is now much disputed by Chinese
scholars, and is increasingly doubted by Western scholars. Cf. Forke, *Geschichte
der alten chinesischen Philosophie*, 1927, pp. 249-255, where it is held that at
the latest Lao-tzŭ belonged to the period of Mo-tzŭ. Similarly, Y. L. Fung
(*History of Chinese Philosophy* i, 1937, pp. 170-172) places the founder of
Taoism in the same post-Confucian period, and holds that this founder, whose
name was Li-Ěrh, has been confounded with a legendary figure, Lao Tan.
Cf. also A. Waley, *The Way and its Power*, 1934, pp. 86, 101 ff., and E. R.
Hughes, *Chinese Philosophy in Classical Times*, 1942, p. 144, the former dating
the *Tao Tê Ching* in the third century B.C., and the latter somewhat hesitat-
ingly at the end of the fourth century B.C. In close agreement with this last
date is the view of H. Dubs, who places Lao-tzŭ *circa* 300 B.C. (*Journal of the
American Oriental Society*, lxi, 1941, pp. 215 ff.; cf. the subsequent discussion
with D. Bodde, *ibid.*, lxii, 1942, pp. 8 ff., 300 ff., and lxiv, 1944, pp. 24 ff.).
Geisser (*Mo Ti*, 1947, p. 140) also decides for the fourth century B.C. Krause
(*Ju-Tao-Fo*, 1924, pp. 136, 544) questions the tradition in a far more hesitating
way. Cf. also Karlgren, in *Illustreret Religionshistorie*, ed. by Johs. Pedersen,
1948, p. 666, and Masson-Oursel, in *Histoire générale des religions*, iv, 1947,
p. 455*b*. Some go so far as to doubt whether such a person as Lao-tzŭ ever
existed, and declare the authorship of the *Tao Tê Ching* an insoluble problem
(cf. E. R. and K. Hughes, *Religion in China*, 1950, p. 25; L. Giles, *apud* S. D.
Champion, *The Eleven Religions and their Proverbial Lore*, 1943, p. 273). Cf.
H. Maspero, *Le Taoïsme*, 1950, p. 229: 'Lao-tseu n'est qu'un nom, et le
petit traité qui est attribué tantôt à lui, tantôt au mythique Empereur
Jaune, le *Tao-tŏ-king*, date probablement du début ou du milieu du ive siècle.'
The challenge to the traditional view was first made in 1886 by H. A. Giles, and
repeated in his *Confucianism and its Rivals*, 1915, pp. 129 ff., 145 ff. It was
firmly rejected by Legge (cf. *supra*, p. 77), and even violently rejected by
Parker, who said 'it is monstrous for Europeans, possessing at best a mere
smattering of this vast body of literature, to come forward with the ridiculous
theory that neither Lao-tsz nor his book ever in fact existed, but are, on the
contrary, mere creatures of imagination and forgery subsequent to the beginning of our era. The real fact is, this outrageous theory was first broached
without reflection or ripe study, with the apparent objective of attracting
attention and gaining notoriety' (*The Imperial and Asiatic Quarterly Review*,
3rd series, xxii, 1906, p. 331). It was rejected also by Maclagan (in Hastings'
Encyclopædia of Religion and Ethics, xii, 1921, p. 197*b*; cf. *Chinese Religious*

but the name of Mo Ti[1] is little known. In Hastings' *Encyclopædia of Religion and Ethics* he received brief mention in a single column.[2] Until 1922 the books associated with his name were untranslated into any European language, save for the chapters on Universal Love—which Legge had printed in Chinese and rendered into English in the Introduction to the second volume of his edition of the Chinese Classics[3]—and a few selected passages incorporated in translation in some of the relatively few books and articles devoted to Mo-tzŭ. Yet he is described by a distinguished contemporary Chinese scholar as 'perhaps one of the greatest souls China has ever produced'.[4]

In 1922 Forke translated into German the surviving texts called by his name, and prefaced the translation with a long and valuable Introduction.[5] Five years later Tomkinson issued an English translation of a larger selection of the chapters than had appeared before in English, together with a brief Introduction[6], and in 1929 Mei Yi-pao published an English

---

Ideas, 1926, pp. 70 f.), and so recently as 1927 Forke could observe that he knew of but one adherent of the view, and his support was not weighty (*Geschichte der alten chinesischen Philosophie*, p. 256). Since then fresh adherents have appeared in east and west to present the view in various forms. Eberhard (*Archiv für Religionswissenschaft*, xxxiii, 1936, p. 318) cites a Chinese author who challenged the traditional view, and added 'Die Fragen sind also noch im Fluss'.

[1] The name of this philosopher stands in a great variety of forms in European works, as will be seen in the references below. The first word stands variously as Mo, Mê, Mei, Meh, Mih and Mu, while the second stands as Ti, Tih or Teih. He is also frequently referred to as Mo-tzŭ, which means the philosopher Mo, and here again we find Motze, Motse and various other forms. A latinized form, Micius—formed on the same principle as Confucius from K'ung-tzu and Mencius from Mêng-tzŭ—is also found in some works.

[2] See under Micius in vol. viii, 1915, pp. 623 f. This article is by P. J. Maclagan. Couling's *Encyclopædia Sinica*, 1917, contains less than a column on Mo-tzŭ (p. 383), while the German encyclopædia, *Die Religion in Geschichte und Gegenwart*, 2nd ed., 5 vols., 1927-1931, contains no article devoted to him.

[3] Cf. 'The Opinions of Mih Teih', in *The Chinese Classics*, ii, *The Works of Mencius*, 1861, Prolegomena, pp. 103-125; or 'The Opinions of Mo Tî', in the second edition of the same, 1895, pp. 100-122. (The second edition of this work will alone be cited below.)

[4] Cf. Hu Shih, *The Development of the Logical Method in Ancient China*, 1928, p. 55.

[5] Cf. A. Forke, *Mê Ti, des Sozialethikers und seiner schüler philosophische Werke*, 1922.

[6] Cf. L. Tomkinson, *The Social Teachings of Meh Tse* (Transactions of the Asiatic Society of Japan, 2nd series, iv, 1927).

version of most of the surviving chapters,[1] followed a few years later by a separate volume of Introduction.[2] More recently a Swiss dissertation by Geisser has been devoted to a study of the sage.[3] In addition to these works, however, there are a number of shorter studies in European languages, mediating some knowledge of the philosopher and his work. The earliest book by a European writer devoted entirely to the exposition of Mo-tzŭ's teaching was published in German by E. Faber,[4] while articles in journals or sections of books appeared at very rare intervals from 1859 to 1896.[5] More recently a few short monographs have been published,[6] while a number of general works have devoted some pages to

---

[1] Cf. Y. P. Mei, *The Ethical and Political Works of Motse*, 1929. The chapters on Logic and Defence have not been included in this translation.

[2] Cf. *id.*, *Motse: the Neglected Rival of Confucius*, 1934.

[3] Geisser, *Mo Ti, der Künder der allgemeinen Menschenliebe*, 1947. The author has some valuable pages (pp. 10 ff.) dealing with Chinese teachers who have been held to be predecessors of Mo-tzŭ in his characteristic doctrines.

[4] Cf. Faber, *Die Grundgedanken des alten chinesischen Sozialismus, oder die Lehre des Philosophen Micius*, 1877. This work contains extracts from the chapters, together with the translator's observations. It was translated into English in 1897 by Dr. Kupfer, but I have not had access to this translation.

[5] Cf. J. Edkins, 'Notices of the character and writings of Mêh Tsî', in *Journal of the North China Branch of the Royal Asiatic Society*, ii, 1859, pp. 165-169; S. Cognetti de Marţiis, 'Un Socialista Cinese del V secolo av. C., Mih Teih', in *Memorie della R. Accademia dei Lincei*, 4th series, Classe di Scienze morali, iii, 1887, pp. 248-281; J. J. M. de Groot, *The Religious System of China*, ii, Book i, 1894, pp. 664-685; C. de Harlez, 'Mi Tze, le philosophe de l'amour universel', in *Giornale della Società Asiatica Italiana*, viii, 1894, pp. 103-126; *id.*, 'Mi Tze: l'amour universel', *ibid.*, ix, 1895-1896, pp. 81-126 (continuing the foregoing, and incorporating translations of considerable portions); L. de Rosny, 'Une grande lutte d'idées dans la Chine antérieure à notre ère, Meng-tse, Siun-tse, Yang-tse et Meh-tse', in *Études de Critique et d'Histoire* (Bibliothèque de l'École des Hautes Études : Sciences Religieuses, vii), 1896, pp. 277-301. (Forke (*Mê Ti*, pp. 14 f.) notes one or two others to which I have not had access.)

[6] Cf. Alexandra David, *Socialisme Chinois: le Philosophe Meh-Ti et l'idée de Solidarité*, 1907; Hoang Tsen-yue, *Étude comparative sur les philosophies de Lao Tseu, Khong Tseu, Mo Tseu* (Annales de l'Université de Lyon, N.S. ii, Fasc. 37), 1925—the pages devoted to Mo-tzŭ being pp. 95-149; H. R. Williamson, *Mo Ti: a Chinese Heretic*, 1927; J. Witte, *Mê Ti, der Philosoph der allgemeinen Menschenliebe und sozialen Gleichheit im alten China*, 1928; S. Holth, *Micius: a brief Outline of his Life and Ideas*, 1935; W. H. Long, *Motze, China's Ancient Philosopher of Universal Love*, n.d.

this sage,[1] and a few short articles have appeared in journals[2] and elsewhere.[3]

It is more surprising that Mo-tzŭ has been little known in China until modern times. There were a few scattered references to him in the writings of Mencius and other ancient authors, but the texts in which his teachings were enshrined lay forgotten and neglected. Yet there was a time when his influence rivalled that of Confucius. Han-Fei-tzŭ, who lived in the third century B.C., says the two most famous schools of philosophy in his day were those of Confucius and Mo-tzŭ,[4] and the *Lü Shih Ch'un*

---

[1] Cf. D. T. Suzuki, *Brief History of Early Chinese Philosophy*, 1914, pp· 92-100; L. Wieger, *Histoire des croyances religieuses et des opinions philosophiques en Chine*, 1922, pp. 207-212 (English translation by E. C. Werner, 1927, pp. 207-212); R. Wilhelm, *Die chinesischen Literatur*, 1926, pp. 56-61; A. Forke, *Geschichte der alten chinesischen Philosophie*, 1927, pp. 368-395; Hackmann, *Chinesische Philosophie*, 1927, pp. 110-122; Hu Shih, *Development of the Logical Method in Ancient China*, 1928, pp. 53-82; Liang Ch'i-ch'ao, *History of Chinese Political Thought*, 1930, pp. 93-112; L. Wieger, *Textes philosophiques*, 2nd ed., 1930, pp. 175 f. (containing two brief extracts of the Chinese text of Mo-tzŭ, together with French translation); M. Granet, *La pensée chinoise*, 1934, pp. 490-500; Y. L. Fung, *History of Chinese Philosophy*, 1937, pp. 76-105; A. Waley, *Three Ways of Thought in Ancient China*, 1939, pp. 163-181; E. R. Hughes, *Chinese Philosophy in Classical Times*, 1942, pp. 43-67; F. T. Cheng (Chêng T'ien-hsi), *China Moulded by Confucius*, 1946, pp. 110-116; Y. L. Fung, *The Spirit of Chinese Philosophy*, 1947, pp. 34-44.

[2] Cf. H. Maspero, 'Notes sur la logique de Mo-tseu et de son école', in *T'oung Pao*, xxv, 1928, pp. 1-64; W. Wallace, 'Religious Elements in the Writings of Motse', in *Chinese Recorder*, lxii, 1931, pp. 557-561; C. O. Simpson, 'Motse and Fatalism', *ibid.*, pp. 638-645; G. Kennedy, 'Ethical and Social Teachings of Moti', *ibid.*, pp. 695-702; F. Rawlinson, 'The Ethical Values of Micius', *ibid.*, lxiii, 1932, pp. 93-102; L. Tomkinson, 'Pacifist and Socialist Intellectuals in the "Warring States"', *ibid.*, lxvii, 1936, pp. 286-296; W. Corswant, 'Le philosophie chinois Mê Ti et sa doctrine de l'amour mutuel', in *Revue de Théologie et de Philosophie*, xxxiv, 1946, pp. 97-124.

[3] Cf. Z. L. Yih, 'Introduction to Mo-Tzu', in *Hirth Anniversary Volume*, 1923, pp. 613-619. There have also been a few short contributions in Russian, but these are inaccessible to me by reason of their language. I have dealt with some aspects of the teaching of Mo-tzŭ in 'The Chinese Sages and the Golden Rule', *supra*, pp. 94 ff., and *Submission in Suffering: a comparative study of Eastern Thought*, *supra*, pp. 46 f., 66 ff.

[4] This is the opening sentence of chapter 1 of *Han-Fei-tzŭ*. The English translation of W. K. Liao, *The Complete Works of Han Fei Tzŭ*, has only reached chapter xxx. I am indebted to Dr. H. R. Williamson for the loan of a Chinese text of this work, and also for the loan of Forke's *Mê Ti* and Tomkinson's *Social Teachings of Meh Tse*. I may take this opportunity of acknowledging that it was the hearing of Dr. Williamson's lecture on Mo Ti, delivered in Tsinanfu in 1926 and published the following year, which first aroused my interest in Mo-tzŭ.

Ch'iu,[1] an important work compiled in the middle of the same century for Lü Pu-wei,[2] says the followers of Confucius and of Mo Ti were in every part of the empire,[3] while Mencius, in the fourth century B.C., says 'the words of Yang Chu and Mo Tî fill the country. If you listen to people's discourses throughout it, you will find that they have adopted the views either of Yang or of Mo'.[4] It was alarm at the spread of these two doctrines, indeed, both of which he regarded as heretical and dangerous, that moved Mencius to expound and defend the principles of Confucius. Yet despite their prevalence at that time they early fell into neglect,[5] and for some two thousand years the writings in which Mo-tzǔ's teachings are set forth appear to have been preserved, in so far as they have been preserved, by the Taoists, whose interest was in a small amount of alchemy which they contained, and who preserved the whole for the sake of this.[6] With the edition of Mo-tzǔ's works by Pi Yüan, Governor of Shensi, in 1783, an important step was taken in the rescue of the sage from neglect, and Forke observes that with this event there began a new era in the study of Mo-tzǔ.[7] Further important work was done by Sun I-jang, who published a critical edition in 1894.[8] Neither of these editions has been accessible to me. Nor have I been able to use the more recent expositions

[1] This has been translated into German by R. Wilhelm, *Frühling und Herbst des Lü Bu We*, 1928. I am again indebted to Dr. H. R. Williamson for the loan of a copy of the Chinese text.

[2] For an account of the life of Lü Pu-wei, cf. D. Bodde, *Statesman, Patriot and General in Ancient China*, 1940, pp. 1-22.

[3] Cf. *Lü Shih Ch'un Ch'iu*, II, iv: 'The followers of Confucius and Mo-tzǔ, whose fame and influence are felt by all men everywhere, are innumerable.' Cf. also XXV, iii. For German translation, cf. Wilhelm, *op. cit.*, pp. 24, 437.

[4] *Mencius*, III, ii. 9—translation of Legge, *The Chinese Classics*, ii, 2nd ed., p. 282. Cf. Couvreur, *Les Quatre Livres*, 2nd ed., 1910, p. 453. Both of these editions contain the Chinese text. R. Wilhelm, *Mong Dsi*, 1921, p. 70, gives a German translation without the Chinese text, closely agreeing with Legge. L. A. Lyall, *Mencius*, 1932, p. 96, gives the not very lucid rendering: 'The words of Yang Chu and Mo Ti fill all below heaven. The words of all below heaven come home to Mo, if they do not come home to Yang.' To render *kuei* by *come home* in this context is less satisfactory than to give it its idiomatic as well as literal equivalent *go back to*.

[5] Wang Ch'ung in the first century of our era tells us that the teaching of Mo-tzǔ had already fallen into neglect (cf. A. Forke's translation of Wang Ch'ung's *Lun Hêng*, i, 1907, p. 461).

[6] Cf. Williamson, *Mo Ti*, pp. 9 f.   [7] Cf. *Mê Ti*, p. 8.

[8] Other Chinese editions are recorded by Forke, *op. cit.*, pp. 6-11.

of Mo-tzŭ that have appeared in Chinese,[1] of which there have been a considerable number.[2] The only edition of the Chinese text of Mo-tzŭ to which I have had access is that edited by Chang Shun-i, and published in Shanghai in 1936. The present study has therefore been based mainly on the European studies to which reference has been made.

The long neglect that Mo-tzŭ suffered may seem the more surprising when we recall some of the things that modern students have said about him. His teachings have been described as socialism,[3] and he has been hailed as an anticipator of Rousseau's 'social contract' theory of the state.[4] He has been described as a forerunner of John Stuart Mill in his utilitarianism.[5] As a logician he is thought to have anticipated Aristotle, who has been regarded as the Father of Logic,[6] while as a moral and political teacher he has been declared infinitely superior to the greatest of the Greeks.[7] The severity of his life has earned for him the name of Puritan,[8] and he has frequently been called a pacifist. While this is certainly going too far, his strong opposition to all aggressive war has made him appear singularly modern.[9] As one who gave his ideas on this subject practical expression, and who harnessed his scientific knowledge to the service of his ideas, he may be said to have anticipated Archimedes.[10] Finally, as an exponent of the principle

---

[1] Forke lists a number of Chinese and Japanese writers who have written on the teachings of Mo-tzŭ, and some supplementary titles are given by Mei, *Motse, Rival of Confucius*, p. 203.

[2] Tomkinson (*Chinese Recorder*, lxvii, 1936, p. 286) observes that there had been a noticeable fall in Mo-tzŭ's stock in China, and ascribed it to a recrudescence of militarism.

[3] Cf. the titles of the works by E. Faber, Cognetti de Martiis and Alexandra David, noted above.

[4] Cf. F. T. Cheng, *op. cit.*, p. 114. So, too, Liang Ch'i-ch'ao (cf. Mei, *op. cit.*, and Tomkinson, *Social Teachings of Meh Tse*, p. 14).

[5] Cf. *Encyclopædia Sinica*, p. 383*b*: 'His chief doctrine is Utilitarianism of the kind associated with John Stuart Mill'.

[6] Cf. Williamson, *op. cit.*, pp. 15 f.

[7] Cf. de Harlez, *loc. cit.*, viii, 1894, p. 103.

[8] Cf. Mei, *op. cit.*, p. 140; Cheng, *op. cit.*, p. 110.

[9] Cf. Cheng, *op. cit.*, pp. 110 f.: 'It is remarkable that at a time distant from the present by nearly twenty-five centuries, he should have forestalled the Kellogg Pact'.

[10] By his mechanical skill Archimedes successfully delivered Syracuse from its siege, while Mo-tzŭ, as will be seen below, was able to prevent an attack by his resource in invention.

of universal love, he has seemed a forerunner of Christ,[1] and one writer has declared that apart from his political teaching, the doctrine of Mo-tzŭ could be described as the twin sister of Christianity,[2] while another has said that he is the only Chinese who can be said to have founded a religion.[3]

So many-sided and versatile a person might have been expected to live in the memories of his fellow-countrymen, rather than to have been known for many centuries only from the brief attacks on him in the writings of better known sages. Many reasons for his eclipse have been suggested. Arthur Waley attributes his neglect to the style in which his teachings are written. He says:[4]

'The *Analects* of Confucius are forcible and pointed; at times they even rise to a sort of austere beauty. *Mencius* contains some of the subtlest and most vivid passages in Chinese literature. The *Tao Tê Ching*, most frequently translated of all Chinese books, is an occultist kaleidoscope, a magic void that the reader can fill with what images he will; *Chuang Tzu* is one of the most entertaining as well as one of the profoundest books in the world. Whereas *Mo Tzu* is feeble, repetitive, heavy, unimaginative and unentertaining, devoid of a single passage that could possibly be said to have wit, beauty or force . . . If Mo Tzu is neglected in Europe it is because he expounds his on the whole rather sympathetic doctrines with a singular lack of æsthetic power.' This infelicity of style was noted in China. For Han-Fei-tzŭ already drew attention to it, and thought

---

[1] Cf. Faber, *op. cit.*, p. 27. Williamson (*op. cit.*, p. 38) quotes Liang Ch'i-ch'ao's description of him as 'a big Marx and a little Christ'. Cf. Liang's *Chinese Political Thought*, p. 110: 'he evolved a religious system very similar to Christianity'. Other writers, however, dispute this similarity. Edkins (*loc. cit.*, p. 167) observes that 'his views, while resembling Christianity in form, are much more akin in reality to the opinions of Bentham and Paley, who, had he lived in their day, would doubtless have claimed him as an ally'. Cf. Cognetti de Martiis (*loc. cit.*, p. 261): 'Tuttavia, malgrado la identità estrinseca della formola de Mih con l'evangelica, non v'ha identità intrinseca. La lèttere è in entrambe la medesima, ma lo spirito è diverso.'

[2] Cf. Hoang Tsen-yue, *op. cit.*, p. 143: 'La doctrine de Mo tseu, sauf la politique, a tant de ressemblance avec celle du Christianisme que l'on peut les prendre comme deux sœurs jumelles.'

[3] Cf. Hu Shih, *Development of the Logical Method*, p. 57. Cf. Wilhelm, *Die chinesischen Literatur*, p. 57.

[4] Cf. *Three Ways of Thought*, pp. 163 f.

that it was deliberate. He says:[1] 'The king of Ch'u said to T'ien Chiu, "Mo-tzŭ was a famous teacher, yet though he was all right in himself his style was prolix and loose. Why was this?" He replied: "There was once a noble of Ch'in who married his daughter to the son of the duke of Chin. He requested Chin to provide the deckings and the garments, whereupon he sent seventy beautifully dressed bridesmaids to Chin. The bridegroom fell in love with a bridesmaid and despised the noble's daughter. The noble may be said to have excellently married the maid, but can hardly be said to have excellently married his daughter. There was a man of Ch'u who sold pearls in Chêng. He made a casket of fragrant wood, perfumed with cassia and spices, adorned with pearls and jade, bedecked with roses, and beautiful with feathers. A man of Chêng bought his casket but gave him back the pearls. This merchant may be said to have excellently sold the casket, but can hardly be said to have excellently sold the pearls. The discussions of the present day all emphasize stylistic and rhetorical qualities, so that men enjoy their elegance and forget their content. Mo-tzŭ's teaching expounded the ways of the ancient kings and discussed the words of the sages. In teaching men had he cultivated lucidity of style, he feared they would have cherished it for its literary worth and would have forgotten its inner truth. For the sake of the style they would have lost the content, and this would have been like the man of Ch'u selling pearls and the noble of Ch'in marrying his daughter. Therefore was he verbose and obscure." '

It is improbable, however, that this is the cause of the neglect of Mo-tzŭ in either East or West. His neglect in the West has been due to the inaccessibility of his works in European languages until recently, and that in turn rests in part on the long neglect of him in China.[2] His neglect in China, however, can hardly be due to the style in which his teachings have been preserved. For there was a time, as has been said, when his fame spread throughout China, and his teachings had a

---

[1] *Han-Fei-tzŭ* xxxii. This chapter has not yet appeared in Liao's translation.

[2] This is, indeed, recognized by Waley, who says (*op. cit.*, p. 164): 'Of course part of the obscurity of Mo-tzŭ in the West is due to the fact that he was till recently very little studied in China.'

considerable vogue. Various other causes have been suggested, which may in part have contributed to his eclipse. Hu Shih suggests that his utilitarianism acted as a boomerang and brought about its own downfall,[1] since its doctrines of universal love and anti-militarism were incompatible with the needs of the age. Tomkinson, on the other hand, cites the view that with the passing of the feudal aristocracy of the period of the Warring States, the *raison d'être* of Moism was gone, and hence it no longer survived.[2] The same writer makes an alternative suggestion, that the main doctrines of Moism were incorporated into rival systems, and notably the pacifism of Mo-tzŭ was taken into the teaching of Mencius and thus into Confucianism, and hence the separate existence of Moism was now superfluous.[3] On the other hand de Harlez thought that it was the bitter hostility of Mencius to the teachings of Mo-tzŭ which effectively terminated its influence.[4] But Moism continued to flourish for some time after Mencius, and neither this nor any of these suggestions is very convincing.

It is possible that the divisions that broke out amongst the followers of Mo-tzŭ in the century after his death may have had some effect on its fortunes and helped to bring about its eclipse. For Mo-tzŭ organized his followers under a head who has been likened to the Roman Pope. He himself was doubtless the first holder of this office, to which the title of Chü-tzŭ was attached, and within thirty years of his death he was succeeded by Mêng Shêng, T'ien-Hsiang-tzŭ and Fu Tun. It has been suggested that the holders of this office formed a sort of 'Suicides Club'.[5] Before the end of the fourth century B.C. there were three sectional heads, under the Chü-tzŭ, each in charge of a geographical area, and all quarrelling among themselves and scheming for the succession to the chief office. Han-Fei-tzŭ says:[6] 'After the death of Mo-tzŭ there was the Moist school of

---

[1] *Development of Logical Method*, pp. 61 f.
[2] Cf. *Chinese Recorder*, lxvii, 1936, p. 294.   [3] *Ibid.*, p. 296.
[4] Cf. *Giornale della Società Asiatica Italiana*, viii, 1894, p. 103; 'L'oubli complet dans lequel il est resté, bien plus cette espèce de reprobation dont il a été frappé dans sa patrie, sont dus aux anathèmes prononcées contre lui par Meng-tze.'   [5] Cf. Tomkinson, *loc. cit.*, p. 292.
[6] Cf. *Han-Fei-tzŭ* l, This chapter is not included in Liao's translation yet. The Chinese text of this passage, which stands near the beginning of the chapter, is quoted in Forke, *Mê Ti*, p. 75.

Hsiang Li, the Moist school of Hsiang Fu, and the Moist school of Têng Ling. Hence, after the time of Confucius and Mo-tzŭ, Confucianism split into eight schools and Moism into three, disagreeing in what they accept and reject, and each claiming to be the true school.' The differences within Moism seem to have been more acute than those within Confucianism, perhaps in part because of the organization of the former, and the personal ambitions that accentuated the differences. From Chuang-tzŭ, the great exponent of Taoism, we learn of these ambitions. He says:[1] 'The followers of Hsiang Li Ch'in such as Wu Hou and the Moists of the South such as K'u Huo, Chi Tz'u and Teng Ling, all recite the same scriptures of Moism but interpret them differently, calling each other heretics of Moism. They criticize one another for their notions of solidity, whiteness, similarity, and dissimilarity; they argue with one another about the contradiction or non-contradiction between the odd and the even. All, however, regard the Elder Master[2] as the Wise Man, aspiring to be his medium in order to become his successor. They cannot come to an agreement even at this time.' This would suggest that even Mo-tzŭ's own professed followers were more concerned with trifling academic disputes than with the great principles which Mo-tzŭ proclaimed. It could hardly be expected therefore, that they would commend his principles to their contemporaries.

Long makes the improbable suggestion[3] that 'in the final chapter of feudal China, which saw the triumph of Ch'in over its rival neighbors, and the consequent union of China, the Mohist schools may have been blotted out through slaughter

---

[1] *Chuang-tzŭ*, XXXIII, iii. 11. The above rendering is that of Y. P. Mei (*op. cit.*, p. 167). Cf. the renderings of Legge (*Sacred Books of the East*, xl, 1891, pp. 220 f.), and Giles (*Chuang Tzŭ : Mystic, Moralist and Social Reformer*, 1926, pp. 442 f.). The Chinese text with French translation is given in Wieger, *Taoïsme*, ii, 1913, pp. 500 f., while Forke gives the Chinese text of part of the passage (*op. cit.*, p. 75).

[2] I.e. Chü-tzŭ, the head of the Moists. Giles (*loc. cit.*) treats this as a proper name here—'Chü Tzŭ was their Sage, and they wanted to canonise him as a saint, that they might carry on his doctrines in after ages'—and Forke (*op. cit.*, pp. 75 f.) says that this is following Kao Yu, who takes this erroneous view. Legge failed to understand the title, and rendered: 'They regarded their most distinguished member as a sage, and wished to make him their chief, hoping that he would be handed down to future ages' (*loc. cit.*).

[3] Cf. *Motze, China's Ancient Philosopher of Universal Love*, pp. 37 f.

following the unsuccessful defense of the invaded states'. It is very unlikely that the Moist schools, which were now geographically scattered and which were divided amongst themselves, were reunited in such a supreme act of self-sacrifice without leaving any trace in tradition. Of one such act of heroism we learn,[1] and it is very doubtful if so much more striking an example of the same spirit would have been left to a baseless modern conjecture to resurrect.

Other important suggestions to explain the failure of Moism are made by Granet and Waley. The former thinks that its excessive challenge of the strongly rooted family tradition of China militated against its success,[2] while the latter thinks its psychological weakness, in failing to understand the complexity of the human heart, was a serious weakness.[3] While there may be a measure of truth in these suggestions, they do not explain why it was that Moism once had the hold in China it is said to have had, and then lost it. This still remains obscure, and the total eclipse of this once influential teaching until its revival in modern times remains an unexplained fact.

Because of this long neglect, little is known of Mo-tzǔ's life. Some of the few facts and incidents mentioned in the records will be noted below in the account of his teachings.[4] Here it may be noted that Ssǔ-ma Ch'ien, the father of Chinese history, devotes but twenty-four words to him in the course of his great work, though there is a further reference in the Preface, to which we shall return. The twenty-four words say: 'Mo Ti was a great officer in the state of Sung. He was skilful in military defence and taught economy. Some say that he was contemporary with Confucius, others that he was after him.'[5] That he lived after Confucius is now generally agreed, while it

---

[1] Cf. below, p. 135.   [2] Cf. *La pensée chinoise*, p. 500.

[3] Cf *Three Ways of Thought*, pp. 180 f.

[4] It may interest the curious to know that Mo-tzǔ is credited with the invention of the kite. Huai-Nan-tzǔ says that he made a wooden kite which he flew for three days without its coming down (cf. de Groot; *loc. cit.*, p. 665). The same story is referred to by Wang Ch'ung (cf. *Lun Hêng*, translated by A. Forke, i, 1907, pp. 498 f., ii, 1911, p. 353).

[5] The section of Ssǔ-ma Ch'ien in which this passage stands is not included in the translation of Chavannes, *Les Mémoires historiques de Se-ma-Ts'ien*, 5 vols., 1895-1905. The twenty-four characters are quoted by Forke, *op. cit.*, p. 25.

is certain that he lived before Mencius. His life fell therefore within the century 480-380 B.C., though more exact agreement cannot be secured.[1] At that time China was under the nominal rule of an emperor of the Chou dynasty whose power was slight, and the rulers of the separate states into which the land was divided[2] were for all practical purposes independent rulers giving no more than nominal allegiance to the emperor and warring amongst themselves. The period is therefore known as the age of the Warring States. The more powerful princes plundered the states of the weaker, and the miseries of the common people, who were called to shed their blood in these useless wars, and to see their homes destroyed and plundered, were intense. On the other hand, luxury and extravagance flourished at the courts of the more powerful princes and there were great extremes of poverty and wealth. The evils of the time are reflected in the writings of Mencius no less than in the work of Mo-tzŭ. In Mencius we find:[3] 'Now the state of things is different. A host marches in attendance on the ruler, and stores of provisions are consumed. The hungry are deprived of their food, and there is no rest for those who are called to toil. Maledictions are uttered by one to another with eyes askance, and the people proceed to the commission of wickedness. Thus

---

[1] Wieger says he probably died before 400 B.C. (*Histoire des croyances*, p. 207=E.T., p. 207); Hu Shih (*Development of Logical Method*, p. 56) dates him from 500 to 420 B.C.; Wilhelm (*Die chinesischen Literatur*, p. 57) from 500-490 B.C. to 425-415; Z. L. Yih (*Hirth Anniversary Volume*, p. 613) 'somewhere between 500-416 B.C.'; Forke (*Mê Ti*, p. 27 ; cf. *Geschichte der alten chinesischen Philosophie*, p. 369) assigns him to the period 480-400 B.C.; Ch'ien Mu (cf. Fung, *op. cit.*, p. 76) to the period 479-381 B.C.; Sun I-jang (cf. Fung, *ibid.*) to 468-376 B.C.; Liang Ch'i-ch'ao (cf. Mei, *Motse, Rival of Confucius*, p. 31) reaches the conclusion that his life ran from 466-459 B.C. to 390-382 B.C.; while Y. P. Mei (*op. cit.*, pp. 31 ff.) 'for convenience of memory' uses the dates 470-391 B.C. Hoang Tsen-yue does not define the date of his birth, but concludes that he died somewhere between 392 and 382 B.C. C. de Harlez (*Giornale della Società Asiatica Italiana*, viii,1894, p. 104) assigns him to the period between the last years of the fifth century and the last quarter of the fourth century, but this must surely be a century later than de Harlez really meant, or else 'last ' must stand for 'first'.

[2] It should be remembered that the southern and western parts of what is China to-day consisted then of barbarian tribes outside the Chinese empire.

[3] *Mencius* I, ii. 4 (translation of Legge, *The Chinese Classics*, ii, 2nd ed., pp. 159 f.). Cf. Couvreur, *Les Quatre Livres*, p. 333; Lyall, *Mencius*, p. 22. Wilhelm (*Mong Dsi*, p. 15) omits this from his translation, as he holds it to be an interpolation.

9

the royal ordinances are violated, and the people are oppressed, and the supplies of food and drink flow away like water. The rulers yield themselves to the current, or they urge their way against it; they are wild; they are utterly lost:—these things proceed to the grief of the inferior princes.'

Some have supposed that Mo-tzŭ belonged to the state of Sung, which fell within what is now known as Honan. This may be because of Ssŭ-ma Ch'ien's reference to his official position there. It is generally held to be more probable that he was a native of the state of Lu, which comprised an area in the western part of the modern Shantung.[1] In that case he belonged to the same state as Confucius. It is not even certain that we know his name.[2] For Mo is a very uncommon surname, and various suggestions have been made as to how he came to be known by it. One is that he lived for a time at a place called Mo near to Tsingtao, and later adopted this name,[3] while another is that it was a term of contempt bestowed upon him by others. In ancient China the punishment of branding and reduction to slavery was denoted by the term *mo*, and it is suggested that it was because of the austere frugality advocated by Mo-tzŭ that this term was used in contempt.[4] In his Preface Ssŭ-ma Ch'ien says: 'Mo-tzu lived in a small house built of rough unworked timbers, with a thatched roof. He used none but earthenware utensils, and partook of the coarsest food. His clothing was of the simplest, of skin or grass according to the season. He was buried in a plain coffin of thin boards.'[5]

Whether Mo-tzŭ was ever an official of Sung, as Ssŭ-ma Ch'ien states, is much disputed by modern scholars,[6] but Fung Yu-lan thinks[7] his teaching is best explained if he were a native of Lu, who first came under the influence of Confucian teachings,

[1] Cf. Y. L. Fung, *op. cit.*, p. 77; Forke, *Mê Ti*, p. 29.

[2] Cf. Fung, *op. cit.*, pp. 79 f.

[3] Cf. Williamson, *op. cit.*, p. 1.

[4] Cf. Fung, *op. cit.*, p. 79.

[5] Translation quoted from Williamson, *op. cit.*, p. 3. This passage is not included in Chavannes' translation, and I have not had access to the Chinese text of the *Shih Chi* of Ssŭ-ma Ch'ien.

[6] Cf. Forke, *Mê Ti*, p. 30; Williamson, *op. cit.*, p. 3; Tomkinson, *Social Teachings of Meh Tse*, p. 6.

[7] *Op. cit.*, p. 78. Cf. Mei, *Motse, Rival of Confucius*, p. 45; Wilhelm, *Die chinesischen Literatur*, p. 57.

and later became an official of Sung, where he adopted some of
the Sung ideas and ideals, which have been found to be much
akin to his teaching. This view would scarcely seem to require
that he became an official of Sung. That he visited Sung is
generally agreed, and a visit, especially if it were a long one,
could as well bring him into contact with Sung thought as an
official position. That Mo-tzŭ was first a Confucianist is stated
by Huai-Nan-tzŭ, who says:[1] 'Mo-tzŭ studied the profession of
the Confucianists and received the arts of Confucius. But he
considered that the rites (of the Confucian school) were trouble-
some and displeasing, its stress on elaborate funerals was
wealth-consuming and impoverished the people, and its practice
of lengthy mourning periods was injurious to the living and
harmful to human affairs. Thereupon he turned his back on the
Chou dynasty practices and made use of the methods of
government of the Hsia dynasty'.

The collection of writings which bears Mo-tzŭ's name did
not all come from his pen, though it is probable that it gives a
reliable summary of his teachings.[2] The surviving chapters are
distributed amongst fifteen books, and this agrees with the
oldest information we have. There have, however, been some
losses from these books. For they once contained seventy-one
chapters, and at a later date sixty-one, while to-day no more
than fifty-three are extant. These have all been included in
Forke's German translation, but the English rendering of
Y. P. Mei omits what he describes as the chapters on Logic and
Defence, and Tomkinson's omits certain other chapters in
addition. By the chapters on Logic Mei means six chapters
contained in Books X and XI, sometimes referred to as *Mo
Pien*, or Mo-tzŭ's Discussions. The first two of these are Ching,
or Canon, and are the most difficult to interpret of all the
chapters.[3] The other four chapters are commentary and
appendix, or illustrations. Hu Shih holds that these have
nothing to do with Mo-tzŭ, but contain the work of a later

[1] Translation of D. Bodde in Fung, *op. cit.*, p. 77, where the passage is
quoted. It is also translated by Mei, *op. cit.*, p. 42. Cf. Williamson, *op. cit.*,
p. 4.
[2] Cf. Forke, *op. cit.*, pp. 15 ff.; Mei, *op. cit.*, pp. 52 ff.
[3] Mei observes that Forke's rendering of these chapters not infrequently
misses the meaning of the original (*Motse, Rival of Confucius*, p. 57).

distinct school of scientific and logical Neo-Moists.[1] Others attribute the first two chapters to Mo-tzŭ himself, the commentary to a disciple—possibly Têng Ling—and the remaining two chapters to later hands,[2] while Tomkinson observes that 'it still seems possible, on the evidence available, to regard these chapters as the work of Meh Tse himself or of his earliest disciples, and not necessarily as produced by the Sophists of a considerably later age'.[3]

The chapters on Defence comprise the last eleven surviving chapters, and these again are full of technical terms and very hard to understand or to translate.[4] Preceding them is a chapter which Mei and Tomkinson translate, and which is believed to have been an introduction to these chapters.[5] It contains an account of an interview of Mo-tzŭ with an official of the state of Ch'u, who gives his name to the chapter, Kung Shu. At some of the contents of this chapter we shall have occasion later to look.

Of far greater importance and interest are the chapters known as the Synoptic Chapters. This is because they survive in three versions—or in some cases one or two, though probably there were originally three—and it has been surmised that these were the forms accepted by the rival schools above referred to.[6] This is speculative and doubtful, and is hardly supported by the above cited passage which tells of these divisions. For it declares that the various groups all cherished the same scriptures, but quarrelled about their interpretation. Tomkinson says that 'the general trend of opinion amongst scholars seems to be that the versions are the work of three disciples, or three groups of disciples, not, however, the three

---

[1] Cf. *Development of Logical Method*, pp. 59 f. Hu Shih refers to these chapters as 'Books 32-37'. They are numbered as chapters xl-xlv in the translations of Forke and Mei, and in the Chinese text to which I have had access.

[2] Cf. Williamson, *op. cit.*, p. 12; Fung, *op. cit.*, p. 80.

[3] Cf. *Chinese Recorder*, lxvii, 1936, p. 291.

[4] Tomkinson (*The Social Teachings of Meh Tse*, p. 18) says no one has seriously attributed these chapters to Mo-tzŭ, and there is an old but doubtful tradition that they are the work of Ch'in Hua-li, an early disciple.

[5] Cf. Williamson, *op. cit.*, p. 12. Tomkinson and Mei, however, connect this chapter rather with the four chapters of 'Mo-tzŭ Analects' noted below.

[6] Cf. Mei, *op. cit.*, p. 54; Williamson, *op. cit.*, p. 13.

groups mentioned by Han Fei Tse'.[1] He himself prefers to think that they all come from Mo-tzŭ's own hand, and represent his treatment of the subjects at different periods of his life. It is in these chapters that we have the main teachings of Mo-tzŭ set forth. They deal with:

1. the Exaltation of the Virtuous (*shang hsien*);
2. the Promotion of Unity (*shang t'ung*);
3. Universal Love (*chien ai*);
4. Against Aggressive War (*fei kung*);
5. Economy of Expenditure (*chieh yung*);
6. Economy in Funeral Rites (*chieh tsang*);
7. the Will of Heaven (*T'ien chih*);
8. the Existence of Spirits (*ming kuei*);
9. Against Music (*fei yo*);
10. Against Fatalism (*fei ming*);
11. Against Confucianism (*fei ju*).

Of the thirty-two chapters originally devoted to these subjects twenty-four are extant, two only on Economy of Expenditure having survived, and one each on Economy in Funeral Rites, the Existence of Spirits, Against Music, and Against Confucianism. It would appear that there were never more than two versions of the last. Not all of these chapters are accepted as authentic, and Tomkinson relegates the chapters Against Music, and Against Confucianism to the category of the questionably authentic.[2] In the latter case doubt is especially widely shared.

Four other chapters form an important group, rather after the style of the Confucian *Analects*. These contain memories of Mo-tzŭ and accounts of incidents in his life and illustrations of his methods of teaching. They are held to be generally reliable. The titles of three of them give little indication of their contents, while the fourth has something of the flavour of Amos about its title. These chapters are called:

1. Kêng Chu (a proper name);
2. the Importance of Righteousness (*kuei i*);
3. Kung Mêng (a proper name);
4. the Inquiry of Lu (i.e. of the ruler of Lu).

[1] Cf. *The Social Teachings of Meh Tse*, p. 21.
[2] Cf. Mei, *op. cit.*, p. 55.

The remaining seven chapters stand first in the collection, but these are regarded as of questionable authenticity or spurious. They are all included in Mei's translation, and the last four of them, which are less firmly rejected and which are more closely related to Mo-tzǔ's principal teachings, are included in Tomkinson's translation. It will be seen, therefore, that in general we should rely on the Synoptic Chapters and the Mo-tzǔ 'Analects' for the study of the sage's teaching. It is here that his characteristic ideas are expounded.

Of his logic little can here be said.[1] He was impatient of shallow thought that played with words. In the chapter Kung Mêng we read: 'Mo-tzǔ asked a Confucianist, saying: "What is the purpose of Music?" He replied: "Music is for music's sake."[2] Mo-tzǔ answered: "You have not yet answered my question. If I were to ask what is the purpose of a house, and you replied that it was to give protection against the cold in winter and against the heat in summer, and to separate men from women, you would have given me the reason for building a house. But when I ask what is the purpose of music and you answer that music is for music's sake, it is like answering the question what a house is for by saying 'A house is built for the sake of a house.' " '[3]

A more penetrating observation is contained in Mo-tzǔ's comment on a saying of Confucius's. We read: 'Tzǔ Kao, the Duke of Shê, asked Chung Ni[4] about government, saying: "What is the good governor like?" Chung Ni replied: "The good governor draws near those who are afar, and reforms what

---

[1] Cf. Hu Shih, *Development of Logical Method*, pp. 63 ff., and H. Maspero, 'Notes sur la logique de Mo-tseu et de son école', in *T'oung Pao*, xxv, 1928, pp. 1–64.

[2] Hu Shih (*op. cit.*, p. 65) renders here 'Music is an amusement', giving to the repeated character two different senses and relieving the tautology. The word can, indeed, have the second sense, and in the opening chapter of the Confucian *Analects* it has that sense, where Legge (*The Chinese Classics*, i, 2nd ed., 1893, p. 137) renders 'Is it not *delightful* to have friends coming from distant quarters?' It is likely that the second sense was in the mind of the Confucianist, so that we have a pun (cf. Fung, *op. cit.*, p. 86), but it is clear from the reply that Mo-tzǔ understood it to be completely tautologous. Cf. Forke, *Mê Ti*, p. 570 n.

[3] *Mo-Tzǔ* xlviii. Cf. Forke, *op. cit.*, p. 570; Tomkinson, *op. cit.*, pp. 139 f. Mei, *The Ethical and Political Works of Motse*, p. 237.

[4] I.e. Confucius.

is obsolete."[1] When Mo-tzŭ heard this, he observed: "Tzŭ Kao, the Duke of Shê, did not put his question right, nor did Chung Ni give a correct reply. For how could Tzŭ Kao, the Duke of Shê, fail to know that the good governor draws near those who are afar, and reforms what is obsolete? What he wished to know was how to effect this. The answer did not tell him what he did not know, but only what he already knew." [2] Here, as throughout Mo-tzŭ's teaching, we find a practical application of his logical faculties. He is never content to think he has solved a problem when he has given a name to it, and empty words have no meaning for him. He said: 'Teaching that can be expressed in deeds may be constantly given; what cannot be given effect should not be constantly taught. When what cannot be given effect is constantly taught, we have but idle words.'[3]

His appeal is constantly to the reason. This is well illustrated by his condemnation of aggressive war. 'To kill one man is said to be criminal and to merit the death penalty. To kill ten men then is tenfold criminal and merits the death penalty tenfold. To kill a hundred men is a hundredfold criminal and merits the death penalty a hundredfold. All the gentlemen of the world know this, and pronounce these things to be criminal. Yet when we come to the greatest crime, the attacking of a state, they do not know that they should condemn it, but on the contrary applaud it and pronounce it righteous. . . . If there were a man who on seeing a little blackness said it was black, but on seeing a lot of blackness said it was white, we should certainly consider that he was unable to distinguish between white and black. If he were to taste a little bitterness and pronounce it bitter but on tasting a lot of bitterness should pronounce it sweet, we should certainly say that he was unable to distinguish between sweet

---

[1] This saying of Confucius's is not preserved in quite this form in the Confucian *Analects*, where we find: 'The Duke of Sheh asked about government. The Master said, "Good government obtains, when those who are near are made happy, and those who are far off are attracted" ' (*Analects* xiii. 16, translation of Legge, *The Chinese Classics*, i, 2nd ed., p. 269; cf. Couvreur, *Les Quatre Livres*, p. 216).

[2] *Mo-tzŭ* xlvi. Cf. Forke, *op. cit.*, pp. 542 f.; Tomkinson, *op. cit.*, p. 126; Mei, *op. cit.*, p. 216.

[3] *Mo-tzŭ* xlvi. Cf. Forke, *op. cit.*, p. 544; Tomkinson, *op. cit.*, p. 126; Mei, *op. cit.*, p. 217. This saying is repeated in chap. xlvii.

and bitter. So they who reckon a small crime to be worthy of condemnation, but who do not condemn the greatest crime, even the attacking of a state, but on the contrary applaud it and pronounce it righteous, may be said to be incapable of distinguishing between right and wrong.'[1]

Mo-tzŭ's opposition to the wanton aggression that led to the innumerable wars of his day was fundamental, and it dictated one of the principal elements of his teaching. He stressed the point just illustrated that it failed to apply on the grand scale standards universally recognized on the small. 'The gentlemen of the world recognize trifles but not great things', he said. 'If a man steals a dog or a pig, he is held to commit a sin against humanity; if he steals a state or a city, this is held to be right-eous.'[2] The same thing is said by Chuang-tzŭ, but with nothing of the moral earnestness of Mo-tzŭ. For Chuang-tzŭ spoke as a satirist rather than as a reformer when he observed: 'One man steals a purse and is punished; another steals a state and becomes a Prince.'[3] But Mo-tzŭ was less the keen observer than the prophet of reform. He not alone denounced the criminality of war, but also its futility. 'When great states attack small states', he said, 'it is like children playing at horses. Children playing at horses only tire and weary themselves. When a great state attacks a small one, the farmers of the state attacked cannot attend to their ploughing and the womenfolk cannot attend to their weaving, since all are engaged on defence. Similarly the farmers of the attacking state cannot attend to their ploughing and the womenfolk cannot attend to their weaving, since all are engaged on attack. Hence, when great states attack small states, it is like children playing at horses.'[4]

This appeal to utilitarian motives was also characteristic of Mo-tzŭ. But he went far beyond this and stripped off the veneer

---

[1] *Mo-tzŭ* xvii. Cf. Forke, *op. cit.*, pp. 267 f.; Tomkinson, *op. cit.*, pp. 60 ff.; Mei, *op. cit.*, pp. 99 f. The whole of this chapter is quoted in Hu Shih, *Development of Logical Method*, pp. 69 ff.

[2] *Mo-tzŭ* xlix. Cf. Forke, *op. cit.*, p. 582; Tomkinson, *op. cit.*, p. 147; Mei, *op. cit.*, p. 246.

[3] *Chuang-tzŭ* X, ii. 3, translation of Giles, *Chuang Tzŭ*, 1926, p. 114. Cf. Legge, *Sacred Books of the East*, xxxix, 1891, p. 285. The Chinese text with French translation is found in Wieger, *Taoïsme*, ii, 1913, pp. 278 f.

[4] *Mo-tzŭ* xlvi. Cf. Forke, *op. cit.*, pp. 543 f.; Tomkinson, *op. cit.*, p. 126; Mei, *op. cit.*, pp. 216 f.

of glory that successful wars were thought to bring, and exposed the hollow nature of so many of the victories. For he held that aggression brought nemesis, which the victory of to-day is powerless to avert. When the state of Ch'i was going to attack its neighbour Lu, Mo-tzŭ pointed his criticism by saying: 'Formerly the king of Wu attacked Yüeh in the east and drove his people to Kuei Chi for refuge. In the west he attacked Ch'u and shut up King Chao in Sui. In the north he attacked Ch'i and took the Crown Prince[1] prisoner to Wu. Then the nobles exacted vengeance, and his own people were wretched and exhausted and refused to serve him, so that the state came to disaster, and the king himself was executed.'[2]

He knew how to prick the bubbles of high motive with which the aggressors sought to disguise their selfish ends. When he sought to dissuade Prince Wên from attacking the state of Chêng, he was asked 'Why should you, sir, prevent me from attacking Chêng? For three generations have the people of Chêng slain their ruler.[3] Heaven has visited them with punishment and caused the harvest to fail for three years. I am only helping Heaven to punish them.' To this Mo-tzŭ replied: 'Suppose there were a man whose son was bad tempered and good for nothing, so that his father thrashed him. If his neighbour's father took up a cudgel and struck him, and said "I am only striking him in accordance with his father's will", would not this be very foolish?'[4]

Nor did he rely on moral suasion alone. He employed his inventive wit to devise measures of defence. For Mo-tzŭ was not a pacifist, who refused to countenance any form of warfare. He opposed aggressive war,[5] but found no wrong in

[1] This rendering follows Forke, taking the characters *kuo tzŭ* to mean 'state son', i.e. Crown Prince. Alternatively they are taken to refer to Kuo Shu, who was a general of Ch'i.

[2] *Mo-tzŭ* xlix. Cf. Forke, *op. cit.*, p. 579; Tomkinson, *op. cit.*, p. 144; Mei, *op. cit.*, pp. 242 f.

[3] Literally *father*. Tomkinson understands it to mean that three generations of rulers had slain their fathers.

[4] *Mo-tzŭ* xlix. Cf. Forke, *op. cit.*, pp. 581 f.; Tomkinson, *op. cit.*, p. 145; Mei, *op. cit.*, pp. 245 f.

[5] In this he stands in the completest contrast to Shang Yang who belonged to the fourth century B.C., and who advocated war for its own sake as an instrument of policy for the satisfactory rule of the home population. Cf. Shang Yang, chap. i, § 3 (Duyvendak, *The Book of Lord Shang*, 1928, pp. 185 ff.).

defence against attack, and on one occasion, on hearing that
the state of Ch'u was about to attack Sung, he travelled to
Ch'u to avert this attack. His appeals at first fell on deaf ears.
The ruler of Ch'u relied on some new invention, called 'cloud
ladders', against which he thought there was no defence, and so
proposed to reap an easy and certain victory. Getting nowhere
with the prince, Mo-tzŭ turned to the inventor of the 'cloud-
ladders', Kung Shu Pan, and taking his girdle to represent the
city wall and a writing tablet to represent military equipment,
he challenged the inventor to capture the city. Nine times
Kung Shu Pan employed his strategy and as many times
Mo-tzŭ foiled his attack, leaving Kung Shu Pan at a loss for
a plan and Mo-tzŭ still with defensive plans in reserve. Then
an ugly thought crossed Kung Shu Pan's mind. 'I know how I
can get the better of you', he said, 'though I prefer not to say.'
'I know what you have in mind', replied Mo-tzŭ, 'but neither
will I say.' The ruler now inquired what this plan was, and
Mo-tzŭ replied: 'Kung Shu Pan's idea is just to have me
murdered. He thinks that when I am dead, Sung will be helpless
in defence, and he can then attack it. But my disciples, Ch'in
Hua-li and others, to the number of three hundred are already
armed with my implements of defence and manning the walls
of Sung, awaiting the brigands of Ch'u. Even though I be
murdered, you will still not cut off my defence.' The ruler of
Ch'u thereupon decided to call off the projected attack.[1]

In this story we have an illustration of the principle of universal love which Mo-tzŭ both advocated and practised, and
which was his cardinal heresy in the eyes of his critics. He was
not actuated by patriotism, since Sung was not his own state,
but simply by the love of men and by his firm anti-aggressive
principles. For Mo-tzŭ held that the ills of society sprang from
partiality and discrimination, and that a world in which all loved
all equally would be an ideal world. He said: 'If we could
cause all men to feel a universal mutual love (*chien hsiang ai*)
so that every man loved all others as himself, would there be
anyone unfilial? If they loved father, elder brother and prince
as themselves, they would hate to display unfilial feeling. . . .

---

[1] *Mo-tzŭ* 1. Cf. Forke, *op. cit.*, pp. 597 f.; Tomkinson, *op. cit.*, pp. 154 f.;
Mei, *op. cit.*, pp. 258 f.

Would there be any thieves or robbers? When men regarded the houses of others as their own, who would rob? When they regarded the persons of others as their own, who would steal? Hence thieves and robbers would be no more. Would there be mutual discord among the families of the great and mutual aggression among the states of the princes? When each loved his neighbour's family as his own, who would create discord? When each loved his neighbour's state as his own, who would invade? Therefore mutual discord among the families of the great and mutual aggression among the states of the princes would be no more.'[1]

Or again he said: 'Suppose there are two men, of whom one adopts the principle of making distinctions (*pieh*) and the other adopts the principle of universality (*chien*). The first will say "How can I consider my friend's person as my own, my friend's kin as mine?" Hence, if he sees his friend in hunger, he will not feed him, or if he sees him cold, he will not clothe him; if he finds him sick, he will not minister to him, if dead, he will not bury him. Such is the language, and such the conduct of the advocate of making distinctions. Quite other will be the language and the conduct of the advocate of universality. He will say: "I have heard that he who would be great among men should consider his friend as himself, his friend's kin as his own, for so alone can he be great among men." Hence, if he sees his friend in hunger, he will feed him, or if he sees him cold, will clothe him; if he finds him sick, he will minister to him, if dead, will bury him. Such is the language, and such the conduct of the advocate of universality.'[2]

It is clear from the whole tenour of this passage that Mo-tzŭ would give to the word 'friend' here as wide a connotation as Jesus did to 'neighbour' in the parable of the Good Samaritan. Of the loftiness and nobility of such teaching there can be no question, and Mei observes that 'it may be regarded as a concrete expression of the Christian Golden Rule'.[3] In his own

---

[1] *Mo-tzŭ* xiv. Cf. Legge, *The Chinese Classics*, ii, 2nd ed., p. 102; Alexandra David, *op. cit.*, pp. 32 f.; Forke, *op. cit.*, pp. 242 f.; Tomkinson, *op cit.*, p. 49; Mei, *op. cit.*, pp. 79 f.

[2] *Mo-tzŭ* xvi. Cf. Legge, *op. cit.*, p. 110; David, *op. cit.*, pp. 45 f.; Forke, *op. cit.*, pp. 255 f.; Tomkinson, *op. cit.*, pp. 54 f.; Mei, *op. cit.*, pp. 89 f.

[3] Cf. *Motse, Rival of Confucius*, p. 92.

day Mo-tzŭ was criticized as doctrinaire. He says: 'The gentlemen of the world say: "While it would be a fine thing if love
could be universal, it is utterly impracticable. It is like taking
up T'ai Shan[1] and leaping over the Huang Ho or the River
Chi." '[2] To this Mo-tzŭ replied that the ancient kings had practised his principles, and that therefore they were practicable.
Elsewhere we read that he defended himself against the charge
that his teaching would not work by saying: 'If it were not
practicable, then even I would reject it. Is it possible that
anything should be good and yet impracticable?'[3] The criticism
of impracticability was renewed by Chuang-tzŭ, who granted
that Mo-tzŭ himself could carry out his own teachings, but who
doubted if the ordinary man was capable of such heights of
conduct.[4] Similarly Wang Ch'ung observed: 'The Confucian
doctrine has come down to us, that of Mê Ti has fallen into
desuetude, because the Confucian principles can be put in use,
while the Mêhist system is very difficult to practise.'[5]

That Mo-tzŭ did in fact put his principles into practice is
admitted by all. 'The philosopher Mo loves all equally',
said Mencius. 'If by rubbing smooth his whole body from the
crown to the heel, he could have benefited the kingdom, he
would have done it.'[6] When he journeyed to Ch'u to prevent
the attack on Sung, he travelled at great discomfort in his
unselfish desire to avert a needless war. 'The following story'
says Hu Shih, 'told in numerous sources, best portrays the
spirit of Mohism and the character of its founder. Kung Shu
Pan, the State Engineer of Chu, had just completed his new
invention of a "cloud ladder" for besieging walled cities, and
the King of Chu was planning an invasion into the State of

---

[1] A sacred mountain in Shantung, often visited by Confucius.

[2] *Mo-tzŭ* xv. Cf. Legge, *op. cit.*, p. 106; David, *op. cit.*, p. 39; Forke, *op.
cit.*, p. 248; Tomkinson, *op. cit.*, p. 51; Mei, *The Works of Motse*, p. 84.

[3] *Mo-tzŭ* xvi. Cf. Legge, *op. cit.*, p. 110; David, *op. cit.*, p. 45; Forke,
op. cit., p. 255; Mei, *op. cit.*, p. 89. (Tomkinson, *op. cit.*, p. 54, omits the quoted
sentence.)

[4] *Chuang-tzŭ* XXXIII, iii. 11 Cf. Legge, *Sacred Books of the East*, xl, p.
219; Giles, *Chuang Tzŭ*, p. 441; Wieger, *Taoïsme*, ii, pp. 500 f. (where the
Chinese text is also given).

[5] Cf. *Lun Hêng* (translated by Forke), i, p. 461.

[6] *Mencius* VII, i. 26, translation of Legge, *The Chinese Classics*, ii, 2nd ed.,
pp. 464 f. Cf. Couvreur, *Les Quatre Livres*, p. 620; Wilhelm, *Mong Dsi*, p. 164;
Lyall, *Mencius*, p. 212.

Sung. When Mo Ti learned of this he started out from his native state and travelled ten days and ten nights all on foot, arriving at the capital city with sun-burnt face and battered feet.'[1] This story is found in the *Lü Shih Ch'un Ch'iu*, where it is added that he was forced to tear up his clothes to bandage his blistered feet.[2] Little wonder that Chuang-tzŭ should describe him as 'one of the best men in the world, which you may search without finding his equal. Decayed and worn his person might be, but he is not to be rejected—a scholar of ability indeed.'[3]

It was not because his teaching was thought to be impracticable, however, that it was so bitterly opposed by Mencius and regarded as a serious menace to society. What is impracticable may be trusted not to be practised. But Mencius was seriously afraid that Mo-tzŭ's teaching might be taken seriously. He classed him with Yang Chu as a dangerous heretic. To Christian readers it seems at first sight odd that Yang Chu, who is said by Legge to be 'about "the least erected spirit" who ever professed to reason concerning the life and duties of man',[4] should be classed with Mo-tzŭ, who is so frequently compared with Christ.[5] For Yang Chu advocated only the most naked selfishness, and complete indifference to every interest but one's own.[6] To Mencius, however, both seemed to menace the foundations of society, though in such different ways. For Yang Chu's pure individualism denied any idea of a duty towards others, while Mo-tzŭ's undiscriminating love ignored the special claims of kindred. 'Yang's principle', said Mencius, 'is "each one for

---

[1] Cf. *Development of Logical Method*, p. 57.

[2] Cf. *Lü Shih Ch'un Ch'iu*, XXI, v. For German translation cf. Wilhelm, *Frühling und Herbst des Lü Bu We*, pp. 382 f.

[3] *Chuang-tzŭ* XXXIII, iii. 11, translation of Legge, *Sacred Books of the East*, xl, p. 221. Cf. Giles, *Chuang Tzŭ*, p. 443; Wieger, *Taoïsme*, ii, pp. 502 f. Cf., too, the rendering given by Liang Ch'i-ch'ao, *History of Chinese Political Thought*, p. 105.

[4] Cf. *The Chinese Classics*, ii, 2nd ed., p. 92.

[5] For some account of the teachings of Yang Chu, cf. Legge, *op. cit.*, pp. 92-99; Forke, *Yang Chu's Garden of Pleasure*, 1912; *id.*, *Geschichte der alten chinesischen Philosophie*, pp. 356-367; Fung, *History of Chinese Philosophy*, pp. 133-143; *id.*, *The Spirit of Chinese Philosophy*, 1947, pp. 29-34.

[6] Cf. Krause, *Ju-Tao-Fo*, 1924, p. 87: 'Er ist Sensualist und Epikureer, sein system ein egoistischer Individualismus, der theoretischen Pessimismus und praktische Eudaimonologie vereinigt.'

himself", which does not acknowledge the claims of the sovereign. Mo's principle is "to love all equally", which does not acknowledge the peculiar affection due to a father. But to acknowledge neither king nor father is to be in the state of a beast. . . . If the principles of Yang and Mo be not stopped, and the principles of Confucius not set forth, then those perverse speakings will delude the people, and stop up the path of benevolence and righteousness. When benevolence and righteousness are stopped up, beasts will be led on to devour men, and men will devour one another.'[1]

What Mo-tzŭ said, as we have seen, was that universal love would include the love of parent and friend. He was trying to lift the love of all to the same high level that Confucius and Mencius demanded for the nearest and dearest. Yet in denying that there were any with special claim on us he seemed to Mencius to be a peril. For to Mencius the corollary of the principle that my neighbour's parents have as great a claim on me as my own was that my parents have no greater claim on me than my neighbour's. He was, therefore, loosening the special ties of kindred, which belonged to the very foundations of society.[2] Fundamentally the same criticism is made by Hsün-tzŭ, who says: 'Micius has insight about what is universal but not about the individual. . . . If one considers the universal, but not the particular, then the government cannot operate.'[3] The whole essence of the Confucian view of man lay in its balanced estimate of his nature and duty. Extreme selfishness and extreme unselfishness were alike to Mencius in being extremes, and extremes have a tendency to meet. And indeed, as we have seen, they did soon meet in the chief followers of Mo-tzŭ. When his followers split into sections whose leaders were each ambitious to become the Chü-tzŭ, it is hard not to find the principle of selfishness, and 'each one for himself' at work.

Moreover the teaching of Mo-tzŭ is frequently criticized in

[1] *Mencius* III, ii. 9, translation of Legge, *The Chinese Classics*, ii, 2nd ed., pp. 282 f. Cf. Couvreur, *Les Quatre Livres*, pp. 453 f.; Wilhelm, *Mong Dsi*, pp. 70 f.; Lyall, *Mencius*, p. 97.

[2] Cf. Wilhelm, *Die chinesischen Literatur*, p. 58: 'Mo Ti mit seiner allgemeinen Liebe kenne keinen Vater, d.h. keinen Familienorganismus.'

[3] *Hsün-tzŭ* xvii. 20, translation of H. Dubs, *The Works of Hsüntze*, 1928, pp. 184 f.

that there was in it an appeal to self-interest. For combined with the principle of universal mutual love (*chien hsiang ai*) we find the principle of the mutual conferring of profit (*chiao hsiang li*), and the idealism of Mo-tzŭ is held to become a mere utilitarianism. This was another element in the criticism of Hsün-tzŭ, who flourished a little later than Mencius. He observed that 'if we consider life from the standpoint of utility, it will merely be seeking for profit'.[1] The same complaint has been made by modern writers too.[2] For if unselfishness is pursued because it pays, then its pursuit is rooted in its anti-thesis. It is true that Mo-tzŭ emphasizes the material benefits that would, he believed, follow the adoption of his principles, and sometimes gave the impression that he was a mere pragmatist. Already we have noted a saying which suggests his belief that the good was the useful. 'Is it possible that anything should be good and yet impracticable?'[3] And in the *Mo-tzŭ Classic*, or *Canon*, we find 'Righteousness is profit',[4] which could easily be represented as the view that 'righteousness is merely what pays'. It is only fair to Mo-tzŭ to say that if it is true that mutual love is mutually beneficial, the paradox is in experience and it is but clearsightedness to perceive it and simple truth to enunciate it. In the teaching of the Bible the will of God is the only basis for the well-being of man, and more than one passage describes the incomparable beauty of a world in which that will should be perfectly done. Yet the selfish, who are only concerned for their own well-being, and eager to possess that world, can never do the will of God. It should not be forgotten that Mo-tzŭ taught the love of others, whose corollary rather than whose source was mutual good. E. R. Hughes says: 'His utilitarian mind made him construe love in terms of doing good, being useful to your fellow men.'[5] That this is true cannot be gainsaid, and it was probably due in

---

[1] Cf. *Hsün-tzŭ* xxi. 5, translation of H. Dubs, *The Works of Hsüntze*, 1928, p. 264.

[2] Cf. Krause, *Ju-Tao-Fo*, 1924, p. 89: 'Die Menschenliebe ist bei ihm aber nur ein Mittel, um den möglichsten Frieden des eignen Lebens zu geniessen. Das Motiv ist kein rein humanitäres, wie der gleiche Grundsatz in der christlichen Ethik, sondern ein utilitaristisches.' [3] *Mo-tzŭ* xvi.

[4] *Mo-tzŭ* xl (' *I li yeh* '). Cf. Forke, *op. cit.*, p. 415. This chapter is untranslated by Tomkinson or Mei.

[5] Cf. *Chinese Philosophy in Classical Times*, p. 45.

no small measure to the conditions of his time. Christian missionaries have been known in times of famine to spend their time in famine relief, and have not been ashamed of so doing. And if in times of desperate ills Mo-tzŭ was moved with pity for the sufferings of men we need not be surprised or condemn him. He neither preached nor practised a cold, calculating search for profit, but inculcated a self-forgetting love whose profit would only be universal when its practice was universal. Nor did he ever suggest that the individuals who followed him could begin to enter into the dividends at once. The dividends could only accrue when the practice was general, and until then he offered self-sacrifice and suffering rather than profit. Liang Ch'i-ch'ao says: 'Motze's theory does not consider the individual at all. According to him nothing is profitable unless it profits the whole of mankind. To secure this mutual profit it is necessary that all individuals should sacrifice their personal profits.'[1] That Mo-tzŭ sought love for its own sake and not for any profit it could bring him is clear from the fact that it brought him no profit, but only pain, and that he gladly embraced it. Liang Ch'i-ch'ao says again 'if men had nailed him to a cross, he would certainly not have regretted it, but would have endured it with a smile'.[2] It was love that Mo-tzŭ taught, and love that merely seeks its own gain is not love.

The main criticisms launched against him were that his love was too all-embracing, and not that it was too calculating. We read that on one occasion when he was journeying from the state of Lu to the state of Ch'i he met an old friend who said to him: 'Nowadays there is none who practises righteousness; you alone at the cost of suffering practise it. You should give it up.' Whereupon Mo-tzŭ replied: 'There was a man who had ten sons, of whom one worked on the land while the other nine idled. The one who worked on the land, therefore, had to work all the harder. Why? Because there were many to feed and few to cultivate. Nowadays there is none who practises righteousness. You should therefore urge me on. Why should you stop me?'[3] Here is no sordid seeking after profit.

[1] Cf. *Chinese Political Thought*, p. 102.
[2] Quoted in Holth, *Micius*, p. 3.
[3] *Mo-Tzŭ* xlvii. Cf. Forke, *op. cit.*, p. 551; Tomkinson, *op. cit.*, p. 130; Mei, *op. cit.*, p. 222.

Nor did Mo-tzŭ's first followers seek their own profit. Huai-Nan-tzŭ says he had a bodyguard of a hundred and eighty men, who would willingly go to death by fire or sword at his command,[1] and Chuang-tzŭ assures us that the Ch'in Hua-li, to whom reference has been already made, shared his Master's self-sacrificing spirit. He says: 'The idea of Mo Tî and *Kh*in Hwa-lî[2] was good, but their practice was wrong. They would have made the Mohists of future ages feel it necessary to toil themselves, till there was not a hair on their legs, and still be urging one another on.'[3] Moreover, the *Lü Shih Ch'un Ch'iu* narrates the story of the heroic but futile self-sacrifice of Mo-tzŭ's successor as Chü-tzŭ and a hundred and eighty-three of his followers,[4] 'actuated', as Williamson observes,[5] 'by no other motive than fidelity to the principle of defending the oppressed'. Neither Mo-tzŭ nor his immediate followers were under any illusions about quick returns from the practice of love.

There was, indeed, an ascetic strain in his teaching and practice. Hsün-tzŭ complained that 'Mo-tzŭ's one-sided doctrine of utility made him ignore the significance of culture and refinement'.[6] This was because he advocated the severest economy in public and private expenditure, and especially in the matter of funerals, and opposed music. 'Whatever adds to expense', he said, 'but adds nothing to the profit of the people, the Sage-Kings did not countenance.'[7] Or again, 'To cut out useless expenditure is to walk in the way of the Sage-Kings'.[8]

---

[1] Cf. Fung, *op. cit.*, p. 82, where the passage is translated.

[2] This is merely a different romanization of the name Ch'in Hua-li.

[3] *Chuang-tzu* xxxiii, translation of Legge, *Sacred Books of the East*, xl, p. 221. Cf. Giles, *Chuang-Tzu*, p. 443; Wieger, *Taoïsme*, ii, pp. 500 ff. (where the Chinese text is also given).

[4] Cf. *Lü Shih Ch'un Ch'iu*, XIX, iii. For German translation cf. Wilhelm, *Frühling und Herbst des Lü Bu We*, pp. 327 f. Cf. also Fung, *op. cit.*, p. 83; Williamson, *op. cit.*, pp. 25 f.; Waley, *Three Ways of Thought*, pp. 178 ff. (Fung and Williamson give the number as eighty-three; the Chinese text to which I have had access gives one hundred and eighty-three, and so Wilhelm and Waley.)   [5] *Ibid.*, p. 26.

[6] *Hsün-tzŭ* xxi. 5, translation quoted by Kennedy (*Chinese Recorder*, lxii, 1931, p. 696) without acknowledgment of its source. Dubs, *loc. cit.*, has 'Micius was prejudiced towards utility and did not know the elegancies of life.'

[7] *Mo-tzŭ* xxi. Cf. Forke, *op. cit.*, p. 296; Tomkinson, *op. cit.*, p. 75; Mei, *op. cit.*, p. 122.

[8] *Mo-tzŭ* xx. Cf. Forke, *op. cit.*, p. 292; Tomkinson, *op. cit.*, p. 73; Mei, *op. cit.*, p. 119.

Whether in public or in private expenditure all that is merely ornamental he held to be waste, and advocated the severest economy and austerity. 'What are clothes for?' he asked. 'In winter to keep out the cold, in summer to keep out the heat. The test of good clothing is therefore whether it adds warmth in winter and coolness in summer. What is merely decorative but does not so add should be cut out.'[1] He goes on to illustrate the same principle in regard to houses, boats and vehicles. Only the useful is the good, and all that is merely æsthetic is not useful.

Again it is only fair to see this against the background of his time, with the great social inequalities which faced him on every side. He saw labour that was urgently needed for the necessities of the many being dissipated on the luxuries of the few, and hence saw luxury as the enemy of the well-being of the people. Similarly in the context of idle rich he urged the importance of honest and unremitting toil in a way that would satisfy the most exacting of our modern politicians. 'Whatsoever thy hand findeth to do, do it with thy might'[2] would have delighted him as a motto. Everyone, be he statesman, judge or labourer, should not grudge a full day's labour. The rulers should devote themselves from morning till night to the duties of their office, the lesser officials to all the multitudinous tasks of administration, the farmers from the crack of dawn till sundown should toil in the fields with unremitting diligence, and the women should rise betimes to spin and weave, and should continue their tasks till late at night.[3]

All this was probably due to the conditions of the times, and did not mean that Mo-tzŭ thought that all luxury and ornament were wrong *per se*.[4] Fung Yu-lan quotes from Liu Hsiang a story about Mo-tzŭ, which, if true, would show that he did not

---

[1] *Mo-tzŭ* xx. Cf. Forke, *op. cit.*, p. 289; Tomkinson, *op. cit.*, p. 71; Mei, *op. cit.*, p. 117.

[2] Eccl. ix. 10.

[3] *Mo-tzŭ* xxxii. Cf. Forke, *op. cit.*, p. 370; Tomkinson, *op. cit.*, p. 159; Mei, *op. cit.*, p. 179.

[4] Cf. Corswant, *Revue de théologie et de philosophie*, N.S. xxxiv, 1946, p. 105: 'Non pas qu'il dédaigne en eux-mêmes les beaux habits, les joies de la table, les maisons bien construites. Déclarer que Mê Ti était parfaitement insensible à l'art, c'est aller au delà de sa pensée. Les circonstances seules l'obligent à faire passer l'utile avant l'agréable et le beau.'

regard these things as inherently evil, but only relatively so compared with the more urgent needs. The story tells how Mo-tzŭ once in answer to a question said: 'Suppose that in a year of bad times, someone wished to give you the pearl of the Marquis of Sui, yet would not allow you to sell it, but only to keep it as a valuable decoration. Or that he wished to give you a *chung* of grain. If you would get the pearl you would not get the grain, and *vice versa*. Then which would you choose? To which the reply came: 'I would choose the grain, for with this I could rescue myself from my extremity.' Mo-tzŭ replied: 'Truly so. So then why strive after lavishness? The Sage does not hasten to exalt what is without use and to delight in frivolity and licence. Therefore one's food should always be sufficient before one seeks to have it fine tasting; one's clothing should always be warm before one tries to make it beautiful; and one's dwelling should always be safe before one tries to make it pleasure giving. . . . To put what is fundamental first and external decoration secondary: this is what the Sage concerns himself with.'[1] Since this story comes from so late a time as the first century B.C., it cannot be accepted without reserve, though it probably rightly relates Mo-tzŭ's austerity to the rigour of the times, when so many had not the bare necessities of life.

So was it also with his opposition to music. It was because music drew men from their labour that Mo-tzŭ opposed it. It is again only fair to point out that to say Mo-tzŭ was against music gives a false impression to the modern ear. 'It should be remembered', says Yih, 'that the term "Music" has here a much wider application than that generally understood. The term is applied to engravings, delicious food and beautiful houses. In fact it means all sorts of luxuries, arts and pleasure-seeking.'[2] Similarly Waley says: 'What Mo-tzu had in mind were elaborate and costly danced rituals, demanding expensive costumes, the maintenance of large companies of dancers and musicians, all of which were paid out of the public funds.'[3] It would be a better translation into modern idiom to say that he was against

[1] Cf. Fung, *op. cit.*, pp. 104 f.
[2] Cf. *Hirth Anniversary Volume*, p. 617.
[3] Cf. *Three Ways of Thought*, p. 169.

amusements, and that because they were a form of extravagance, breeding waste and idleness, and leading to selfishness. Nevertheless it remains true that life as Mo-tzŭ conceived it was a dreary business, and there was little millennial quality about the 'mutual conferring of benefits' that he called for. It consisted alone in a life of unceasing toil, without colour or relief, and rewarded by the barest necessities of existence. Liang Ch'i-ch'ao says 'Motze's opposition to music is like a man who builds a house but deplores the space within the walls as waste.'[1]

Similarly Mo-tzŭ's demand for simplicity in funerals was born of his horror at all the waste imposed by the tyranny of funeral customs.[2] He declaims against the customs of his day, with their costly coffins and periods of mourning extending to as much as three years and declares that the funeral of a nobleman was calculated to empty the treasury of the state, and that of a peasant to reduce his family to poverty.[3] His rule for funerals was: 'The coffin should be three inches thick, sufficient to hold the bones. The shroud should be of three pieces, sufficient to cover the flesh. The grave should not be of such a depth as to reach water, yet deep enough to ensure that no odours will arise. The mound should be just high enough to be identified. Weeping is permissible on the way to and from the interment, but then there should be a return to work to produce clothing and food.'[4]

But custom is hard to defy, and Mencius tells us that even Mo-tzŭ's disciples who continued his teaching had not strength to put them into practice. We read: 'The Mohist, Î Chih, sought, through Hsü Pî, to see Mencius . . . Mencius said . . . 'I have heard that this Î is a Mohist. Now Mo considers that in the regulation of funeral matters a spare simplicity should be the rule. Î thinks with Mo's doctrines to change the customs of the

---

[1] Cf. *Chinese Political Thought*, p. 103.

[2] De Groot (*loc. cit.*, pp. 666-682) gives the text of the chapter on Economy in Funeral Rites, together with a translation. This is the earliest translation of this chapter into any European language.

[3] *Mo-tzŭ* xxv. Cf. Forke, *op. cit.*, p. 300; Tomkinson, *op. cit.*, pp. 76 f.; Mei, *op. cit.*, p. 125. See also de Groot, *loc. cit.*, pp. 668 f.

[4] *Mo-tzŭ* xxv. Cf. Forke, *op. cit.*, p. 312; Tomkinson, *op. cit.*, p. 83; Mei, *op. cit.*, p. 134. See also de Groot, *loc. cit.*, p. 681.

kingdom—how does he regard them as if they were wrong, and not honour them? Notwithstanding his views, Î buried his parents in a sumptuous manner, and so he served them in the way which his doctrines discountenance.'[1]

Of Mo-tzǔ's own sincerity and consistency there can be no doubt, however, and it is clear that the frugality and asceticism that he both practised and inculcated was not born of a dour spirit that loved asceticism for its own sake, or that sought to mortify the flesh, but rather of his eagerness for service and his recognition of the claims of others.

Passing over other aspects of the teaching of this sage, including his political theory which has reminded modern authors of the 'social contract' theory,[2] we must look finally at the religious element in his thought. Hu Shih says he is the only Chinese who can truly be said to have founded a religion,[3] and Wieger that he is the only Chinese writer of whom one can suppose that he believed in God.[4] His term for God is Heaven —a term which is already found frequently on the lips of Confucius. But Confucius was certainly not profoundly religious, and Mo-tzǔ seems to fill the term with more content than he did. It is true that there are passages which indicate that Confucius thought of Heaven as a conscious and purposive power that was cognizant of human affairs,[5] but his belief in God was not the spring of life for him. He preferred to keep at a respectful distance from God and to let the world of the spiritual be left as far as possible out of his conversation.[6]

---

[1] *Mencius* III, i. 5, translation of Legge, *The Chinese Classics*, ii, 2nd ed., pp. 257 f. Cf. Couvreur, *Les Quatre Livres*, pp. 430 f.; Wilhelm, *Mong Dsi*, p. 59; Lyall, *Mencius*, p. 82.

[2] *Mo-tzǔ* xi. Cf. Forke, *op. cit.*, pp. 214 f.; Tomkinson, *op. cit.*, pp. 36 f.; Mei, *op. cit.*, pp. 55 f.

[3] *Development of Logical Method*, p. 57.

[4] Cf. *Histoire des croyances*, p. 207=E.T., p. 207): 'Le seul écrivain chinois dont on puisse penser qu'il crut en Dieu, le seul apôtre de la charité et chevalier du droit que la Chine ait produit.' Granet (*La pensée chinoise*, p. 492 n.) comments on this: 'Dans ce dithyrambe imprudent, il y a, pour le moins, quelque légèreté.' Hoang Tsen-yue (*op. cit.*, p. 95) adopts Wieger's words and even goes beyond him: 'Mo tseu ou Mécius est, avant Jésus, le seul apôtre de l'altruisme et le plus grand chevalier du droit qu'ait produit le monde.'

[5] Cf. *supra*, p. 92.

[6] Cf. *Analects* vi. 20: 'To give oneself earnestly to the duties due to men, and while respecting spiritual beings, to keep aloof from them, may be called

With Mo-tzŭ, however, it is otherwise. His appeal is frequently
to the will of Heaven. Aggressive war is condemned because it
is contrary to the will of Heaven,[1] and to love all men is
declared to be but obedience to the same will.[2] Moreover
Heaven not alone wills that men should love, but exemplifies
that love. For Heaven loves the whole world, and proves that
love by visiting with calamity those who sin against their
fellows.[3] For Mo-tzŭ firmly held the view that all sin of man
against man is yet more profoundly sin against Heaven.

It is not without interest to observe that in his thought the
divine punishment of human wickedness is an expression of the
love of Heaven. In this he is at one with Old Testament prophets, with whom he has, not surprisingly, been compared.[4]
When Amos said in the name of God: 'You only have I known
of all the families of the earth: therefore will I visit upon you
your iniquities',[5] he perceived that a God who was indifferent
to human sin would not be a God of love. And Mo-tzŭ perceived
the same truth.

From this it is clear that for him Heaven is personal.
Rawlinson observes: 'Micius seems to have conceived of T'ien[6]
as a person though he does not explicitly say so. He did however, refer to him in personalistic terms. T'ien is, for instance,
interested in the welfare of men.'[7] In my view this could be
stated with much more emphasis. The Heaven that is marked
by a loving will, and that cherishes a moral purpose, and that
not alone makes high demands of men but exemplifies the

wisdom' (translation of Legge, *The Chinese Classics*, i, 2nd ed., p. 191); *Analects*
vii. 20: 'The subjects on which the Master did not talk were extraordinary
things, feats of strength, disorder, and spiritual beings' (translation of Legge,
ibid., p. 201).

[1] *Mo-tzŭ* xxvii. Cf. Forke, *op. cit.*, pp. 322 ff.; Tomkinson, *op. cit.*, p. 89;
Mei, *op. cit.*, pp. 142 f.

[2] *Mo-tzŭ* xxviii. Cf. Forke, *op. cit.*, p. 333; Tomkinson, *op. cit.*, p. 95;
Mei, *op. cit.*, p. 153.

[3] *Mo-tzŭ* xxviii. Cf. Forke, *op. cit.*, p. 334; Tomkinson, *op. cit.*, p. 96;
Mei, *op. cit.*, pp. 153 f.

[4] Cf. Wallace, *Chinese Recorder*, lxii, 1931, p. 559: 'His emphasis on the
doctrine of righteousness is comparable to that given it in the old Testament.'
Wilhelm compares Mo-tzŭ with Savonarola (*Die chinesischen Literatur*, p. 56).

[5] Amos iii. 2.

[6] I.e. Heaven.

[7] Cf. *Chinese Recorder*, lxiii, 1932, p. 95.

qualities it asks of them, is no mere impersonal force, but a living and personal Power.[1]

This would seem to be implied too, by Mo-tzǔ's vigorous opposition to any belief in blind, impersonal Fate. 'Fatalism is disastrous to the world' he said.[2] He urged that, instead of supposing their misfortunes were due to the whims of Fate, men should recognize that there was a moral Power behind the universe. 'He who obeys the will of Heaven', we read, 'entering into the universal mutual love (*chien hsiang ai*) and the mutual conferring of benefits (*chiao hsiang li*), will obtain rewards, while he who resists the will of Heaven, being moved with a discriminating mutual hatred (*pieh hsiang wu*) and the mutual doing of injury (*chiao hsiang tsê*), will incur punishment.[3] Heaven is therefore righteous, and the will of Heaven for man is that he should do righteousness.[4] The will of Heaven is therefore as compasses to the wheelwright, and the square to the carpenter.'[5]

[1] Cf. Williamson, *op. cit.*, p. 35: 'In fact, it would seem that the personal interpretation is the only one which meets the case'; Wilhelm, *Die chinesischen Literatur*, p. 57: 'Sein Glaube an einen persönlichen Gott'; Forke, *Mê Ti*, p. 40: 'Der Himmel ist für Mê Ti das höchste Wesen, Gott . . . Mê-tse sieht im Himmel nicht nur das sich über uns ausbreitende Himmelsgewölbe mit den Gestirnen, sondern ein anthropomorphes Wesen'; Krause, *Ju-Tao-Fo*, 1924, p. 89: 'Die oberste Kraft des Himmels erhält, bei Mo Ti einen neuen Sinn, nicht nur als unpersönliche Naturgewalt, sondern als ein höchstes Wesen im Sinne, eines allmächtigen Gottes'; Witte, *Mê Ti*, p. 11: 'Vom Himmel selbst und seinem Wirken wird bei Mê Ti in solchen Ausdrücken geredet, dass man fast zu dem Urteil kommen könnte, der Himmel sei nach Mê Ti eine persönliche Gottheit, ähnlich wie in den ältesten, chinesischen heiligen Schriften von der obersten Gottheit, Schang-ti, gesprochen wird.' Witte, however, holds that Mo-tzǔ was a pantheist, rather than a theist (*ibid.*). Eberhard (*Archiv für Religionswissenschaft*, xxxiii, 1936, p. 316) criticizes Witte sharply as one whose observations sometimes reveal 'eine Unkenntnis des chinesischen Charakters', and says the question is not so simple as Witte supposes. Corswant (*Revue de théologie et de philosophie*, N.S. xxxiv, 1946, p. 116) rejects Witte's view, but holds that both Confucius and Mo-tzǔ can better be described as Deists. It will be apparent that the present writer is scarcely more satisfied with this.

[2] *Mo-tzǔ* xxxvi. Cf. Forke, *op. cit.*, p. 387; Tomkinson, *op. cit.*, p. 96; Mei, *op. cit.*, pp. 153 f.

[3] *Mo-tzǔ* xxvi. Cf. Forke, *op. cit.*, p. 317; Tomkinson, *op. cit.*, p. 86; Mei, *op. cit.*, p. 137.

[4] *Mo-tzǔ* xxvi. Cf. Forke, *op. cit.*, p. 316; Tomkinson, *op. cit.*, p. 85; Mei, *op. cit.*, p. 136.

[5] *Mo-tzǔ* xxvi. Cf. Forke, *op. cit.*, p. 320; Tomkinson, *op. cit.*, p. 87; Mei, *op. cit.*, p. 140.

It seems therefore surprising that many modern writers depreciate Mo-tzǔ as a religious teacher. De Rosny set him down as a very mediocre teacher, and went on to declare that it could not be otherwise with a thinker who appears to have been devoid of any idea of God.[1] Similarly Alexandra David found Mo-tzǔ's Heaven to be a pale substitute for God.[2] Others have maintained that his Heaven was but a lay figure to be clothed with his own ideas. Mei reaches the conclusion that 'with Motze religion is functional and social, and an organic part of his ethics'[3] and that he 'personified social values for their pre-servation and enhancement. He threw a religious halo around his fundamental ethical convictions, and lifted his doctrines to the commanding position of creeds.'[4] Similarly Wallace: 'Motse's argument is always a utilitarianism, and the thing is then given an additional reference to Heaven, which is so nominal that the argument is not strengthened by it.'[5]

All this seems to me to be much less than fair to Mo-tzǔ, and to rest on an exaggerated emphasis on his utilitarianism and a gross under-estimate of his teaching of Heaven. Mei observes that 'what Heaven desires is just what Motse has been teaching himself'.[6] But how could it be otherwise? If Mo-tzǔ believed that in the will of God was the supreme law for man, then he would necessarily set forth what he believed to be the content of that will. It can scarcely be maintained that he would have proved himself more truly religious if he had said 'The will of Heaven is one thing, but what I advocate is another'!

[1] Cf. *Études de critique et d'histoire* (Bibliothèque de l'École des Hautes Études: Sciences Religieuses, vii), 1896, p. 299: 'La doctrine de Meh-tse . . . est d'une assez mediocre portée . . . Il ne pouvait d'ailleurs en être autrement chez un penseur qui semble n'avoir pas eu la moindre aperception de l'idée de Dieu et qui, par conséquent, n'a pu concevoir un motif d'Amour supérieur aux appels de la chair et du sang.'

[2] Cf. *op. cit.*, p. 142: 'Si l'on nous y propose l'imitation du Ciel "dont les dons généreux se répandent sur tous" c'est uniquement pour nous donner un haut exemple, celui de la nature et nous ne pourrions, quelque désir que nous en ayons, rien y trouver qui ressemble au commandement d'une Puissance supérieure.'

[3] Cf. Motse, *Rival of Confucius*, p. 157.

[4] *Ibid.*, p. 158. Cf. Holth, *op. cit.*, p. 48; Kennedy, *Chinese Recorder*, lxii, 1931, p. 698.

[5] Cf. *Chinese Recorder*, lxi, 1931, p. 560. Cf. Suzuki, *Brief History of Early Chinese Philosophy*, 1914, p. 100.

[6] Cf. *Motse, Rival of Confucius*, p. 149.

It is true that he emphasizes only certain sides of religion. He is not much interested in the forms of worship. But neither were the Old Testament prophets. Yet they are allowed to have been religious teachers. Mo-tzŭ accepts the current forms, but with something of the spirit of the prophets he demands that these forms should be validated by obedience to the will of God in daily life. In his day he found hollow sacrifices being offered. Says Fung: 'The Confucian school, or at least a part of it, did not believe in the existence of supernatural beings, yet at the same time stressed the performance of sacrifice in order to give emotional satisfaction. Looked at from the point of view of Mohist utilitarianism, performance of sacrifices under such circumstances is meaningless.'[1] Mo-tzŭ himself said: 'To hold that there are no spirits and yet to learn the sacrificial rites is like refusing to entertain a guest and yet studying the forms of hospitality, or like denying the existence of fish and yet making a fishing net.'[2] Mo-tzŭ's emphasis is not on the forms of religion, because he did not think the urgent need of the world was for a reform of those forms, but for a life which conformed to the will of God and a character that reflected God's love.

As a religious teacher he is to be criticized rather in that his Heaven is too remote. His character and will are made known to men, but His fellowship is not offered them as the living fountain of their strength to obey His will. Mo-tzŭ himself did not come to men with a 'Thus saith the Lord', proclaiming a word which he had received in the immediacy of fellowship with God. Nor does he call upon men to love God with a love that responds to His own. As a religious teacher he is cold and rational. Yet that should not make us withhold from him appreciation of the greatness of his spirit and of the loftiness of his teaching.[3] God hath not left Himself without witness amongst men of many races, and though we may find their witness to be 'by divers portions

---

[1] *Op. cit.*, pp. 90 f.

[2] *Mo-tzŭ* xlviii. Cf. Forke, *op. cit.*, p. 569; Tomkinson, *op. cit.*, p. 139; Mei, *Works of Motse*, p. 236.

[3] Cf. Corswant, *Revue de théologie et de philosophie*, N.S. xxxiv, 1946, p. 123: 'Mê Ti n'est pas le plus grand penseur de la Chine, ni un génie, et encore moins le Jésus-Christ chinois! Mais il n'est pas non plus un esprit superficiel et il ne saurait être rabaissé au rang d'un vulgaire et déplaisant démagogue. Il appartient de droit à cette élite d'hommes parfaitement intègres, courageux

and in divers manners' we may honour their memory for their greatness. Few amongst them attained the heights of self-sacrifice and unselfishness that Mo-tzŭ attained, and none was more earnest in his desire for a world in which the will of God should be perfectly done. His conception of that world was forbidding and unlovely, in that it was a comfortless world of unceasing toil, and he insufficiently recognized the place of the natural relationships of men. In both respects his over-emphasis finds its justification in the setting of his times, and if Mo-tzŭ can scarcely be thought of as the universal teacher for all ages, he can be recognized to have been a teacher whose message was urgently needed in his own day. Perhaps that is why his words filled the empire in his own age, and then suffered neglect.

et désinteréssés, à ces sages de l'Empire du Ciel qui ont consacré leur vie entière, tous leurs efforts, toutes les ressources de leur intelligence et de leur cœur aux problèmes de la morale individuelle, politique et sociale, et partant, au bien de leur pays. Son nom mérite d'être tiré de l'oubli pour former . . . une lumineuse constellation au ciel de l'histoire de la Chine.'

LIST OF WORKS CONSULTED

The following list of books consulted in the preparation of these studies contains some to which no reference will be found in the foot notes. For the texts of Hinduism, Jainism and Buddhism the writer has been compelled to depend wholly on translations, but for the texts of Judaism and Islam, and of Chinese writers, he has consulted the original wherever it has been available. Quotations from published translations of texts have been normally employed.

A. CHINESE RELIGIONS

i. *Texts and Translations*

The Four Books (Ssŭ Shu): Chinese text and English translation in J. Legge, *The Chinese Classics,* i and ii, 1861, Hongkong; 2nd ed., 1893, 1895, Oxford; Chinese text and French and Latin translations in S. Couvreur, *Les Quatre Livres,* 2nd ed., 1910, Hokienfu; translation only in M. G. Pauthier, *Doctrine de Confucius, ou les Quatre Livres traduits du chinois,* n.d., Paris.

The Analects (Lun Yü): Text and translation in W. E. Soothill, *The Analects of Confucius,* 1910, Yokohama; translation only in A. Waley, *The Analects of Confucius,* 1938, London; German translation in R. Wilhelm, *Kung-Futse Gespräche,* 1923, Jena.

The Great Learning and the Doctrine of the Mean (Ta Hsüeh and Chung Yung): translation by E. R. Hughes, in *The Great Learning and the Mean-in-action,* 1942, London.

Mencius: translation only in L. A. Lyall, *Mencius,* 1932, London; German translation in R. Wilhelm, *Mong Dsi,* 1921, Jena.

Shu Ching: Chinese text and English translation in J. Legge, *The Chinese Classics,* iii, 2 vols., 1865, Hongkong; Chinese text and French translation in S. Couvreur, *Chou King,* 1916, Hsien Hsien; translation only in W. G. Old, *The Shu King, or the Chinese Historical Classic,* 1904, London.

Shih Ching: Chinese text and English translation in J. Legge, *The Chinese Classics,* iv, 2 vols., 1871, London, and in B. Karlgren, *The Book of Odes,* 1950, Stockholm; Chinese text and French and Latin translations in S. Couvreur, *Cheu King,* 3rd ed., 1934, Hsien Hsien; translation only in W. Jennings, *The Shi King,* 1891, London, and A. Waley, *The Book of Songs,* 1937, London.

Li Chi: Chinese text and French and Latin translations in S. Couvreur, *Li Ki,* 2 vols., 1913 (2nd ed.), 1899, Hokienfu; translation only by J. Legge in *Sacred Books of the East,* xxvii and xxviii, 1885, Oxford; German translation in R. Wilhelm, *Li Gi, das Buch der Sitte des älteren und jüngeren Dai,* 1930, Jena.

I Li: Chinese text and French translation in S. Couvreur, *Cérémonial,* 1928, Hsien Hsien; translation only in J. Steele, *The I-Li, or Book of Etiquette and Ceremonial,* 2 vols., 1917, London.

K'ung tzŭ-Chia Yü : Translation of Sections 1-10 in R. P. Kramers, *K'ung Tzŭ Chia Yü,* 1950, Leiden.

Tao Tê Ching: Chinese text and Legge's English translation in *The Original Chinese Texts of the Confucian Analects . . . and the Works of Lao-tsze, with their Japanese translation and their English translations and notes,* Tokyo: Chinese text and French translation in L. Wieger, *Taoïsme,* ii, 1913, Hsien Hsien; translation only by J. Legge in *Sacred Books of the East,* xxxix, 1891, Oxford; Ch'u Ta-kao, *Tao Tê Ching,* 1937, London; A. Waley, *The Way and its Power,* 1934, reprinted 1942, London; R. Wilhelm, *Laotse: Tao Te King,* 1923, Jena.

Lü Shih Ch'un Ch'iu: Chinese text edited by Chün I-shu, 26 chüan, 1921, Shanghai; German translation in R. Wilhelm, *Frühling und Herbst des Lü Bu We,* 1928, Jena.

Chu Hsi, *The Philosophy of Human Nature,* translated by J. P. Bruce, 1922, London.

Chuang-tzŭ, *Works,* Chinese text and French translation in L. Wieger, *Taoïsme,* ii, 1913, Hsien Hsien; translation by Legge in *Sacred Books of the East,* xxxix and xl, 1891, Oxford; translation by H. A. Giles in *Chuang Tzŭ, Mystic, Moralist and Social Reformer, translated from the Chinese,* 1926, Shanghai.

Han-Fei-tzŭ, *Works,* Chinese text edited by Tung Shên-hsing, 20 chüan, 1875, reproduction of edition of Sung period of the reign of Ch'ien Tao, 1165-1174; translation only (Chapters i-xxx) in W. K. Liao, *The Complete Works of Han Fei Tzŭ,* i, 1939, London.

Hsün-tzŭ, *Works,* translated by H. H. Dubs in *The Works of Hsüntze, translated from the Chinese,* 1928, London.

Lieh-tzŭ, *Works,* Chinese text and French translation in L. Wieger, *Taoïsme,* ii, 1913, Hsien Hsien. For Chinese text and English translation of Lieh-tzŭ (part of) Chapter vii, see Legge, *The Chinese Classics,* ii, Prolegomena, Chapter iii, Section 1.

Mo-tzŭ, *Works,* Chinese text edited by Chang Shun-i, 1936, Shanghai; translated by L. Tomkinson in *The Social Teachings of Meh Tse* (Transactions of the Asiatic Society of Japan, 2nd series, iv), 1927, Tokyo, and by Y. P. Mei in *The Ethical and Political Works of Motse,* 1929, London; German translation by A. Forke in *Mê Ti, des Sozialethikers und seiner Schüler philosophische Werke,* 1922, Berlin.

Shang Yang, *Works,* translated with Introduction and Notes in J. J. L. Duyvendak, *The Book of Lord Shang,* 1928, London.

Ssŭ-ma Ch'ien, *Shih Chi,* translated by E. Chavannes in *Les Mémoires historiques de Se-ma-Ts'ien,* 5 vols., 1895-1905, Paris.

Wang Ch'ung, *Lun Hêng,* translated into English by A. Forke in *Lun Hêng,* 2 vols., 1907, 1911, Leipzig, Berlin.

Wang Yang-ming, *Works*, translated with a biographical introduction in F. G. Henke, *The Philosophy of Wang Yang Ming*, 1916, London and Chicago.

L. Wieger, *Textes philosophiques: Confuciisme, Taoïsme, Buddhisme*, 2nd ed., 1930, Hsien Hsien (containing selected texts in Chinese with French translation).

ii. *Interpretations*

D. Bodde, *Statesman, Patriot and General in Ancient China*, 1940, New Haven.

D. Bodde, 'The New Identification of Lao Tzŭ proposed by Professor Dubs', in *Journal of the American Oriental Society*, lxii, 1942, pp. 8-13, New Haven.

D. Bodde, 'Further Remarks on the Identification of Lao Tzŭ: a Last Reply to Professor Dubs', *ibid.*, lxiv, 1944, pp. 24-27.

J. P. Bruce, *Chu Hsi and his Masters*, 1923, London.

F. T. Cheng (Chêng T'ien-hsi), *China Moulded by Confucius*, 1946, London.

S. Cognetti de Martiis, 'Un Socialista Cinese del V secolo av. C., Mih Teih', in *Memorie della R. Accademia dei Lincei*, 4th series, Classe de Scienze morali, iii, 1887, pp. 248-281, Rome.

W. Corswant, 'Le philosophe chinois Mê Ti et sa doctrine de l'amour mutuel', in *Revue de théologie et de philosophie*, N.S. xxxiv, 1946, pp. 97-124, Lausanne.

S. Couling, *Encyclopædia Sinica*, 1917, London.

H. G. Creel, *Confucius : The Man and the Myth*, 1951, London.

Alexandra David, *Le philosophe Meh-Ti et l'idée de solidarité*, 1907, London.

R. K. Douglas, *Confucianism and Taouism*, 1879, London.

H. H. Dubs, *Hsüntze, the Moulder of Ancient Confucianism*, 1927, London.

H. H. Dubs, 'The Date and Circumstances of the Philosopher Lao-Dz', in *Journal of the American Oriental Society*, lxi, 1941, pp. 215-221, New Haven.

H. H. Dubs, 'The Identification of the Lao-Dz: a reply to Professor Bodde', *ibid.*, lxii, 1942, pp. 300-304.

W. Eberhard, 'Neuere Forschungen zur Religion Chinas 1920-1932' in *Archiv für Religionswissenschaft*, xxxiii, 1936, pp. 304-344, Leipzig and Berlin.

J. Edkins, 'Notices of the Character and Writings of Mêh Tsî' in *Journal of the North China Branch of the Royal Asiatic Society*, ii, 1859, pp. 165-169, Shanghai.

E. Faber, *Die Grundgedanken des alten chinesischen Sozialismus, oder die Lehre des Philosophen Micius*, 1877, Elberfeld.

A. Forke, *Yang Chu's Garden of Pleasure*, 1912, London.

A. Forke, *Die Gedankenwelt des chinesischen Kulturkreises*, 1927, Munich and Berlin.

A. Forke, *Geschichte der alten chinesischen Philosophie*, 1927, Hamburg.

A. Forke, *Geschichte der mittelalterlichen chinesischen Philosophie*, 1934, Hamburg.

A. Forke, *Geschichte der neueren chinesischen Philosophie*, 1938, Hamburg.

Fung Yu-lan, *A History of Chinese Philosophy*, translated by Derk Bodde, i, 1937, Peiping and London.

Fung Yu-lan, *The Spirit of Chinese Philosophy*, English translation by E. R. Hughes, 1947, London.

F. Geisser, *Mo Ti, der Künder der allgemeinen Menschenliebe*, 1947, Berne.

H. A. Giles, *Confucianism and its Rivals*, 1915, London.

M. Granet, *La pensée chinoise*, 1934, Paris.

J. J. M. de Groot, *The Religious System of China*, 6 vols., 1892-1910, Leiden.

H. Hackman, *Chinesische Philosophie*, 1927, Munich.

C. de Harlez, 'Mi Tze, le philosophe de l'amour universel', in *Giornale della Società Asiatica Italiana*, viii, 1894, pp. 103-126, Florence.

C. de Harlez, ' Mi Tze : l'amour universel', *ibid.*, ix, 1895-96, pp. 81-126.

F. Hartmann, *Theosophie in China: Betrachtungen über das Tao-Teh-King*, n.d., Leipzig.

Hoang Tsen-yue, *Étude comparative sur les philosophies de Lao Tseu, Khong Tseu, Mo Tseu* (Annales de l'Université de Lyon, N.S. ii, Fasc. 37), 1925, Lyons.

Sverre Holth, *Micius: a Brief Outline of his Life and Ideas*, 1935, Shanghai.

E. R. Hughes, *Chinese Philosophy in Classical Times*, 1942, London.

E. R. and K. Hughes, *Religion in China*, 1950, London.

Hu Shih, *The Development of the Logical Method in Ancient China*, 1928, Shanghai.

G. Kennedy, ' Ethical and Social Teaching of Moti ', in *Chinese Recorder*, lxii, 1931, pp. 695-702, Shanghai.

F. E. A. Krause, *Ju-Tao-Fo*, 1924, Munich.

Liang Ch'i-Ch'ao, *History of Chinese Political Thought during the Tsin Period*, translated by L. T. Chen, 1930, London.

Lin Yu Tang, *The Wisdom of Confucius*, n.d., Shanghai.

W. H. Long, *Motze, China's Ancient Philosopher of Universal Love*, n.d., Peking.

P. J. Maclagan, *Chinese Religious Ideas*, 1926, London.

H. Maspero, ' Notes sur la logique de Mo-tseu et de son école ', in *T'oung Pao*, xxv, 1928, pp. 1-64, Leiden.

Y. P. Mei, *Motse, the neglected Rival of Confucius*, 1934, London.

E. H. Parker, ' Taoism ', in *The Imperial and Asiatic Quarterly Review*, 3rd series, xxii, 1906, pp. 311-333.

F. Rawlinson, 'The Ethical Values of Micius', in *Chinese Recorder*, lxiii, 1932, pp. 93-102, Shanghai.

L. de Rosny, 'Une grande lutte d'idées dans la Chine antérieure à notre ère, Meng-tse, Siun-tse, Yang-tse et Meh-tse', in *Études de critique et d'histoire* (Bibliothèque de l'École des Hautes Études: Sciences religieuses, vii), 1896, pp. 277-301, Paris.

C. O. Simpson, 'Motse and Fatalism', in *Chinese Recorder*, lxii, 1931, pp. 638-645, Shanghai.

W. E. Soothill, *The Three Religions of China*, 3rd ed., 1929, Oxford.

D. T. Suzuki, *Brief History of Early Chinese Philosophy*, 1914, London.

L. Tomkinson, 'Pacifist and Socialist Intellectuals in the "Warring States"' in *Chinese Recorder*, lxvii, 1936, pp. 286-296, Shanghai.

A. Waley, *Three Ways of Thought in Ancient China*, 1939, London.

W. Wallace, 'Religious Elements in the Writings of Motse', in *Chinese Recorder*, lxii, 1931, pp. 557-561, Shanghai.

L. Wieger, *Histoire des croyances religieuses et des opinions philosophiques en Chine*, 2nd ed., 1922, Hsien Hsien; English translation by E. C. Werner, 1927, Hsien Hsien.

R. Wilhelm, *Die chinesischen Literatur*, 1926, Wildpark-Potsdam.

R. Wilhelm, *A Short History of Chinese Civilization*, English translation by Joan Joshua, 1929, New York.

H. R. Williamson, *Mo Ti: a Chinese Heretic*, 1927, Tsinan.

H. R. Williamson, *Wang An Shih*, 2 vols., 1935, 1937, London.

S. Wells Williams, *The Middle Kingdom*, 2 vols., 1883, London.

J. Witte, *Mê Ti, der Philosoph der allgemeinen Menschenliebe und sozialen Gleichheit im alten China*, 1928, Leipzig.

Z. L. Yih, 'Introduction to Mo-Tzu', in *Hirth Anniversary Volume*, 1923, pp. 613-619, London.

Z. K. Zia, *The Confucian Civilization*, 1925, Shanghai.

B. Brahmanism and Hinduism

i. *Texts in Translation*

Upaniṣads: F. Max Müller, *The Upanishads*, in *Sacred Books of the East*, i and xv, 1879, 1900, Oxford: R. E. Hume, *The Thirteen Principal Upanishads*, 2nd ed., 1934, Oxford; J. N. Rawson, *The Kaṭha Upaniṣad*, 1934, Oxford; P. Deussen, *Sechzig Upanishad's des Veda*, 1897, Leipzig; R. Otto, *Die Kaṭha-Upanishad übertragen und erläutert*, 1936, Berlin.

Bhagavadgītā: translation by L. D. Barnett in *Hindu Scriptures*, ed. by N. Macnicol (Everyman's Library), 1938, London; E. J. Thomas, *The Song of the Lord*, 1931, London; R. Otto, *The Original Gītā*, translated by J. E. Turner, 1939, London; S. Prabhavananda and C. Isherwood, *The Song of God*, 1947, London.

Laws of Manu: G. Bühler, *The Laws of Manu,* in *Sacred Books of the East,* xxv, 1886, Oxford.

Mahābhārata: P. C. Rāy, *The Mahabharata translated into English Prose,* 1884-1896, Calcutta.

Sarva-Darśana-Saṃgraha: E. B. Cowell and A. E. Gough, *Sarva-Darśana-Saṃgraha, or Review of the different Systems of Hindu Philosophy,* 1882, London.

ii. *Interpretations*

A. Barth, *The Religions of India,* translated by J. Wood, 1889, London.

S. K. Belvalkar and R. D. Ranade, *History of Indian Philosophy,* ii, 1927, Poona.

S. Cave, *Redemption: Hindu and Christian,* 1919, Oxford.

A. K. Coomaraswamy, *Hinduism and Buddhism,* n.d., New York.

S. Dasgupta, *A History of Indian Philosophy,* 4 vols., 1922-1949, Cambridge.

P. Deussen, *The Philosophy of the Upanishads,* translated by A. S. Geden, 1906, Edinburgh.

P. Deussen, *The System of the Vedânta,* translated by C. Johnston, 1912, Chicago.

J. N. Farquhar, *The Crown of Hinduism,* 1913, Oxford.

J. N. Farquhar, *An Outline of the Religious Literature of India,* 1920, Oxford.

H. D. Griswold, *The Religion of the Rigveda,* 1923, Oxford.

M. Hiriyanna, *Outlines of Indian Philosophy,* 1932, London.

E. W. Hopkins, *The Religions of India,* 1895, Boston.

A. B. Keith, *The Religion and Philosophy of the Veda and Upanishads,* 2 vols., 1925, Cambridge, Mass.

S. Konow and P. Tuxen, *The Religions of India,* 1949, Copenhagen.

J. McKenzie, *Hindu Ethics: a Historical and Critical Essay,* 1922, Oxford.

N. Macnicol, *Indian Theism from the Vedic to the Muḥammadan Period,* 1915, Oxford.

M. Monier-Williams, *Brāhmanism and Hindūism,* 4th ed., 1891, London.

M. Monier-Williams, *Hinduism* (Non-Christian Religious Systems), 1877, London.

S. Radhakrishnan, *Indian Philosophy,* 2 vols., 2nd ed., 1929, 1931, London.

S. Radhakrishnan, *The Philosophy of the Upaniṣads,* 1924, London.

R. D. Ranade, *A Constructive Survey of Upanishadic Philosophy, being a Systematic Introduction to Indian Metaphysics,* 1926, Poona.

C. BUDDHISM

i. *Texts in Translation*

Aṅguttara-Nikāya: F. L. Woodward, *The Book of the Gradual Sayings*, in Pali Text Society's *Translation Series*, xxii, xxiv-xxvii, 1932-1936, London ; Nyāṇatiloka, *Die Reden des Buddha aus dem "Angúttara-Nikāya"*, 5 vols., 1922 (vol. i, 2nd ed., 1923), Munich.

Dhammapada: F. Max Müller, *The Dhammapada*, in *Sacred Books of the East*, x, 1881, Oxford; P. Dahlke, *Suttapitaka, i. Dhammapada*, 2nd ed., 1922, Zehlendorf-West bei Berlin ; S. Radhakrishnan, *The Dhammapada, with Introductory Essays*, 1950, London.

Dīgha-Nikāya: T. W. and C. A. F. Rhys Davids, *Dialogues of the Buddha*, in *Sacred Books of the Buddhists*, ii-iv, 1899-1921, London; P. Grimblot, *Sept Suttas Pâlis*, 1876 (French and English); P. Dahlke, *Suttapitaka, ii. Digha-Nikaya*, 1920, Zehlendorf-West bei Berlin; K. E. Neumann, *Die Reden Gotamo Buddho's aus der längeren Sammlung Dīghanikāyo des Pāli-Kanons*, i, 1907, Munich (the only volume of this work to which I have had access).

Majjhima-Nikāya: P. Dahlke, *Suttapitika, iii, Majjhima-Nikaya*, 1923, Zehlendorf-West bei Berlin; Bhikku Sīlācāra, *The Majjhima-Nikāya: the First Fifty Discourses from the Collection of the Medium-Length Discourses of Gotama the Buddha*, 2nd ed., 1924, Munich.

Milindapañha: T. W. Rhys Davids, *The Questions of King Milinda*, in *Sacred Books of the East*, xxxv, xxxvi, 1890, 1894, Oxford; Nyāṇatiloka, *Die Fragen des Milindo*, 2 vols., 1914-1924, Munich.

Saṃyutta-Nikāya: F. L. Woodward, *The Book of the Kindred Sayings*, in Pali Text Society's *Translation Series*, vii, xiii-xvi, 1917-1930, London; W. Geiger, *Saṃyutta-Nikāya aus dem Pāli Kanon der Buddhisten*, 1-16 (all published), 2 vols., 1930, 1925, Munich.

Suttas: T. W. Rhys Davids, *Buddhist Suttas*, in *Sacred Books of the East*, xi, 1881, Oxford.

Sutta-Nipâta: V. Fausböll, *Sutta Nipâta*, in *Sacred Books of the East*, x, 1881, Oxford.

Visuddhi-Magga: Pe Maung Tin, *The Path of Purity*, in Pali Text Society's *Translation Series*, xi, xvii, xxi, 1923-1931, London.

C. A. F. Rhys Davids, *Psalms of the Early Buddhists*, in Pali Text Society's *Translation Series*, i, iv, 1909, 1913, London.

C. A. F. Rhys Davids, *The Minor Anthologies of the Pali Canon*, i, in *Sacred Books of the Buddhists*, vii, 1931, London.

K. Seidenstücken, *Pāli-Buddhismus in Übersetzungen*, 1923, Munich.

E. J. Thomas, *Early Buddhist Scriptures*, 1935, London.

H. C. Warren, *Buddhism in Translations*, 5th issue, 1909, Cambridge, Mass.

L. Wieger, *Bouddhisme chinois* (Chinese text and French translation), 2 vols., 2nd ed., 1940, Peking.

ii. *Interpretations* (excluding works given under B ii)

S. Beal, *A Catena of Buddhist Scriptures from the Chinese*, 1871, London.
R. S. Copleston, *Buddhism Primitive and Present in Magadha and in Ceylon*, 1908, London.
A. Coomaraswamy, *Buddha and the Gospel of Buddhism*, 1928, London.
P. Dahlke, *Buddhist Essays*, E. Tr. by Bhikkhu Sīlācāra, 1908, London.
J. Edkins, *Chinese Buddhism*, 1880, London.
R. Spence Hardy, *A Manual of Buddhism in its Historical Development*, 1853, London.
C. Humphreys, *Karma and Rebirth*, 1943, London.
A. B. Keith, *Buddhist Philosophy in India and Ceylon*, 1923, Oxford.
G. Mensching, *Die Bedeutung des Leidens im Buddhismus und Christentum*, 2nd ed., 1930, Giessen.
G. Messina, *Cristianesimo, Buddhismo, Manicheismo nell' Asia antica,* 1947, Rome.
M. Monier-Williams, *Buddhism, in its connexion with Brāhmanism and Hindūism*, 1889, London.
H. Oldenberg, *Buddha: his Life, his Doctrine, his Order*, English translation by W. Hoey, 1882, London.
L. de la Vallée Poussin, *The Way to Nirvāna*, 1917, Cambridge.
S. Radhakrishnan, *Gautama the Buddha*, 1938, London.
T. W. Rhys Davids, *Buddhism* (Non-Christian Religious Systems), new ed., 1910, London.
T. W. Rhys Davids, *Lectures on . . . the History of Indian Buddhism*. 2nd ed., 1891, London.
Mrs. Rhys Davids, *Outlines of Buddhism: a Historical Sketch*, 1934, London.
A. Roussel, *Le Bouddhisme primitif*, 1911, Paris.
B. H. Streeter, *The Buddha and the Christ*, 1932, London.
B. L. Suzuki, *Mahayana Buddhism*, 1938, London.
S. Tachibana, *The Ethics of Buddhism*, 1926, Oxford.
E. J. Thomas, *The Life of Buddha as Legend and History*, 1927, London.
E. J. Thomas, *The History of Buddhist Thought*, 1933, London.

D. JAINISM

Jaina Sutras: H. Jacobi, *Gaina Sûtras*, in *Sacred Books of the East*, xxii, 1884, and xlv, 1895, Oxford.
Uvāsagadasāo: A. F. R. Hoernle, *The Uvāsagadasāo, being the seventh Anga of the Jains*, 1885, Calcutta.
J. Jaini, *Outlines of Jainism*, edited by F. W. Thomas, 1940, Cambridge.
C. J. Shah, *Jainism in North India, 800 B.C.-A.D. 526*, 1932, London.
Mrs. S. Stevenson, *The Heart of Jainism*, 1915, Oxford.

E. ISLAM

i. *Texts and Translations*

Qur'ān: G. Flügel, ed. by: *Corani Textus Arabicus*, 3rd ed., 1858, Leipzig, and *Concordantiæ Corani Arabicæ*, 1875, Leipzig; Arabic text and English translation in Muḥammad 'Ali, *The Holy Qur-ān containing the Arabic text with English translation and commentary*, 1920, Lahore; translation only in G. Sale, *The Koran*, 1838 ed., London; J. M. Rodwell, *The Koran* (Everyman's Library), 1913 ed., London; R. Bell, *The Qur'ān translated, with critical rearrangement of the Surahs*, 2 vols., 1937, 1939, Edinburgh ; French translation in E. Montet, *Le Coran : traduction nouvelle et intégrale*, 1949, Paris.

Ḥadith: L. Krehl and T. W. Juynboll, *Le receuil des traditions mahomét-anes par el-Bokhâri*, 4 vols., 1862-1908, Leiden; French translation in O. Houdas and W. Marçais, *El-Bokhâri: Les traditions islamiques*, 4 vols., 1903-1914, Paris; Muslim, *Jami' 'al-Saḥiḥ, with a commentary by Nawawi* (Arabic text), 2 vols., 1885, Delhi.

F. A. Arnold, *Septem Mo'allaḳât Carmina antiquissima Arabum*, 1850, Leipzig; Arabic text and English translation in F. E. Johnson, *The Seven Poems suspended in the Temple of Mecca*, 1894, London.

G. W. Freytag, *Hamasæ Carmina*, 2 vols., 1828, 1847, Bonn.

C. J. Lyall, *Translations of Ancient Arabian Poetry*, 1885, London.

E. E. Salisbury, 'Materials for the History of the Muhammadan Doctrine of Predestination and Free Will', in *Journal of the American Oriental Society*, viii, 1866, pp. 105-182, New Haven.

ii. *Interpretations*

Mirza Ghulam Ahmad, *The Teachings of Islam*, 1921, Lahore.

Muḥammad 'Ali, *The Religion of Islām*, 1936, Lahore.

Encyclopædia of Islām, ed. by M. Th. Houtsma, T. W. Arnold, R. Basset and R. Hartmann, 4 vols., 1913-1934, Leiden.

I. Goldziher, *Le dogme et la loi de l'Islam*, translation by F. Arin, 1920, Paris.

A. Guillaume, 'Some Remarks on Free Will and Predestination in Islam, together with a translation of the Kitabu-l Qadar from the Sahih of al-Bukhari', in *Journal of the Royal Asiatic Society*, 1924, pp. 43-63, London.

A. Guillaume, *The Traditions of Islam*, 1924, Oxford.

T. P. Hughes, *A Dictionary of Islam*, 1895, London.

Sir Mohammad Iqbal, *The Reconstruction of Religious Thought in Islam*, 1934, Oxford.

L. Bevan Jones, *The People of the Mosque*, 1932, London.

H. Lammens, *L'Islam: croyances et institutions*, 1926, Beirut.

11 *

D. S. Margoliouth, *Mohammedanism* (Home University Library), n.d., London.

D. S. Margoliouth, *The Early Development of Mohammedanism*, 1914, London.

H. Ringgren, *Islam 'aslama and muslim*, 1949, Lund.

J. W. Sweetman, *Islam and Christian Theology*, Part I, 2 vols., 1945-1947, London:

W. M. Watt, *Free Will and Predestination in Early Islam*, 1948, London.

F. BABYLONIAN RELIGION

i. *Texts and Translations*

P. Dhorme, 'Ecclésiaste ou Job?' in *Revue biblique*, xxxii, 1923, pp. 1-27, Paris.

H. Gressmann, *Altorientalische Texte zum Alten Testament*, 2nd ed., 1926, Berlin.

B. Landsberger, 'Die babylonische Theodizee', in *Zeitschrift für Assyriologie*, xliii (Neue Folge, ix), 1936, pp. 32-76.

S. Langdon, *Babylonian Wisdom*, 1923, London.

J. B. Pritchard, ed. by, *Ancient Near Eastern Texts relating to the Old Testament*, 1950, Princeton.

R. W. Rogers, *Cuneiform Parallels to the Old Testament*, 1912, New York.

ii. *Interpretations*

C.-F. Jean, *Le Milieu biblique avant Jésus-Christ*, 3 vols., 1922-1936, Paris.

M. Jastrow, *The Religion of Babylonia and Assyria*, 1898, Boston.

M. Jastrow, *Die Religion Babyloniens und Assyriens*, 2 vols., 1905-1912, Giessen.

M. Jastrow, *Aspects of Religious Belief and Practice in Babylonia and Assyria*, 1911, New York.

B. Meissner, *Babylonien und Assyrien*, 2 vols., 1920, 1925, Heidelberg.

J. J. Stamm, *Das Leiden des Unschuldigen in Babylon und Israel*, 1946, Zürich.

G. Widengren, *The Accadian and Hebrew Psalms of Lamentation as Religious Documents*, 1937, Stockholm.

G. JUDAISM AND CHRISTIANITY

i. *The Old and New Testaments*

A. Calmet, *Commentaire littéral sur tous les livres de l'Ancien et du Nouveau Testament*, 8 vols. in 9, 1724-1726, Paris.

M. Poole, *Synopsis criticorum aliorumque S. Scripturæ interpretum*, 5 vols., 1684-1686, Utrecht.

ii. *The Old Testament*

P. Dhorme, *Le Livre de Job*, 1926, Paris.

B. Duhm, *Hiob*, 1897, Freiburg.

S. R. Driver and G. B. Gray, *Critical and Exegetical Commentary on the Book of Job*, 1921, Edinburgh.

R. Levy, *Deutero-Isaiah*, 1925, Oxford.

J. Lindblom, *Boken om Job och hans lidande*, 1940, Lund.

A. S. Peake, *The Problem of Suffering in the Old Testament*, 1904, London.

O. S. Rankin, *Israel's Wisdom Literature: its bearing on Theology and the History of Religion*, 1936, Edinburgh.

H. Ranston, *The Old Testament Wisdom Books and their Teaching*, 1930, London.

H. W. Robinson, *The Cross of Job*, 1916, London.

H. W. Robinson, *The Cross of the Servant*, 1926, London.

H. H. Rowley, *Israel's Mission to the World*, 1939, London.

C. C. Torrey, *The Second Isaiah*, 1928, Edinburgh.

iii. *The Later Period of Judaism*

Mishnah: Hebrew text, edition of 1832-1834, Berlin; Text and German translation in *Die Mischna*, edited by G. Beer and O. Holtzmann, 1912—(in progress), Giessen; English translation in H. Danby, *The Mishnah*, 1933, Oxford.

Pirqē Abōth: Hebrew text and English translation in C. Taylor, *Sayings of the Jewish Fathers*, 2nd ed., 1897, Cambridge; R. Travers Herford, *Pirkē Aboth*, 2nd ed., 1930, New York.

Talmud Babli: Hebrew text, edition of 1862-1868, Berlin; Text and German translation in L. Goldschmidt, *Der babylonische Talmud mit Einschluss der vollständigen Mišnah*, 9 vols., 1897-1935, Berlin; English translation in *The Babylonian Talmud translated into English* (Soncino Talmud), edited by I. Epstein, 32 vols., 1935-1948, London.

Ta'anith: Hebrew text and English translation in H. Malter, *The Treatise Ta'anit of the Babylonian Talmud* (Schiff Library), 1928, Philadelphia.

Berāchōth: English translation in A. Cohen, *The Babylonian Talmūd: Tractate B^erākōt*, 1921, Cambridge.

Sifrē: Hebrew text, edited by M. Friedmann, 1864, Vienna; edited by H. S. Horovitz and L. Finkelstein, 1935—(in progress), Breslau (Corpus Tannaiticum III, 3).

Midrash Rabbah: Hebrew text, edition of 1877, Warsaw; English translation in H. Freedman and M. Simon, *Midrash Rabbah translated*, 9 vols. and Index, 1939, London.

M. Friedmann, *Seder Eliahu rabba und Seder Eliahu zuta* (Hebrew text), 1902, Vienna.

I. Abrahams, *Studies in Pharisaism and the Gospels*, 2 vols., 1917-1924, Cambridge.

J. Bonsirven, *Le Judaïsme Palestinien*, 2 vols., 1934, 1935, Paris.

R. H. Charles, *The Book of Jubilees*, 1902, London.

R. H. Charles, ed. by, *The Apocrypha and Pseudepigrapha of the Old Testament*, 2 vols., 1913, Oxford.

M.-J. Lagrange, *Le Judaïsme avant Jésus-Christ*, 1931, Paris.

C. G. Montefiore and H. Loewe, *A Rabbinic Anthology*, 1938, London.

G. F. Moore, *Judaism in the first centuries of the Christian Era*, 3 vols., 1927-1931, Cambridge, Mass.

S. Schechter, *Studies in Judaism*, First and Second Series, 1938 (2nd ed.), 1908, Philadelphia.

S. Schechter, *Some Aspects of Rabbinic Theology*, 1909, London.

R. Smend, *Die Weisheit des Jesus Sirach*, 1906, Berlin ; *Die Weisheit des Jesus Sirach erklärt*, 1906, Berlin.

iv. The New Testament

A. Durand, *Évangile selon Saint Matthieu*, 1938, Paris.

M.-J. Lagrange, *L'Évangile de Jésus-Christ*, 1936, Paris.

M.-J. Lagrange, *Évangile selon Saint Matthieu*, 8th ed., 1948, Paris.

H. L. Strack and P. Billerbeck, *Kommentar zum Neuen Testament aus Talmud und Midrasch*, 4 vols. in 5, 1922-1928, Munich.

C. C. Torrey, *The Four Gospels: a New Translation*, 1933, London.

C. C. Torrey, *Our Translated Gospels*, 1935, London.

H. GENERAL WORKS

W. F. Albright, *From the Stone Age to Christianity*, 1940, Baltimore.

A. Bentzen, S. Holm, and N. H. Søe, ed. by, *Illustreret Religionsleksikon*, 3 vols., 1949-50, Odense.

S. Cave, *An Introduction to the study of some Living Religions of the East*, 1921, London.

S. Cave, *Christianity and some Living Religions of the East*, 1929, London.

S. D. Champion, *The Eleven Religions and their Proverbial Lore*, 1944, London.

Dictionary of Christ and the Gospels, edited by James Hastings, 2 vols., 1906-1908, Edinburgh.

Encyclopædia of Religion and Ethics, edited by J. Hastings, 12 vols. and Index, 1908-1926, Edinburgh.

M. Goce and R. Mortier, *Histoire générale des religions*, 4 vols., 1944-1947, Paris.

H. H. Gowen, *A History of Religion*, 1934, London.

R. E. Hume, *Treasure House of the Living Religions*, 1933, London.

E. O. James, *Comparative Religion*, 1938, London.

Jewish Encyclopedia, edited by I. Singer, 12 vols., 1901-1906, New York and London.

G. B. King, 'The Negative Golden Rule', in *Journal of Religion*, viii, 1928, pp. 268-279, xv, 1935, pp. 59-62, Chicago.

G. van der Leeuw, *De godsdiensten der wereld*, 2nd ed., 2 vols., 1948, Amsterdam.

G. F. Moore, *History of Religions*, 2 vols., 1914, 1920, Edinburgh.

Johs. Pedersen, ed. by, *Illustreret Religionshistorie*, 1947, Copenhagen.

S. Reinach, *Orpheus: a History of Religions*, English translation by F. Simmonds, 1930, New York.

H. W. Robinson, *Suffering Human and Divine*, 1940, London.

H. J. Schoeps, *Gottheit und Menschheit : die grossen Religionsstifter und ihre Lehren*, 1950, Stuttgart.

F. H. Smith, *The Elements of Comparative Theology*, 1937, London.

INDEXES

(a) Subjects

(b) Modern Authors

Williams, S. Wells, 80 n., 149
Williamson, H. R., 42 n., 68 n., 94, 95, 100, 102, 110 n., 111 n., 112 n., 113 n., 114 n., 120 n., 121 n., 122 n., 135, 141 n., 149
Witte, J., 110 n., 141 n., 149

Wood, J., 150
Woodward, F. L., 22 n., 23 n., 24 n., 25 n., 151
Yih, Z. L., 94, 111 n., 119 n., 137, 149
Zia, Z. K., 85 n., 92 n., 149

(c) REFERENCES

1. OLD TESTAMENT

	PAGE
Exodus	
xxxiv. 7	10 n.
2 Kings	
xx. 19	12 n.
Job	
i. 1	64 n.
i. 8	64 n.
i. 21	53 n.
ii. 10	53 n.
xxii. 5 ff.	4 n.
xxxiii 17 ff.	60 n.
xxxvi. 8 ff.	60 n.
xlii. 5	65 n.
Psalms	
xxxi. 10 ff.	55 n.
xxxvii. 25	2 n.
xxxvii. 35 f.	2 n.
cvii	58
cxix. 71	60 n.
Proverbs	
iii. 11 f.	59 n.
xii. 14	2 n.
xxii. 4	2 n.
xxii. 8	2 n.
Ecclesiastes	
ix. 10	136 n.
Isaiah	
xxxix. 8	12 n.
l. 6	65 n.
liii. 3 ff.	66 n.
liii. 7	66 n.
liii. 9	66 n.
liii. 10	66 n.
Jeremiah	
xxxi. 29 f.	10 n.
Lamentations	
v. 7	10 n.
v. 22	12 n.

	PAGE
Ezekiel	
xviii. 4	11 n.
Amos	
iii. 2	140 n.
Obadiah	
15	2 n.

2. APOCRYPHA AND PSEUDEPIGRAPHA

Tobit	
iv. 15 (Vulg. 16)	74, 75
Wisdom	
iii. 1, 4 ff.	62 n.
Ecclesiasticus	
ii. 1 f., 4 ff.	61 n.
xi. 14	50 n.
Jubilees	
iv. 31	3 n.
2 Maccabees	
v. 9 f.	3 n.
4 Maccabees	
vi. 28 f.	72 n.

3. NEW TESTAMENT

Matthew	
v. 43-48	106
v. 44-48	80
v. 44 f., 48	105
vii. 12	74
xix. 19	106
xxii. 39	106
xxv. 31-46	96
xxvii. 52	2 n.
Mark	
x. 33 f.	70 n.
x. 45	71 n.
xii. 29 ff.	106